CONVERSATIONS WITH VALERIA

CONVERSATIONS WITH VALERIA

Discovering Moscow's past and present, and its curious links with Scotland

Robbie Strachan

V
PRESS

VULPINE
PRESS

Published by Vulpine Press in the United Kingdom in 2023

ISBN: 978-1-83919-472-6

www.vulpine-press.com

To Helen

Preface

Similar to all great cities Moscow has many faces. Some are familiar only to native Muscovites, or those whose affairs draw them to little-known corners of city life. Others are famous worldwide – the great landmarks and historic sites recognisable to tourists and TV viewers alike. For Western observers there's also a Moscow of the popular imagination that has been shaped by decades of journalistic clichés. It's the city viewed through lenses of high-level international politics, or of Russia as a freak-show. A lurid narrative of plotting behind the Kremlin walls, of cybercrime, greedy oligarchs, political murders, official misdeeds and astonishing corruption. None of which is untrue. And it's impossible to live in Moscow without being aware of its dark and troubling sides. Yet although I occasionally caught glimpses during my years in the city, they remained largely off-stage, and never became central to my experience.

As a foreigner I approached Moscow with an outsider's eyes, but unlike tourists or media professionals, I was there not to observe, but to work – as an employee of a large Russian company. I had a job to go to, and my discovery of the city was therefore shaped as much by the unplanned events of daily existence as by deliberate exploration. With no news-desk or editor to satisfy back home, I pursued whatever happened to catch my interest, however idiosyncratic or eccentric. Inevitably I visited the iconic tourist sites, but I was equally fascinated by the quirks of ordinary life, by the city's

1

day-to-day challenges and its quiet, timeless satisfactions. Moscow is many-layered, and some of its most rewarding features low-key and largely unseen. Above all, I was drawn especially to its Soviet past and felt fortunate to have arrived at a time when this was still alive and thriving.

During my four years in Moscow – in the first decade of this century – the city sat uneasily between two worlds. The new, emerging Russia had officially abandoned its communist heritage and embraced modern capitalism. That was, after all, the reason I was there. But the transition had not been easy, and the social and economic chaos of the 1990s continued to scar the nation's psyche. At the same time, the old Soviet world was still near enough to touch. Its habits, values, and assumptions deeply ingrained in the fabric of Russian society, and in the souls of even the youngest of my Russian acquaintances. And while Moscow's physical face was changing, the city's huge, often ugly, urban sprawl was still largely a Soviet creation. It remains so today.

As I got to know Moscow and reflected on what I encountered, I also read widely – on Russian history, particularly of the Soviet-era – determined to understand the background and context to what was happening around me. This new-found knowledge enriched my appreciation of the city, and some of it has found its way into these pages. My personal Moscow therefore embraced both the present and the past, history and imagination as well as contemporary reality. Consequently, this memoir is not a record of what's conventionally important, but of what I found curious, amusing, shocking and admirable. I have not attempted a rounded portrait but a collection of snapshots illuminating what I believe are some of the city's essential characteristics.

My employer was a major Russian company, but I have omitted any details that would allow its identification. Although I found its many peculiarities maddening at the time, I remain grateful that it hired me, welcomed me into its organisation, and gave me the opportunity to experience Moscow. Its identity is in any case unimportant, as what I encountered was typical of so many Russian businesses of the time. Similarly, I have changed the names of some of the individuals who appear in these pages. Most still live and work in Moscow and would not wish to see themselves in print.

1

The reaction in the office to my resignation was predictably downbeat.

"You're kidding – *Moscow?*" I heard innumerable times. "Don't think I'd fancy that."

Well it's not you that's bloody going!

I'd mutter this to myself, yet despite exasperation with all the negativity, I remained civil and put on a show of optimism, largely to reassure myself about the wisdom of my decision, for I was less confident than I let on.

"*Moscow?*" my boss said, screwing his face quizzically. "Isn't it a bit, well – *dangerous?*"

"It's not what people imagine. Things have calmed down a lot since Putin took over."

"Well, rather you than me."

"It's a chance," I said. "An adventure. They don't come along too often at our age."

"And how does Helen feel about it?"

"She had some reservations. But we've talked them through. I'll go out myself first – then when our daughter finishes school she'll join me."

My wife had initially taken some convincing; her idea of the city echoed my colleagues. A mixture of Soviet-era clichés and horror-stories from the Yeltsin years. Gloom, crime, corruption – and interminable queues. But the money, I reminded her more than once, was pretty good. And if we didn't like it, we could just leave. After all, people went there on holiday. So it couldn't be that bad – could it?

For the most part, the gloom-merchants spoke from positions of ignorance. But there was one lady in our Finance Department who claimed more authority. Her brother-in-law, she told me, had recently worked in Moscow. Then taking me aside, she warned me – in all seriousness – about predatory Russian women.

"Take care!" she said in the kind of low, solemn voice favoured by those with grave news to impart. "They're dangerous, and they'll do anything to hook a Western man. You hear so many stories of men taken in by young floozies!"

According to her sister, secretaries and translators were apparently the primary seductresses.

"It's all too easy to end up having an affair," she said. "Or worse."

Worse?

"Don't worry" I said, "I'm far too old to be a great catch."

"Yes. But that won't stop them if they think you've got money."

Ouch! But I nodded wisely and muttered something about remaining on guard.

But her warning, although intended otherwise, cheered me up. Maybe Moscow wasn't as dark and miserable as everyone supposed. A further rare uplift came when I told my mother what I'd done. "Moscow?" she said. "That's a surprise! Good for you. Be sure to visit St. Basil's and Lenin's tomb."

***

On my second day in Moscow, in my new office in Bolshaya Tatarskaya Street, near Red Square, I was introduced to Norman Petroni.

"Where are you living?" he said.

"The Hyatt – but they're showing me apartments tomorrow."

Norman was an American accountant, and one of a small handful of Western colleagues in the company that employed me. A girl from HR had brought him to my office, recognising that a fellow English-speaker could advise me about life in Moscow.

"A rental agent's taking me on a tour," I said. "Any suggestions? Where do most foreigners live?"

"Somewhere central – or else way out. The bit in between – and it's a huge area – isn't popular. Got a map?"

There was one in the induction pack the HR girl had given me, and I spread it out on the desk in front of us.

"Here's the Kremlin and Red Square," Norman said, stabbing at a red triangle near the middle. "And here's this office – see how near we are. I live over there at Chisty Prudy," – he moved his finger a couple of inches to the left, indicating an easterly direction. "It's about a mile away. And this whole area here"- he sketched out a central circle which occupied roughly a fifth of the area covered by the map – "is where I guess you'll want to be. *Inside the Garden Ring*. Old Moscow! Some folks say it's the real Moscow."

He hesitated and asked: "Do you mind me asking what rental allowance they're giving you?"

"$4000."

He nodded slowly but said nothing.

"How does it compare?" I said. "Is it enough?"

"It's not great – but OK if you don't expect anything too grand. A couple of years back you'd have got something real classy. But

7

the market went crazy. BP screwed it up by paying silly money. They're in a joint venture with some Russian oligarchs and brought in loads of expats on allowances of eight to ten thousand a month, even for low-level guys. Moscow's huge, but there's still only a limited supply of Western-quality rentals – especially in areas Westerners actually want. So, it's hiked prices."

He shrugged and continued with what was obviously a pet critique of the market.

"The Russian mentality's another problem. They're greedy but commercially naïve. The BP surge is over so rents should have levelled down. But most owners still hold out for ridiculous prices – seven or eight thousand for apartments that should be four or five. They'll leave them empty rather than take less. It happens all the time. I guess it's psychological – some legacy of communism. They don't understand markets or negotiation – that you get what you can get. But seem to think there should be some official price that nobody queries and renters just accept. That's my theory anyway."

I must have looked deflated for he hurried to reassure me.

"No, no, don't worry. There *are* decent places at your price. What do you need?"

"One bedroom's enough but I'd prefer two – in case my daughter wants to come out. They gave me this -."

I handed him the agent's brochure – a *Guide to the Moscow Rental Market* – which outlined the categories of housing available, and the characteristics of different residential districts.

"It's in English" I said. "What do you think? Is it accurate?"

He skimmed the contents, slowing at times to read more closely. "It's the usual realtor bullshit – mega upbeat. But overall, it's pretty good. The main locations and the different kinds of housing are all here. In reality, though, some areas should be avoided."

"Such as?"

He glanced again at the brochure. "Taganskaya. It's there."

He turned to the map and gestured at the central area. Taganskaya was just on the edge of the desirable Garden Ring.

"Yes, it's real close," Norman said. "But it's a mess. Scruffy and run down. New roads built everywhere. Ignore the brochure stuff about the '*lively night life.*' It's second-rate bars and tatty casinos."

"Anywhere else?"

"Leningradsky Prospect. It's not really a district – just a long road. The route out of the city to Leningrad – St Petersburg now. Look -"

And he traced along a line on the map where heavy red ink indicated a key artery running to the Northwest.

"The Prospect's huge and there's masses available to rent. But it's a hassle. Congestion. Noise. And nothing to make you want to live there anyway. If you're going to travel that far every day, you'd be better out somewhere like Rosinka."

"Rosinka?"

I hadn't seen it mentioned in the brochure.

"They don't cover it," Norman said. "It must be with different realtors. It *should* be here because it's one of the main expat locations in Moscow. A long way out maybe – here, off the edge of the map – but personally I like it."

He handed me back the brochure and I scribbled black crosses beside Taganskaya and Leningradsky Prospect. Prompts for my discussions with the rental agent.

"Should I be looking at Rosinka?"

"It's expensive. Difficult on your rental allowance. But it's different from everything else available for foreigners in Moscow.

Here in the centre, apartment living's the norm. Typically, in old blocks that have been done up – like that -"

He gestured to the window where we could see across the street the pink stucco walls of a restored four-storey 19th century tenement.

"Or you might get something more modern – there are some OK post-war blocks. But in general, the nearer the centre the older the building – and the more they're sought after. Most expats without kids want to be central because that's where everything is – theatres, tourist sites, restaurants. But Rosinka's unique. It's a gated community and could be anywhere. New-build, low-rise American-style houses – not like living in Russia at all. All kitted out to a real high standard. Landscaped grounds like a country club, with a swimming pool and sports complex. The problem's the distance. In Moscow's traffic you'll spend a couple of hours getting home every night. And it's not to everybody's taste. Some folks think it's too much of an expat ghetto – a bit *Desperate Housewives*. There's truth in that. Out there in the boondocks. Wives with nothing to do but play tennis and sit around bitching all day. Husbands stuck in cars, getting home after nine at night. Lots of them banging their Russian secretaries because they see more of them than their wives. Guys with families live out there because it's near the international school. And so do a lot of expats who are scared of Moscow."

He noted my questioning glance at this final comment.

"Remember," he said, "not everybody's here by choice. It's not a popular posting. Plenty guys get sent against their will. And most have the typical Western idea of Moscow – all problems and risks. So, their companies stick them in Rosinka to soften the blow. It's a sheltered environment. High-level security, and other foreigners for neighbours. I guess it calms their paranoia about getting robbed or shot in the street. That's something you'll recognise once you've been here a bit – there's a whole bunch of unhappy foreigners just counting the days till they get to leave. Maybe it's even the norm."

This was negative talk to hear on my third day in the city. But I understood it wasn't a deliberate attempt to depress, simply a fellow expat trying to educate me with a mixture of facts and opinion. Foreign residents everywhere wear their local knowledge as a badge of honour; sharing their insights with newcomers becomes a form of self-validation.

"How much do you pay?" I asked Norman.

He shrugged, and for a moment I thought he might avoid answering. But he went on: "A lot less than four thousand – to be exact two thousand five hundred. But you can't compare – my circumstances are different."

***

Despite my surface bravado, when I first set out for Moscow it was against my inclination and better judgment. I knew it to be violent, corrupt and dreary, and I was lured only by money.

A placename alone can be enough to light up the imagination or depress the spirit. Think Bali or the road to Mandalay. Like many Scots I had always looked south – to a promise of warm breezes, palm trees and primary colours. Never once had I felt drawn to Russia. Who yearns for Moscow when they're shivering in Glasgow?

When my Moscow opportunity came it was out of the blue, in disguise, and like many an old-fashioned fictional adventure, started with an advert in *The Times*. A bold headline in Thursday's *Appointments* section announced an **Exciting International Role** for an experienced Human Resources Manager. But otherwise, the details were vague. There was no mention of Moscow, no salary information and no employer's name. Instead, the recruiter spoke coyly of *'a major European city'* and a *'dynamic international organisation'*.

Paris? Barcelona? Maybe Rome? Sunshine would be nice. Although I recognised the job was a long shot – any attractive posting meant strong competition – I saw no harm in trying, and without any great hope sent off a CV. It was acknowledged within a few days, and then there was silence.

I'd forgotten all about it, when several months later a lady from the agency telephoned unexpectedly. "I know it's been some time," she said apologetically. "Unfortunately, we've had some unforeseen delays. Are you still interested?"

Her client was now keen to fill their vacancy. It was a Russian company based in Moscow. My heart sank. She clearly sensed my disappointment, and quickly added: "They're offering an exceptional salary and benefits package."

My aversion to Moscow was only partly due to its public image. As a child of the Cold War, I'd absorbed all the Western stereotypes – food queues, police informers, deplorable living conditions. I knew that the city's glum Soviet citizens had found escape only through vodka or classical music. With the collapse of communism, the details changed, but Moscow's reputation remained steadfastly depressing. Iconic images of military triumphalism (grim-faced party hacks in heavy overcoats on a Red Square podium as missiles rolled past) were replaced on TV by stories of economic chaos, gangsterism and corruption. Moscow unquestionably was still no fun.

Yet my hesitancy was more complicated and personal. I should have known if not better, at least more. Because the spectre of Russia had been a constant presence throughout my childhood and adolescence. At a time when the world behind the Iron Curtain was remote and generally suspect, Russia persistently intruded into our family life – not as a forbidding dictatorship, but as a Promised Land. My parents were enthusiastic Russophiles, part of a surprisingly large contingent in the West of Scotland. As determined socialists they fancied themselves inheritors of Red Clydeside's legendary revolutionary traditions. The regime in Moscow was building socialism, so it deserved their unquestioning support, and I got used to hearing of how good life was in Russia. It seemed that commonplace Scottish problems – universal problems – were unknown there. News reports suggesting otherwise were dismissed by my parents as American propaganda, and when high-profile Russian defectors – ballet dancers, poets, writers – showed up in New York or London, my mother would shake her head sadly and wonder at such talent wanting to escape. *Escape!* Escape from what? Then she'd find comfort in the reflection that their betrayal was of course evidence of moral bankruptcy or mental illness, and that Russia was lucky to be rid of them.

When the Red Army Ensemble appeared on television during its periodic cultural missions to Britain, she'd shoosh away all interruptions, and oblivious to its desperate lack of cool, watch reverentially as they wrestled with accordions and kicked their heels in Cossack dances (The contrast between these clean-cut military figures and our scruffy rock stars was of course proof of Western decadence). Russian entertainment was proper entertainment – serious, grown-up, and unblemished by trashy DJs and smarmy gameshow hosts. She had a particular dislike for American sitcoms,

13

largely I suspect, because the stage-sets depicted ordinary Joes in homes whose space and luxury niggled at suppressed doubts about Russian living conditions.

Mostly I took all this claptrap in my stride, aware even as an adolescent that it wasn't really the Russian people or their history that interested my parents, but rather the *idea* of Russia – or more correctly the USSR. In their eyes Russia and the Soviet Union were interchangeable, and if the beacon of socialism had been Polynesia, they'd have been Polynesian aficionados, and we'd have been regaled at the dinner table with the superiority of grass skirts and coconuts over kilts and haggis. Yet in most areas of life, they were ordinary, hard-working, sensible – astute even – members of Scottish society; the Russia thing was their sole eccentricity. I found it crazy and profoundly embarrassing (in the same category as membership of a weird religious sect or an obsession with extra-terrestrials) but usually simply ignored it. Only occasionally did my touchiness get the better of me, and with an adolescent's merciless eye for parental stupidity I was deliberately confrontational: *What about the prison camps? Or queueing for hours to buy anything?* But invariably my barbs achieved nothing more than an exasperated repetition of a familiar mantra: *It's all American lies. Invented to discredit communism.*

Yet in these exchanges I was also aware of the darker side of their Russian infatuation – their ruthless selectivity. Their wilful determination to believe only what suited them – however removed from reality. The comic nonsense of their cultural pronouncements went hand in hand with a grim denial, even in the face of irrefutable evidence, of whatever horrors didn't fit with their world view.

14

I've never doubted my parents' sincerity. They believed in socialism, and therefore *made themselves* believe in Russia. Throughout the Soviet heyday, and into the tempestuous years that followed its collapse, they stuck with their certainties. When previously undisclosed dirty secrets were exposed, they never wavered. No revelation could shake them. And although their Russian obsession was politically driven, its intensity and longevity saw it develop over the years an almost spiritual dimension, which expressed itself in a sentimental belief that at the human level there was some kind of special affinity between the Scots and the Russians. For me nothing changed. My adolescent aversion to all things Russian remained intact well into the post-Soviet era. Until, that is, decades later it was overcome by the unexpected offer of a job at double my UK salary and a flat-rate income tax of 13%. It's one of the great ironies of my life that I became the one in our family to set out for a life in Moscow.

***

Valeria, my new secretary, was a robust, dark-haired girl in her mid-twenties who had clearly not been hired for her looks but because she could speak English. She was too tall and heavy-set to be considered pretty. But she had a cheerful personality and seemed genuinely determined to help me. The colleague back home who had warned about Russian women, would have been relieved. There was no danger our relationship would be anything but solidly professional.

And there was further comfort on my first morning, as Valeria set the scene for me.

15

"There are three of us who'll support you," she said. "Me and Nikolai, your driver. And also a translator. You'll meet them soon."

"Translator?"

"For the complicated work. But you'll share him with the other foreigners."

"*Him?* The translator's a man?"

"Yes – Dmitri Katoshin."

"Ah…" More danger averted.

Nikolai Surakov, my driver, was a Muscovite in his fifties. He was friendly and obliging but had minimal English. The Head of the Car Pool had given him a Russian-English phrase book and expected us to cope. In the West a driver is the preserve of the very wealthy, government ministers or senior corporate types. But in Russia their wages are low, and the perk's available even to mid-level bureaucrats and junior managers. My car was a leased black Mercedes saloon, with tinted windows. These were ubiquitous on Moscow's streets, and once the preferred vehicles of the local mafia. But changing fashions have seen the gangsters turn to Hummers, Land Cruisers and other large four-wheel-drives, leaving the Mercs increasingly to ordinary businessmen and private owners.

"You can use it any time," Valeria told me. "Evenings and Saturdays if you wish. Nikolai's paid for the whole week. Only Sunday's free for him."

I became aware early on of tension between Valeria and Nikolai. She had an office-worker's disdain for those with irregular hours, and what appeared to be less demanding responsibilities. There was also a measure of envy.

"Of course Nicolai has nothing to do all day," she grumbled more than once. "Except smoke and sleep! But his salary's more than mine!"

I also suspected Nikolai's lack of English was a factor in their discord. In our early days my instructions were filtered through Valeria, who no doubt put her own slant on them. Later, as my understanding of Russian improved, I would recognise my own mild requests to Nikolai become imperious orders in Valeria's mouth. He must have found this galling. Nevertheless, they were my immediate circle, and become a loyal little group.

In particular Valeria and I became good friends. She would be my ally, my eyes and ears, and a key interpreter of events around me. I appreciated her clear-headed cynicism, and her sharp grasp of the realities of life in our company, and I came to value her as a sounding board for anything controversial or political. Above all she was protectively loyal. This was partly innate decency – looking out for a foreigner who didn't know the territory. But professionally she also guarded the reputation of a boss whose failure would reflect badly on all his subordinates – including her. There's something very Russian in this. Personal loyalty – loyalty to individuals rather than institutions – is particularly strong in Russia. This is unsurprising, since institutions – the state, its organs and its officials – were the chief oppressors of the population for the best part of the last century. Moreover, a version of the Stalin-era principle of guilt by association still survives. In the past the families and friends of condemned officials might also be shot. Now, managers and their teams succeed or fall together, and when a senior employee is fired it's common for his department to be immediately purged. Conversely, when a manager resigns, he routinely takes his associates with him to his next company.

Of course, none of this is unknown in the West. But it's markedly more prevalent in Russia, where loyalty overrides any Anglo-Saxon notions of merit, fairness or professionalism. Time

17

and again I would see it in action and witness the negative results. The wrong people promoted, key policies ignored, mistakes and incompetence accepted as inevitable. Paradoxically, it operated in the face of what I came to recognise as a defining characteristic of the Russian business world – a fixation with following processes rather than chasing goals.

During my first week in Moscow, I encountered a trivial instance, when Valeria informed me my claim for reimbursement of baggage costs had not been approved.

"Why? It's in my contract. How can there be a problem?"

"Rusalka says it's not valid."

"Who's Rusalka?"

"She's in the accounts department. And looks *as if she has sucked a lemon.*" Valeria's careful enunciation suggested she'd just learned this new English expression. "Wait -" she went on. "I've called Katoshin to explain. He's speaking directly with Rusalka."

Valeria was perfectly capable of explaining herself, but I guessed that in this early stage of our acquaintanceship she wanted the translator's moral support with bad news. Dmitri arrived clutching an email printout in Russian and proceeded to paraphrase in English.

"Rusalka says it's impossible to pay your claim, because there's no company policy on baggage expenses. Without a written policy the regulations forbid any payments. Nothing can be done."

"Nonsense! My contract clearly says – in writing – that I'll be reimbursed. What's Rusalka's answer to that?"

"Mr. Strachan," Dmitri said with elaborate patience, "you must understand two things. First: that Rusalka's an awkward, difficult, obnoxious person – I believe that's the correct English description. Second: she doesn't pick on you alone – she acts the same with everybody. She's got the old Russian mentality – and believes the most important thing's loyalty to her boss. It's more important than doing what's correct or fair. Because her boss is the Finance Director – Mr. Pryadkin – loyalty means saving the company's money. For Rusalka the Accounts Department doesn't exist to make payments, but to stop payments. I think it's better if you send a note directly to Pryadkin. He's a reasonable man and he'll make sure you get what your contract says."

I was surprised by Dmitri's open hostility towards Rusalka, and once he'd gone, I asked Valeria why the company put up with her behaviour.

"Mr. Pryadkin knows what she's like, and often overrules her. But she's useful to him. She checks everything carefully, so people are afraid to cheat."

"But look at the trouble she causes."

Valeria shrugged. "Pryadkin doesn't care. She's loyal and that's the important thing. Of course, her personality's not good. I think she pretends to be loyal just because she enjoys upsetting people. There must also be people like that in England."

I had to agree. Rusalka was a universal type – an embittered, officious jobsworth who would not have been out of place in a British town hall or the lower ranks of the civil service.

2

"My name's Yulia," the woman from the rental agency said. "I've selected seven apartments for you."

She had arrived at the office with a car and driver which the agency had hired for the day to take us to our viewings. This had provoked mild protests from both Valeria, who thought she should be coordinating my search, and Nikolai, who expected to drive us. We compromised on Valeria accompanying me on the viewings, but we agreed to stick with the agency car since the driver was already familiar with the location of our target properties.

It was raining heavily, and in my rush to keep dry I closed the door of the old Volkswagen with some force. The driver shot me a sour look and snapped something in Russian.

"What did he say?" I asked.

"He said take care with his car," Yulia answered. "The lock on your side's not good and he's afraid you'll damage it even more."

"Sorry!"

Valeria shot me a smug look that said *of course this is what comes of using their car.*

Yulia handed me a sheaf of property schedules, and as I leafed through them, I concentrated on the locations, rather than the photographs of apartment interiors. In preparation for this tour, I'd bought a guidebook, and done my homework on the city's topography. Moscow, I discovered, is built on a radial plan with the Kremlin, the heart of the old city, sitting at the very centre. It's encircled by four major roads, each progressively a bit further out, like the rings on a dartboard. The innermost road is the *Boulevard Ring*, a chain of tree-lined 19th century boulevards, which according to the guidebook follows the line of Moscow's now-vanished 16th century city walls. The name's misleading, for the road does not extend south over the Moscow River to truly complete a ring but stops on the north bank making only a horseshoe. I had walked part of the *Boulevard Ring* close to my hotel the day before. It was an attractive park-area bordered by grand Victorian buildings, and I concluded I'd be happy with a place there.

Another half mile or so further out is the *Garden Ring Road*, of which Norman had spoken. This time the route does cross the river, and loops back again in a genuine circle. For Muscovites the *Garden Ring* has special resonance. Today it's a traffic-choked ten lane highway, with no pastoral quality whatever, yet it neatly separates the old city from the mass of Moscow's post-war sprawl. The name derives from the gardens that once flourished here, and they marked what for most of Moscow's existence was its outer boundary. For many Russians the area inside the *Garden Ring* is the real Moscow, the prestigious heart of Russian civilisation.

The next circle is the *Third Ring Road*, a nondescript modern highway completed in 2003 in an attempt to alleviate traffic congestion. And finally, on the outer perimeter of the city is the *MKAD*, the Moscow orbital road, 101 kilometres in circumference. When it opened in 1961, the *MKAD* marked the administrative limits of the modern city, but during the 1980s, Moscow began to encroach on land even further out, and now the city's development straggles a long way beyond. In the 90s, the *MKAD* underwent a major upgrade, expanding from four to ten lanes. Rosinka is just outside the *MKAD*, but for the purposes of my house hunt the

whole area between Rosinka and the Garden Ring was badlands –
on Norman's advice off-limits and to be ignored. I had told the
agency as much. I wanted to concentrate only on the city centre.

Our first viewing was inside the *Boulevard Ring*, a two-bedroom
apartment on the fourth floor of a five-storey building on
Tverskaya Street. The property schedule described it as 'five
minutes from the Kremlin' – which was only a very slight
exaggeration. In communist times, under its former name of Gorky
Street, Tverskaya was Russia's premier shopping thoroughfare.
Today it's eclipsed by the new international-style malls which have
sprung up throughout the city. Yet its proximity to the Kremlin
ensures it remains a prestigious location, and at street level, it is
home to an array of both high-end luxury-brand retailers and mid-
market fashion stores. Tverskaya runs from the edge of the Kremlin
at Revolution Square up to Pushkin Square, then beyond to
Triumphal Square, where its name changes to Tverskaya-Yamskaya
Street and it heads out, almost in a straight line, into the suburbs.
Historically this was one of Moscow's key arteries, the route to the
Tver region and Northwest Russia. It's still the main road to St.
Petersburg, and after it passes Belorusskaya Station, a couple of
miles out from the Kremlin, reverts to its Soviet title of
Leningradsky Prospect.

The apartment itself was a severe disappointment. There was no
entrance from the street, as a sushi bar and shoe-shop occupied the
whole frontage, and we had to approach via a muddy yard at the
back of the building. Here a group of scruffy middle-aged men
lounged against the wall of a brick outhouse, smoking as they
sheltered from the rain under the overhang of its corrugated iron
roof. A bottle was being passed around, and between gulps they
shot us hostile glances as Yulia struggled with the key to a heavy

steel security door. Their presence was more dispiriting than intimidating, but it set the tone for our visit. I looked up at the grey stone tenement walls, the bottom level scarred with graffiti, and had a sudden vision: welcome to Glasgow circa 1973. It was a prophetic moment, for it was the first of many echoes of the Scottish city I'd experience during my years in Moscow.

A rackety lift took us to the fourth floor and, ominously, another steel door. Inside, the apartment was cramped and tatty, and Valeria pulled a face when we crossed the threshold. The bedrooms, their windows overlooking the back court, were small but adequate. However, the lounge at the front of the building was a makeshift affair – clearly part of what had once been a bigger room, but now partitioned off with plasterboard to make space for a windowless kitchen, accessed via an open archway reminiscent of a Spanish holiday-let. It was an old building, and I guessed that at one time there must have been a proper kitchen, but I couldn't see where. Later, after many similar viewings, I understood that the whole apartment had been carved out of a much grander house and that other rooms, now part of a separate residence, must have lain hidden behind bricked-up doorways, invisible under plaster and decades of wallpaper.

"What do you think?" Yulia asked.

I thought: *$4000 for this – are they joking?* But my reply was non-committal.

"I'd like to see others – to compare. And what about furniture? There's none."

"They'll buy when someone takes the apartment."

As an introduction to Moscow living this first property was a huge let-down. I struggled to believe it was $4000 a month and suspected an estate agency trick – showing the worst properties first to soften me up for the real deal later on.

Back in the car I remarked that four thousand seemed high for the quality on offer.

"Many foreigners say that," Yulia said. "Don't worry – you'll see more before you decide. The next one's very near – in Gazetny Pereluk." (Gazetny Lane.)

Moscow regularly features in surveys of the world's most expensive cities for Western companies relocating staff. Expats hoping for generous compensation naturally welcome its designation as a hardship posting. Yet this is misleading. Rents for Western-standard housing are certainly high, but these apart, the real cost of living is significantly lower than most Western capitals. How could it be otherwise in a city of over twelve million, where more than 95% of inhabitants have incomes well below Western norms?

Gazetny Pereluk was only a couple of hundred yards away, and we could have walked in less time than the car took in Moscow traffic. But the heavy rain filled the potholes in the pavements, and collected in pools on the roads, so we drove.

"Today's not the best for travelling in the city," Yulia said.

According to the brochure I'd reviewed with Norman, there were five categories of accommodation suitable for Western residents. In date order, starting with the oldest, they were: 1) *Pre-Revolutionary* properties – 19th century residential buildings that had survived various waves of the city's redevelopment. These were often fine, ornate relics of old Moscow. 2) *Stalin Blocks* – monumental apartment complexes built between the 1930s and 1950s to house the Soviet elite. They not only provided spacious, comfortable accommodation, but in their heavy architecture –

characterised by huge slabs of grey stone and concrete – made a deliberate political statement about the power and solidity of the communist state. 3) *Khrushchyovka* – cheaply built, prefabricated five-storey blocks erected by the Khrushchev regime to address Moscow's post-war housing shortage. The *Khrushchyovka* got a brief mention in the brochure and were included only for completeness. There were a few examples renovated to a Western standard, and available for rent, but they were not generally recommended for foreigners.

The final two categories were *Ministerial* and *Modern*. The former were 1970s and 80s tower blocks – typically of 12 stories, faced in orange brick – located usually in central areas and originally intended for government employees. The final category was the myriad of new developments completed since the fall of communism – anything from luxury penthouses on the seventieth or eightieth floors of skyscrapers, with views that stretched to the edge of the city, to more modest new-builds that speculators had slotted into vacant lots in established residential districts. The majority of the modern properties however shared two characteristics: they were usually well outside the central area I preferred; and the rents were significantly higher than my limit.

The flat in Gazetny Pereluk turned out to be an improvement on the first one I'd seen. It was on the 8th floor of a block of indeterminate age, and though small, was nicely decorated and furnished. The drawback was its single bedroom. At a pinch I could have lived there, but it was too early in the viewing process to settle for less than I'd hoped.

"This is a special house," Yulia told me, meaning the whole building. "In Soviet times it was the *House of Musicians*. Shostakovich for example lived here."

"The composer? *He lived in this apartment?*"

"Not this exact apartment. But in this building. The Bolshoi's just round that corner. Many musicians still live here."

I was surprised such a famous name had such a modest home.

"Surely Shostakovich's flat was bigger?"

"No," Yulia said. "The same. We're going to Arbat next, and then to Patriashy Prudy."

A conversation in Russian ensued between Valeria and Yulia, and while I understood not a word, I knew from the tone that sharp comments were being exchanged.

"I've asked Yulia," Valeria said in English, "if we'll be visiting some apartments in more healthy locations. These are very close to the centre."

"The centre's exactly what I asked for."

"I told her that," Yulia said.

Valeria frowned but said nothing. However, as we drove to our next prospect in Arbat she broke the silence:

"Do you know Robbie – the air here's not fresh? I think it's better if you live away from the centre. My friend's a teacher in a school near Tverskaya, and she's stopped the children playing outside to protect them."

Valeria's concern had a solid basis. Moscow has genuine problems with air quality, and for the first few weeks after my arrival my eyes itched and my face stung whenever I was outside. Eventually I became acclimatised and would notice the all-pervading choke of traffic fumes only on exceptionally bad days.

Arbat is one of Moscow's most historic districts, a picturesque enclave of largely 19th century properties situated between the *Boulevard Ring* and the *Garden Ring*. It has a bohemian air and its main street – *The Arbat*, now pedestrianized – is a favourite with tourists. The apartment was not in one of the old buildings, but on the third floor of a *Ministerial* block that had been tucked into a vacant site during the Late-Soviet era. The previous tenants – foreigners – had just left, and I was told the landlord would clean throughout, and also redecorate the living room. It could have been a British council flat, and it would have been acceptable to me. I mentally noted it as a possibility. But Valeria, after inspecting the kitchen and bathroom, cautioned me to think carefully.

"There's no boiler," she said. "That's serious. Do you know what it means?"

I didn't.

"It means your hot water for baths and heating comes directly from the government. You can't control it. When it's turned off there's no hot water without a boiler."

This was my introduction to one of Moscow's domestic peculiarities, its unique system of centrally supplied heating – a Soviet innovation dating back to 1931. The majority of the city's homes remain linked to this municipal system, provided via a complicated network of more than 9000 kilometres of pipework. The operator, Mosenergo, Moscow's main power company, does not heat the water directly, but supplies very hot steam to a number of heat exchange stations located in different areas of the city. These in turn heat water for circulation to domestic users – without the steam and the domestic water ever coming into direct contact. During the summer months Mosenergo turns off the supply to radiators entirely, and for a few weeks, while maintenance is done on the system, also stops providing hot water for washing. The most-modern properties, and some of the more expensively refurbished older ones, have their own private heating systems, but millions of Muscovites continue to rely on the old Soviet supply.

Many however also choose to install a separate small boiler to provide enough hot water for warm baths during the summer weeks when the system is closed.

"You must insist on an apartment with a boiler," Valeria continued, "or you'll wash in cold water in summer."

We saw one more flat in Arbat (scruffy furniture) then drove the short distance to our next viewing in Patriarshy Prudy.

"You'll like this location" Yulia said. "Russians think it's a special place."

The name, so the brochure advised, literally means the Patriach's Ponds, and it was once a swampy pond area belonging to the Orthodox Church. Today it's a city square with a small lake in the centre, the water edged in concrete and bordered by gardens, trees and park benches. Although – like Arbat – it's within the Garden Ring, Patriarshy Prudy has a peaceful air that contrasts strongly with the usual rush and noise of the rest of central Moscow. The water undoubtedly helps, as do the high buildings on all sides, which provide shelter from the traffic noise of the Garden Ring Road. These are an eclectic mix of styles – spacious Victorian apartments originally built for wealthy merchants, which during the Soviet era became communal housing for ordinary Russians; art nouveau mansions; and several Soviet blocks erected from the 1930s to the 1950s. Increasingly the area has been colonised by affluent Russians attracted by its tranquility, and by foreigners who can afford the rising rents as its older properties are refurbished. I liked it instantly and could imagine myself living there – even before I'd seen the apartment on offer.

This turned out to be a small two-bedroom flat in an Early-Soviet block on the north end of the square. For the first time in our tour the owner was present at the viewing and provided a commentary in Russian as we moved through the rooms. At one point he had an extended conversation with Valeria. The interior was nothing special – about the size of the flat in the Shostakovich building, though less recently decorated. But purely for the location I was ready to take it. Again, however Valeria struck a note of caution, and whispered that I should make no quick decision.

"No boiler?" I asked, once we had taken our leave and were back out in the street.

"There *is* no boiler – but that's not the problem." She dropped her voice and edged me out of Yulia's hearing. "The owner says he'll install one if you rent it. But you can't trust him. He said he'll pay me half of a month's rent if I get my boss to take the apartment. Maybe you should consider somewhere healthier – away from the centre."

I was determined to live centrally despite her concerns. In any case, I reasoned a daily commute of several hours through Moscow traffic to reach clean country air would be equally hazardous to health. But I'd no wish to debate with Valeria, so I changed the subject.

"Valeria," I said. "Tell me why so many front doors are covered with cloth."

This curious detail had struck me repeatedly as we toured our selected properties. On every staircase the entrances to most apartments were heavy steel doors, clad in some quilted fabric – like a bedspread or a ski-suit.

"For security of course."

"I don't understand. The steel door – yes. But the quilting? How does it help security? Surely, it's the opposite? If a door's getting smashed down quilting cuts the noise. And stops neighbours calling the police."

Valeria pondered a moment. She'd clearly never considered this – and just as clearly had no interest now.

"Maybe the reason's to stop noise. I don't know. I think it's not so important." She shrugged dismissively and I gave up on the conversation. Fortunately, Yulia then announced that we had one more appointment to keep.

"Across the river. In Serafimovich Street" she said. "It's not far and won't take long."

Months later, when the padded doors had become a fact of life and I no longer noticed, a casual conversation with a long-term English resident shed more light. My acquaintance chuckled.

"Remember when they sold off the council houses in the UK? And owners changed the front doors? The same happened here when Yeltsin privatised the housing stock. New steel doors signalled ownership. Partly pride – but also fortress mentality. It was a difficult time. Lots of crime – and property scams. So, as well as deterring criminals, the doors were security against anyone who might try to claim your apartment. Once you'd got title to a property you were desperate to hang on to it."

"But the padding?"

"Deafening! All that metal on every landing. Stone steps and cement walls. Imagine it with nothing to kill the noise. Stairways clattering like jail cells. Quilting *is* a tad dramatic – but at least it's getting more modest. You should've seen it early on – in the first flush of post-communist excess. Moscow then equated glamour and the good life with red velvet. Anybody with cash decorated their home in it: wallpaper, sofas, bed-heads – the lot. And inevitably stuck it on external doors. *Brothel chic.* I guess sociologists would say it's an over-the-top reaction to decades of communist drabness."

Yulia's estimate of the time needed to drive to Serafimovich Street turned out to be seriously wrong. Our difficulties started at Bolshoi Kamenny Bridge, where we were to cross the river. On a day which had become one of exploration and discovery, Moscow revealed another of its defining characteristics – its truly awful traffic congestion.

We joined the tail-end of a queue at the bridge's approach and waited – utterly motionless – for twenty, twenty-five, thirty-five minutes. Then progressed less than four metres. Three of the four lanes going in our direction, on the bridge and as far as we were able to see on the road beyond, were at a standstill. We were caught in one of the ubiquitous jams that make Moscow one of the world's worst cities to get around in by car. The fourth lane to our left however was surprisingly empty, and I was about to ask why when a convoy of half-a-dozen black saloons, blue lights flashing on their roofs, appeared on it and swept past. Our driver raised his hands from the steering wheel in a gesture of disgust and muttered loudly.

"What did he say?" I asked.

"That they are bastards," Valeria replied. Then she hesitated. "And that…he wishes…some bad things to happen to them."

"Can't we just do the same – drive there?"

"Yes. Some people do. But it's the *Priority Lane* and the police may catch us. It's only for special people. Official people."

At that moment, as if on cue, with the bigshots' vehicles speeding into the distance, a couple of cars from behind us nipped into the empty lane and quickly took off.

Two and a half hours later we arrived at our destination – a journey we could have walked in twenty minutes or driven in four or five on a clear road. This episode foreshadowed a recurring frustration of my years in Moscow – I had access to a car and driver but using them was often more trouble that it was worth. On evening commutes from the office, I'd routinely give up waiting in traffic, and abandon the car to Nikolai and walk home.

Moscow's traffic shocks visitors and infuriates Muscovites. Reports of drivers marooned in gridlocked streets for hours are commonplace. The week I arrived a disgruntled German businessman made the pages of the *Moscow Times*, complaining that he'd spent eight hours in a taxi attempting to cross the city from Sheremetyevo Airport to attend a meeting in the city's Zyablikovo district. He gave up without ever reaching his destination and vowed never to set foot in Moscow again. Traffic congestion is of course a fact of modern life, and cities everywhere wrestle with its challenges. But as I'd experience time and again, in Moscow it's at its most hellish.

***

For those who didn't know better – including myself and Valeria – the official address of our next rental prospect suggested a modest flat. But Number 2 Serafimovich Street was the grandest and also strangest of all the properties I would view. It turned out to be a whole pre-war block of over 500 apartments, standing on the bank of the Moscow River directly across from the Kremlin. My first impression was not favourable. If one imagines an archetypal grim, Soviet building, this was it – concrete-grey, ugly, gloomy and forbidding. Oddly, a huge rotating Mercedes star, obviously a recently added advert, was sited on the roof.

Our appointment, Yulia advised, was to see two flats – on the second and tenth floors. As the driver pulled into a dark courtyard that housed the complex's entrance, I heard Valeria take a sharp breath. Before she could say anything however, Yulia spoke: "This is a famous Moscow house. Very prestigious. Many important people have lived here. You're lucky to get a chance."

The second-floor apartment was spacious but needed refurbishing. At some time it had undergone a tacky modernisation, with hardboard panels, polystyrene tiles and garish paint. This decor was now disintegrating, and the rooms looked knocked-about and sad. In contrast, the one on the 10th floor, although also shabby, was completely unmodernised. It was equally large but appeared not to have been touched since the war. The view over central Moscow was stunning, and for this alone I was tempted.

"How long will it take the owner to redecorate?" I asked Yulia.

"I'll find out."

"Are you serious?" Valeria whispered as we made our way back to the car.

"Yes – it's potentially the best we've seen so far."

"Do you know that no Russian will live here without bringing a priest?"

"What do you mean Valeria?"

"To clear it of ghosts."

"Ghosts?"

"Yes. This isn't a good place."

What the agent hadn't said was that we'd just visited one of Moscow's most iconic and notorious buildings. Popularly known as the House on the Embankment, it's more of a residential compound than a conventional apartment block. When I later researched its history I discovered the mixture of repulsion, fear and fascination with which it's regarded by ordinary Russians. Valeria's aversion was typical.

Begun during the late 1920s and built to the highest standards of contemporary design, it was completed and first occupied in 1931. The earliest residents were senior communists, government officials, military men and celebrities from the Soviet culture and arts worlds, all of whom must have delighted in its spacious interiors, state-of-the-art kitchens and bathrooms, and luxurious government-supplied furniture and antiques. Stalin's children lived here. At a time when living conditions for most of the general population were appalling, the building's residents also enjoyed a range of on-site amenities which included a theatre, post office, supermarket, gym and library. There was even a central kitchen that provided low-priced meals on request, and a laundry service to ensure that the wives of the Soviet elite never had to do their own washing.

I told Yulia I'd think seriously about the top flat, and as we drove out of the courtyard I studied our surroundings carefully, taking in details I'd missed when we arrived. An integral part of the structure at street level was a busy *Sedmoi Kontinent* supermarket, but it was the bronze and marble plaques which festooned the walls that grabbed my attention. These are the equivalent of the blue plaques displayed on London houses to commemorate distinguished residents. The number here alone testified to the significance of *The House* in Moscow's 20th century history. I had no time to decipher any inscriptions as we passed, but determined that wherever I decided to live, I'd come here again and do them justice.

During its early years those living in *The House* had an enviably comfortable existence. But as the 1930s progressed and Stalin pursued his purges the mood changed, and fear, paranoia and betrayal blighted the atmosphere. The concentration of leading citizens in one place made them easy to monitor, and the NKVD (the KGB's predecessor) were permanently on site, with one apartment specially equipped to tap every phone in the building. Servants, cleaners and other staff were required to report regularly to the Kremlin on the activities of residents, and the tragic fate of many defined forever the building's sinister reputation. Searches, arrests and sudden disappearances became commonplace, and by the end of the 1930s, 280 of its 500 apartments had been sealed off by the NKVD following the arrest of the occupants. *The House* suffered the highest per capita number of arrests of any building in Moscow, and it is estimated that around 800 residents were seized – of whom 300 were executed. Indeed, historians claim that fully a third of those who lived there during the Stalin era were either executed, committed suicide or were deported to the gulags. At the height of the Great Terror other Muscovites knew instantly when residents were being arrested, as they could see apartment lights come on in *The House* in the middle of the night. Today there's a small museum in one of the apartments commemorating the building's occupants, filled with photographs and memorabilia of those who disappeared. During World War II, when it seemed that Moscow might fall, Stalin had *The House* evacuated and planted with explosives, determined to destroy it rather than let the Germans take posession. Residents returning after the war discovered that in their absence the NKVD had combed every nook and cranny of the building, searching for evidence of disloyalty or treason.

With such a history it's not surprising that even today it has an unsavoury reputation. But for the superstitious there are other troubling details. The site opposite the Kremlin on which it was built, had for centuries served as an enormous graveyard. Originally swampland, it became Moscow's traditional place of execution – it was here for example that Ivan the Terrible had traitors tortured to death – and in the 1920s when the ground was dug for the building's foundations, several truckloads of human bones had to be carted away. With this blood-soaked heritage, it's little wonder that popular rumour has it haunted not only by Stalin's victims, but also contingents of uneasy souls from previous eras. That the communists' favourite residence was literally built on a foundation of human bones became part of the legend.

My direct exposure to such a lurid chapter of the city's past so early in my time in Moscow was unexpected and gratifying. A tiny, vicarious connection to major historical events. I'd been inside a genuine Soviet landmark, inspected its living quarters, used the same lifts and walked the same corridors, as famous men who'd been bundled into cars at midnight never to be seen again. My own experience I knew was unremarkable – with hundreds of flats in the House there were bound to be some for rent at any time – but I nevertheless enjoyed reflecting on it.

Apartments in the *House on the Embankment* are expensive, and beyond the means of most ordinary Russians – even if they can bring themselves to live there. While some descendants of the original tenants are still in residence, most flats have been bought by wealthy foreigners, or members of Russia's nouveau riche. Many of the latter consciously relish supplanting the old Soviet ruling class. But they are also prey to superstitions which never troubled the communists, and when completing their costly refurbishments, as Valeria suggested, frequently engage alongside their plumbers, electricians and decorators, the services of an Orthodox priest to perform precautionary exorcisms.

In the end, after another day inspecting apartments, I settled on one in an old building two minutes from Pushkin Square. The hot water was centrally supplied, but the bathroom was fitted with additional pipework to allow the temporary connection of an electric boiler during the summer. To demonstrate good faith and seal the deal, the owner escorted us to a lock-up garage a couple of blocks away, where he unveiled the actual boiler, wrapped in canvas sheets in a corner. My rental allowance stretched to this prestigious central location only because the apartment had not undergone the extensive modernisation expected by most foreigners or wealthy Russians.

3

The difference in Norman's circumstances was that he had a Russian wife.

A few days after my apartment tour he came to my office to ask about my progress.

"I'm sorted," I told him. "A two-bedroom flat in Bolshaya Bronnaya. Big rooms – although they need a facelift. No furniture yet but the owner's going to kit it out from IKEA *and* do a limited paint job on the walls and ceilings."

"Brilliant! It's a great location. You should celebrate. If you're free let's go for dinner after work tomorrow. I'll get my wife to meet us – it's a chance to introduce you. And another suggestion – have you been on the metro yet? Instead of driving we'll take it. You should get comfortable using it. It's the best way to get around Moscow. Essential if you want to understand the city. I'll be your guide the first time."

"Great idea," I said. "Are we going anywhere particular?"

"There's a place near your new apartment called the *Scandinavia*. It's an expat hangout – a couple of minutes from Pushkin Square metro station."

"And your wife?"

"She'll make her own way. She's working near Volgogradsky Prospect. She might be a bit later as her hours are less predictable than ours."

"What's her name? What does she do?"

"She's an auditor with KPMG. She's called Ina – *Irina* if we're being formal. Of course, you know she's local. It's the reason I'm still here."

The closest metro station to our office was Paveletskaya, on the Zamoskvoretskaya line (green on the metro map). Pushkin Square, Norman told me, was just three stops away, with no change of line required. We'd take less than ten minutes.

"You realise we're model passengers doing this," he said as we bought tickets at the booth. "Loads of folk just dodge on without paying. Look -" He gestured towards the barrier where two women just then were none-too-subtly squeezing through the electronic turnstile on one ticket.

"You'll see whole groups jumping over and running down. Officially there's security but..." He shrugged. "I guess it's too much hassle to give chase for a few roubles. When I came to Moscow at first it was even worse. Cheating was the norm. That was in Yeltsin's time, when everything was collapsing. The mafia took over the economy and ordinary folk took to travelling on the metro for free."

The Moscow metro's iconic status meant it was already on my must-see list. Even during the Cold War Western commentators acknowledged its architectural splendour, scale and history, while at the same time slyly reminding us of the contrast between the palatial underground environment and the drab reality of communist Moscow at street level. Today it's still regularly cited as a wonder of the modern world. Dan Cruikshank in his 2005 BBC documentary series, *Around the World in 80 Treasures* chose it as one of three man-made Russian treasures of world significance.

"Talking about security," Norman said as we descended the escalator to the platform, "forty people were killed in a terrorist attack here a couple of years ago. Some Chechens planted a bomb in a carriage. It went off just as the train came into the station."

Paveletskaya station itself was something of a generic introduction to the whole metro system. With its attractive arched ceiling, marble walls, pillars, and red hammer and sickle motifs, it's grand by international subway standards, without being one of Moscow's more elaborate or interesting. As I travelled the network over the next few years, I found many that were more spectacular, curious or memorable.

The *Scandinavia* was in a back lane just behind Pushkin Square, approached via a gated yard which was set out with tables and sun-umbrellas for al fresco dining.

"There's a bar and restaurant inside," Norman said, "but most people eat out here – even in winter. They light patio heaters and braziers then, and put rugs on the chairs in case you want to wrap up. If you come when it's really freezing – around Christmas and New Year – the yard's decorated with ice sculptures. And they chill the drinks in tubs out here in the open."

We took seats at a table for four, and Norman ordered beers and a carafe of vodka. He continued speaking: "On warm evenings like this it's a great ambience. Calm and peaceful. You can almost forget we're in the middle of the city. The food's reliable too – and not expensive. A lot of Russian restaurants are dodgy – even supposedly good ones. This one's owned by the same people who have *Night Flight* round on Tverskai."

"*Night Flight*?"

"It's a club. High end. Expensive. They've a restaurant, but in reality, the food's incidental. You go for the girls. Have you met John Morrison yet? He's been waiting for you to arrive."

"No. Who is he?"

"One of your countrymen. He works with Dimitrov in Quality Assurance. He's been in Moscow for years. The only other Westerner still in the company. I guess you'd call him a character." He lowered his voice and continued: "I'm not breaking any confidences – because he's open about it himself – but he spent over $15,000 on girls in *Night Flight*. Escorts. Before he got married."

"Why's he waiting for me?"

"To complain – about the holiday issue. Has nobody mentioned it?"

I shook my head.

"In the scheme of things it's not our biggest problem, though Morrison's all fired up. But here's Ina now."

A young woman placed a handbag on the table and dropped a briefcase on an empty chair. Norman rose and offered her his cheek. She wasn't what I'd expected. A good-looking American male, on a Western salary, was an eligible prospect in Moscow. In my imagination a matching wife would have been a glamorous *femme-fatale*. A stereotypical blonde – sultry and voluptuous. Who spoke heavily-accented English, languorously, in a low, husky voice. Ina however was dark-haired, slim and petit. She was quietly dressed in an accountant's sober business attire, and her near-perfect English revealed only a hint of an accent. She looked to be in her mid-twenties which, since Norman was in his late thirties, did at least confirm one cliché – foreign men can punch several levels above their league with Russian women.

Once we had exhausted the obvious topics – how I was finding the city, my new flat, Ina's job, and such like – I ventured a more personal question.

"How did you two meet?"

"At work," Ina said. "I was auditing in a company where Norman was working."

"Oh Ina – it was more romantic than that," Norman said. He was now on his third vodka, and his mood was becoming whimsical. "Tell Robbie about when you first came to Moscow."

Ina sighed. "That old story's not so interesting."

"But it is! And Robbie hasn't heard it. You see, Ina's not a Muscovite. She's a country girl – from way out – from Tomsk. And…"

"Tomsk isn't a village," Ina said with a touch of annoyance. "It's a modern city."

"That's true. But it's not Moscow. Anyway – the point is that she learned English at university, but never actually saw a foreigner in the flesh before she came here. Then in her first week she overheard two Americans speaking in the street and was so curious she followed them. A bit like a KGB tail. When they went into an expensive restaurant she went in too. And sat at a table near them just to listen. Her meal cost a big chunk of the money she'd saved for coming to Moscow. But she still says it was a worthwhile educational expense."

Ina nodded. "It was my first chance to hear English in real life."

"And I guess it's why she ended up marrying me," Norman said. "Those guys became her model of how native-speakers should sound. When we first met my voice must have rung some kind of bell. Lucky for me."

The conversation drifted, then Ina said: "Did Norman tell you about our new house? It's very exciting. We are *building* a house."

"Building? That's great. Where?"

"Not personally," Norman interjected. "We're *having it built*. Well – in a way. A developer's building the external shell – the walls, the roof, etc. – to a standard template. And putting in the utilities. But we get to decide the internal layout, and fit it out ourselves to our own spec. It's in a village called Orlovka – out in the country. But not too far out. About eight km beyond the MKAD. It used to be real rural but they've started building there. Moscow itself's impossible. Too expensive."

They had paid a deposit and construction was in progress.

"My friend Natasha's a designer," Ina said. "She's helping us with plans for the rooms and the decoration. She's very creative and can guide us on what's sensible. And about costs."

"When will it be ready?"

"That's the big question," Norman said. "According to the builder he'll be done by the end of the year. Then we'll finish all our stuff. So, who knows? Fingers crossed for next Spring."

Ina turned and spoke to Norman in Russian, then disappeared to the toilet.

"She likes you," Norman told me. "She says you're not like Mr. Morrison."

"That's nice. What's her problem with Morrison?"

Norman was silent for a moment.

"It's a Russian thing," he said at last. "She just doesn't get him. Finds him a bit *indelicate*."

He chuckled at this, then continued. "But he's an interesting guy. Get him talking. Ask for his insights on the city – and the company. But don't believe everything you hear."

***

When I did meet Morrison, he turned out to be a surprise. I was expecting someone younger. A cocky man-about-town – a bit flash.

But the man in front of me was in late middle age. He was heavy-set, and aside from a weary, careworn air, there was something slightly odd that I couldn't immediately pinpoint.

Was this really the guy who'd spent $15,000 on escorts?

"Another Scotsman," he said as we shook hands. "We're everywhere. How're you finding it here?"

"Just settling in. It's early days yet."

After appropriate pleasantries we got on to the holiday issue Norman had mentioned.

"It's all about pay," Morrison said. "Maybe your Russian staff have mentioned it?"

"Not so far – what's the problem?"

"It's a bit technical. But every time we take a holiday we're out of pocket. Because of how it's managed."

As he spoke, I realised what had seemed odd – the absence of any greying hair on a man of his age. His face was heavily lined, and puffy around the eyes. But his hair and moustache were unnaturally black and glossy. Dyed and coiffed like an American TV host. Incongruous against his battered Glaswegian face.

"They're administering us like local staff," he continued. "Instead of international hires. Using the Labour Code as a benchmark – not our contracts."

He continued with a long-winded analysis of the two different approaches, and while I did my best to show concern, it was clear his complaint was a fuss about very little. Sensing that he'd lost me he retreated into cliché.

"Anyway," he said, "it's not about the money – it's the principle."

I nodded understandingly and promised to look into it. But had no intention of wasting energy or political capital on such a trivial matter. I'd let it vanish into the bureaucracy. His disquiet I put down to expat paranoia – to the stresses of a foreign working environment. And the probability he'd nothing much else to worry about.

4

A few weeks into my stay, a frowning Valeria hesitated at my office door one morning, and I knew something was amiss.

"I've bad news," she said and paused, clearly uncertain how to begin.

"Mr. Plotinsky from the General Affairs Department says you must leave your hotel – today."

My landlord needed time to furnish the apartment, so I'd reconciled myself to longer in a hotel.

"Today? What's the problem?"

"You've been there too long. That's one problem."

"There's more than one?"

She nodded but made no move to elaborate.

"What's the other? Just tell me."

I guessed what was coming. Someone – probably Rusalka – had complained about the cost, and they would now deduct hotel bills from my salary. The Hyatt was not cheap, and I'd been there several weeks already. In truth it wasn't the kind of hotel for a prolonged stay – too luxurious and expensive. I'd been surprised when I was taken there at the start, but I wasn't aware at the time of the severe shortage of hotel rooms in central Moscow. There had been nothing else available.

"So Mr. Plotinsky wants me out," I said resignedly.

"No – it's the Hyatt that wants you out."

My original booking, she explained, had been for a couple of weeks. When I hadn't found a flat in that time it was extended. And then extended again. However, when Plotinsky had tried that week to do the same again, the Hyatt could not oblige. Some longstanding reservations would completely fill the hotel for the next eight days.

I relaxed. This wasn't about money then. I'd unjustly maligned Plotinsky. Like most expatriates, I always expected the worse when dealing with a foreign employer. Some universal law compels local HR and finance staff worldwide to apply scrooge-like vigilance to expatriates' salaries and benefits. The more junior the staff the more miserly, as they make a show of protecting their company from exploitation by greedy, overpaid foreigners.

"What should I do?" I asked Valeria.

"That's the other bad news! You've to go to the Rossiya."

"The Rossiya?"

"There's no vacancies in any of the good hotels. Mr. Plotinsky tried. Only the Rossiya's available."

I knew the Rossiya. Everyone in Moscow did. It was an iconic landmark, the biggest hotel in Europe, with 3500 rooms. It stood just off Red Square, behind St. Basil's Cathedral, overlooking the river.

"What's wrong with the Rossiya?" I asked. In my eyes there was nothing wrong. Why all the fuss?

I knew that for decades it had accommodated Western tourists on package holidays to Moscow organised by *Intourist*, the legendary Soviet travel agency. My mother had photographs of herself standing in front of its main entrance during Russian jaunts in the 1980s.

Architecturally it was a monstrosity: a huge, grey concrete slab, out of keeping with the historic buildings in the immediate area. But it reportedly offered decent, mid-priced rooms.

"It's not the kind of hotel for a businessman," Valeria said.

"Have you ever been inside?"

"No. But I've heard about it. It's very Soviet. And old fashioned."

When later in the day I told Morrison of my impending move he was reassuring.

"Don't worry – the Rossiya's OK. A bit basic maybe, but fine. I stayed there myself when I first came to Moscow. Here's a useful tip: if you go out at night take your room key with you – don't leave it at the desk."

"Why?"

"Just hang on to the key. I'm serious. It's a kind of charm – keeps away evil spirits."

He chuckled heartily and I gave him a quizzical look.

"It's the girls," he said. "If you're in a bar and don't want escorts bothering you, just casually play with the key. It really works. When they see you're at the Rossiya they leave you alone. Gets rid of them without unpleasantness. I guess you've seen the wallflowers haunting every hotel?"

I'd certainly noted a remarkable number of expensively dressed, unaccompanied women lingering in the Hyatt's public areas.

"You can't miss them," Morrison continued, "in every decent bar and hotel reception-lounge in Moscow – but not the Rossiya. They can't get in. Even if you picked one up, she couldn't go back with you. So, they don't waste time trying. The hotel security's like Fort Knox. Won't let them past the door."

When I checked-in I found the security was indeed tight. Not only was there a guard on the main door, but a plain-clothed security man stopped everyone approaching the lifts, demanding sight of room keys and identity papers before allowing them to proceed. Soviet security.

The accommodation was satisfactory. My room a little smaller than the average hotel standard, but clean and comfortable, if a bit overheated. I could live with the absence of a mini-bar. And contrary to Western legend, the ensuite bathroom had plugs in both the bath and the wash basin. (Soviet era tourists, my mother included, invariably mentioned bath plugs in reminisces of their Moscow holidays. *You'll never believe it,* they'd say, as if it were a source of wonder to rival the city's historic sites, *there were no plugs in the baths – you're supposed to take your own!* To be fair, travel agents of the time regularly included it in their *Essential Advice for Travellers,* alongside malaria prophylactics for West Africa, and avoiding uncooked food in India. The notion was ubiquitous enough to feature in a comic scene in a Moscow hotel in a BBC production of Alan Bennett's *An Englishman Abroad.*)

If thin toilet paper and meagre portions of soap hinted at the persistence of Soviet tradition, overall, I found little to complain about in the Rossiya. Surprisingly however, on my second night I was woken by the telephone in my room. The speaker sounded like a ham actress in a bad sitcom.

"Allo meezter!" a female voice said in heavily accented, but intelligible English. That it was English at all indicated this wasn't a random call.

"Yes?"

"You vant massage in your room?"

"Eh – no thank you. It's very late."

"You sure? Is possible now. Very nice. You sleep good."

"No, no. Thank you, but no."

"In morning maybe?"

"No, sorry. No massage."

So much for hotel security. It seemed the ban on external escorts was simply to protect in-house business.

Or was there something more sinister at play? I quickly discounted a film-style KGB honey trap. What intelligence service aims to recruit a minor HR manager with no contacts of any importance? It was more likely that had I accepted, instead of a husky-voiced girl, a hefty male thug would have appeared at my door, beaten the shit out of me, and stolen my cash and credit cards.

A day or two later I told Morrison about the massage offer.

"It's not what you expect in a budget hotel," I said. "Most of the tourists are couples. And the other guests must be cost-conscious or they wouldn't be there. I suppose the girls are a throwback to the hotel's Soviet heyday?"

"Ah," Morrison said. "So they're still there? They're not for foreign tourists. Never have been. Nobody came to the USSR for nookie. They're for Russians from the sticks. The Rossiya was once the biggest knocking shop behind the Iron Curtain. Do you know its story?"

"No."

"Have you been inside the Kremlin yet?"

"Not yet."

"Well, when you go you'll see in the grounds a huge conference-come-concert-hall – the only modern building in there. Khrushchev built it in the sixties to host communist party congresses. The capacity's around six thousand – big enough for every delegate from everywhere in the USSR. They built the

Rossiya at the same time. The idea was that Moscow delegates would stay in their own homes, and out-of-towners would just walk across Red Square to the hotel. So it had to be big. And of course, what does Ivan from Vladivostok do when he's here without his wife? Gets plastered and looks for female company. Imagine thousands of horny, vodka-fuelled party hacks hitting town and expecting fun. After a hard day on your backside feigning interest in the next five-year plan, a nice relaxing massage would have been just the thing."

Morrison paused for a moment, visibly pleased with his evocation of times past.

"Of course the congresses are just a memory, but the Rossiya's still popular with minor-bureaucrats from the provinces. The big shots, and guys with their fingers in lucrative pies, don't stay there. They expect somewhere fancier. But middle-level officials – and most of them are still Soviet at heart – appreciate the low prices and familiar ambience. So, I guess the girls still do good business. They don't get the high rollers, but for sheer numbers, and steady demand – well…"

For the next couple of weeks, I began my day in the Rossiya's 21st floor restaurant. It provided spectacular views over the city, but it was the hotel itself, and the other guests, that interested me most. In the Hyatt or the Marriott, you could be anywhere in the world. But in the Rossiya you knew you were in Russia. Looking back, I see that my brief stay was the closest I came in Moscow to personally breathing the air of the Soviet Union. Its spirit was in the 1960s décor (Soviet-Imperial in the public areas), the food and the people. Internally the hotel's most memorable feature was its huge scale, which meant tramping never-ending corridors to access facilities. Such were the distances that little desks, manned by severe matrons, were positioned like border posts at strategic points along each stretch. Presumably to control movement and to spy on goings-on.

The hotel's buffet-style breakfast was included in the room rate and never varied – bread, chipolata sausages, leaves of processed cheese, unsweetened yoghurt and diluted orange juice. The restaurant felt like a works canteen, as the sheer number of guests made industrial-style catering inevitable. But the food didn't matter, for I entertained myself studying my fellow diners – guessing the likely customers for the massage service and imagining the backgrounds of others. I was conscious above all of the sheer ordinariness of the guests. They were not like the modern Muscovites I worked with – or the fashionable young who populated the streets of central Moscow. But largely middle-aged and conservatively dressed. Ordinary Russians from the provinces. Women with elaborate 1980s hairstyles, and men equally well groomed, smarter than normal for their visit to the capital.

I count myself privileged to have stayed in the Rossiya. And when it came time to leave Valeria brought me some unexpected news.

"Mr Plotinsky congratulates you," she said. "You're one of the last guests to live in the Rossiya. There's been an announcement – it's going to close forever."

It was true. A few months later they started knocking it down to redevelop the site, creating serious problems for the city's tourism industry, as it removed at a stroke several thousand hotel rooms from the market in central Moscow.

5

"Valeria – will you phone Mr. Ivanov's secretary again and ask for an appointment?"

A few minutes later she returned: "Marina wants to know the purpose of your meeting."

"The same as the last time I asked – just to meet him! To discuss what he expects of me. My goals."

Valeria shot me a sceptical glance and retreated. When she reappeared, the message was unchanged. "Mr. Ivanov isn't available. But Marina will call you when it's possible."

I shrugged resignedly.

"Robbie," Valeria said, "you must be patient. This is Russia."

"I guess so."

It was week five of my new job and I'd still not met with my boss. He had publicly welcomed me to my first Weekly Management Meeting, but he had otherwise been elusive.

When I mentioned it to Morrison he smirked knowingly.

"Take it easy," he said. "It's no big deal. Things work differently here. I knew an expat over at Gazprom who waited seven months before he got an audience with his boss. After that he didn't see him again for the rest of his three-year contract. To you and me it's weird – and discourteous. But it's the culture here. Russian managers aren't like us. Some are just assholes of course. Arrogant prats who treat subordinates like shit. But most simply don't get what management's all about. All the usual stuff about communicating, motivating and guiding staff pretty much don't exist. They're more comfortable hiding in their offices issuing orders – preferably in writing. Anyway, how are you finding it in general?"

I was non-committal. "It's still early days," I said. "But I'm beginning to understand how things work. Though I *did* expect to talk to Ivanov about priorities."

"It's not like a Western company. You'll be shocked at what happens. Just accept it, adjust your expectations, and you'll survive. It helps to see yourself as a performer in a bizarre pantomime. You'll want to laugh out loud at times. Don't – be an actor, role-play. Keep a straight face and pretend to take it seriously. Individually most Russians are fine – on a personal level anyway. But collectively – as a company – they're a challenge. They've a huge problem with foreigners. I don't mean hiring us – but *keeping* us. Half a dozen guys in my department have come and gone in the time I've been here. The problem's never about money. It's the whole schizoid working atmosphere. All the mixed messages and changes of direction. It's wearing and gets to everybody in the end."

He paused for a moment, and I said nothing, allowing him to continue at his own pace. "Do you ever wonder why we're here?" he asked. "Why they hired us at all?"

"They said they need more international experience."

"Yes, yes! Officially maybe. But the bottom line is they don't really want us – or trust us. They're curious about Westerners, and they imagine we might know things that are useful to them. But frankly, ultimately, we're just trophies. An expat on the books is a fashion statement. Like owning an exotic bird or an expensive dog. It shows how cosmopolitan and forward-looking they are. Ivanov's mates in other businesses have hired foreigners so he wants some too. It's obvious they don't know how to use us. But the key question's *do they actually want us to do anything?* I struggle with that one. I've been here – in this company – more than three years. Before that, another eight years here in Moscow. And I've still not worked it out. On the one hand they're demanding. Expect the world. A professional job. And talk about cutting edge solutions, etc. On the other – they won't let you *do* the job. Incompetence or bureaucracy usually gets in the way. Sometimes though it's deliberate obstruction. Games and politics. At the best of times, you never know what's really going on – only what they want you to know. Even when they're not up to anything sinister everything's still unclear. Because they won't take the trouble to communicate properly. It's frustrating!"

He paused again. "I know I sound cynical. I'm not trying to depress you. It's just a personal take on the working environment. You'll make up your own mind."

"No, no," I said. "I'm not depressed. It's good to get insights from somebody with local experience. Advice's always welcome."

This was a cue for more on the same theme, but as he spoke, I was surprised at how thoughtful his analysis was. Neither glib comments on workplace annoyances nor predictable expat gripes. On many later occasions, when I reflected on what was happening around me, I recognised Morrison's clarity.

"What I noticed at first when I came to work in Moscow," he continued, "was the – the *comical* – gulf between how companies see themselves and hard reality. There's been a craze for Western management-speak since communism collapsed. Loads of folk went on courses to prepare for the new capitalist world. They picked up business-school jargon but only adopted the language. The ideas themselves proved too difficult. You know the standard stuff – leadership theories, objective setting, performance indicators, and suchlike. But they've just become an overlay on the old Soviet ways of doing things. Those never really changed. The very top managers might believe it – or pretend to – but nobody else does. Ordinary Russians carry on like they've always done. Did you know I used to come here years ago? In communism's dying days."

"Really?"

"Business trips – a few times a year. That's when I started learning Russian. Moscow was different then of course. Duller – although not everything's improved since. You'll be surprised when I say some of the old gentleness has gone. It sounds bizarre – not what you'd expect of a communist dictatorship. But it's exactly the right word. Life really was *gentler*. Slower, more relaxed. A bit stale certainly. Unexciting. None of the frenetic activity – or anxiety – you see today. But there wasn't the same rudeness or arrogance either. People were polite and respectful in business meetings – at least to foreigners. You could have a civilised negotiation. After the collapse, attitudes changed. Business got coarser, and a lot of managers who used to be perfectly agreeable morphed into abrasive smart-asses. Just because they could. Like acting badly made them big shots. It was hard-nosed and important to keep you waiting. Or make ludicrous demands, or abort meetings – that kind of thing. One guy I used to deal with suddenly got a habit of snapping his fingers and pointing threateningly – like he was talking to a school kid.

"But all that's calmed down now. It was a transitional thing. An overreaction by guys learning to cope with the new world. Most settled back into their usual ways.

"To use business-school jargon myself, I'd say the old Soviet approach was *process driven*. It wasn't *what* you did that mattered – but *how* you did it. It was more important to follow a specified process – usually in excruciating detail – than actually achieve a goal. It's the communist thing about controlling people. Prescribing ways of acting instead of letting people think for themselves. Forget initiative or creativity – apply rules and regulations. And the results are still around us every working day. Busy people churning out paperwork, checking approvals, collecting signatures – but not delivering much of value. It's why almost every company in Russia's overstaffed. Ours could run as well with a tenth of the headcount – if everybody genuinely contributed. But most folk just fanny around making a show of following rules – so we need lots of them to get anything done. It's more than just bureaucracy. At the extreme, it's almost about recasting people as automatons – of removing freewill.

"The other big thing's this culture of fear and blame. Russian companies aren't happy places. Forget encouragement or motivation – blame's the key management tool. The communists shamed or terrorised people into compliance, and it's still the favoured approach. Of course, it achieves the opposite. Everybody's so scared of being criticised or punished, they duck and dive and avoid any responsibility. They *expect* to be scolded – usually publicly – so their efforts go into avoiding blame. Take no risks, follow the rules, keep your head down. It's a recipe for stagnation and failure, but it's ingrained in the Russian workplace. And in Russian society. *Understandably!*"

It was, Morrison reminded me, how you survived during the Stalin years. It was no accident when communism collapsed that crooks and gangsters took over the economy. They were the only

Russians who for decades had thought for themselves – or were comfortable casually and routinely breaking rules.

"Do you ever watch those old black and white Soviet movies that pop up on TV?" he said.

I shook my head. "They're too difficult without subtitles."

"You should. Give it a go when your Russian improves. There's a couple of so-called *Classic* channels that show retro stuff. Mostly garbage. But you get an insight into the Soviet mindset. You see attitudes and behaviour you'd recognise today. A lot have workplace settings and pretend to be realistic portraits of ordinary life. There's a scene that crops up in film after film – I guess you'd call it iconic. A meeting's being held. The room's full of smoke and a man's shouting and banging on the table – which shows how serious he is. The louder he shouts the more serious. He's berating his subordinates about something. Then at the height of his rage, having made his point, he drops dead on the spot with a heart attack. Some stirring music strikes up – signalling he's had an honourable death. We're meant to take the dead guy as a role model – because dying on the job shouting shows you really care about building socialism.

"Not exactly subtle. But I've seen so many Russian managers behaving like that. The boss in my last company would scream at his Russian staff – go red in the face sounding off about trivial mistakes. A missing full-stop in a document, or a word spelled wrong. Bad temper? Probably – but I think he also genuinely believed it's how things should be done. Generations of Russian managers were conditioned to think like that. Can you imagine the fuss back home if you or I behaved like that? All those entitled young folk who expect praise just for showing up at work would be mightily offended."

During my Moscow years I often encountered the blame culture's fixation with punishing the pettiest of crimes. It existed not only at work, but like many deep-rooted human characteristics, manifested itself in the most unusual circumstances. Once, in a restaurant just off Arbat, I flicked past the dessert section of the menu and discovered a strange appendix – a detailed tariff of penalties for damage. A broken cup would cost you 300 roubles. A plate 700. A missing teaspoon came in at 250. A knife 600 … and so on. The destruction of a cheese platter – the most serious crime listed – triggered a charge of a full 2500 roubles. (Had this, I wondered, ever actually happened?) The restaurant was a sedate place, frequented by Western expats and respectable-looking Russians. The tables and chairs weren't bolted to the floor, and there were no obvious threats.

"Do they expect a brawl?" I asked my companion, a Russian colleague. "Like in a mining camp canteen? Do they take an inventory after every meal?"

Chernov waved my query away. "It's nothing," he said. "Maybe just a bit old fashioned."

"I've never seen it anywhere else."

"Not now – but it was normal once. We Russians don't trust anybody."

On another occasion, an expat acquaintance working for a Russian oil company showed me a similarly detailed tariff – this time for breaches of company policy. He chuckled ruefully as he summarised the punishments. Losing your security pass would cost you a day's pay. Failure to carry out a direct order – two days' pay. Poor timekeeping might trigger a week's suspension.

"But this one's really bizarre," he said. "*Signing a contract without proper authority – four days' pay!* In BP you'd be fired for that. It's the sheer lack of proportion that's so weird. You're in as much trouble for something silly, as something we'd regard as pretty serious – even verging on criminal. It's a strange mix. Harsh punishments for trivia – and surprisingly mild ones for important stuff. There's an absolute acceptance – expectation even – that people will behave badly. Be dishonest and incompetent as a matter of routine. So, the punishments are ready-made for when the inevitable happens."

6

Expatriate workers often experience an episode of sharp self-doubt early in a new job. An *Oh God what have I done?* moment, when the wisdom of their foreign adventure suddenly seems questionable. Typically, it's when the first flush of novelty and excitement has faded, but not enough time has yet elapsed to have adjusted fully to the new culture and environment. Some incident crashes through their optimism and abruptly changes the mood. Usually the gloom passes quickly, when the positives and negatives of the place settle into a state of comfortable equilibrium. My own moment of doubt appeared a few weeks into the job in Moscow, and it was my first personal encounter with Russia's ubiquitous blame culture.

I had received an official-looking letter in Russian from the company President's Directorate, which I handed to Valeria to translate.

"What's it about?" I asked.

She frowned and hesitated. "It's a punishment."

"A punishment? Who for?"

"For you."

"*Me?* What for?"

She took a few moments to read it through, clearly considering how best to translate the delicate points. "It's an official reprimand. About…your…failure to achieve first quarter goals."

"First quarter goals? What goals? I haven't set any. I've only arrived. You know that."

"The President set your goals."

"But that's ridiculous. I've not even met Ivanov yet. How can I get punished for failing to achieve goals I didn't know existed?"

Valeria was silent for a moment then said: "It *is* very silly of course. But this is Russia."

This is Russia! That phrase again. The habitual verdict of my Russian colleagues on their homeland's shortcomings and absurdities. A mixture of resignation and exasperation.

But I was annoyed and offended.

"Exactly what wasn't achieved – does it say?"

She peered again at the letter: "The recruitment target wasn't met. And the optimisation of the Marketing Organisation wasn't approved."

"Optimisation? What's that about?"

"I don't know," Valeria said. "But I think you must punish Kolbakov and Grishin."

Kolbakov was head of the Recruitment Group and Grishin looked after Organization Development.

This episode was also an insight into the workings of the President's Directorate, the unit that was the command-and-control engine for the company's authoritarian world of arbitrary commands, stylised reprimands, and financial penalties. The Directorate operated a rigid, old fashioned, civil service-type system for issuing, recording and filing management orders, and tracking their implementation. It was astonishingly clunky and bureaucratic – a complicated edifice of numbered memos, time-coded responses and elaborate transmittal documentation. All prepared on paper and processed by hand. A Soviet legacy of course, but versions are still in common use across Russian business. My Russian colleagues accepted it without question as a fact of life.

In time I came to understand how my punishment, far from being arbitrary or mistaken, was in this world strictly logical. My department had been set goals. They weren't met, so someone must be guilty. I had inherited responsibility when I took the job, so I inherited the guilt. While I was personally blameless, I was institutionally responsible. The system required a culprit and the bureaucratic sausage machine that was the President's Directorate spat out a punishment, in the way that an unpaid gas bill generates a computerised warning letter.

Except that the President's Directorate wasn't a computer, but a group of living, breathing individuals. Didn't they comprehend the offensiveness of a letter addressed to me by name, personally reprimanding me for failure? Someone had taken the trouble to draft the document, solicit the President's signature, put ink on an official rubber stamp and apply it to paper. The signature I found particularly infuriating. To my Western eyes it was incredible that a company president would both sanction such a letter, and personally participate in censuring one of his direct reports. Without discussion. For a crime of which he wasn't guilty.

It was a measure of my naivety at the time that any of this surprised me. Later, I would recognise it as comedy, and tell myself I was fortunate to witness the madness of a post-Soviet world that was yet to shake off an inherited obsession with rules, sanctions, procedures, and directives.

I took the President's letter from Valeria and held it theatrically over the waste basket.

"What do I do with this now?" I asked. "What happens next?"

"Nothing," Valeria said. "They'll put a copy in your file. And you'll punish Kolbakov and Grishin. I'll prepare letters for you to sign and pass them to the Directorate."

"No!" I said. "Let me think first."

"But you must! It's expected."

"Call them – Kolbakov and Grishin. Ask them to come and see me – separately of course."

She frowned in disapproval at this eccentricity.

"Are you sure? I think it's better to just send letters."

"No, I want to speak to them."

I hadn't yet been in the job long enough to establish relationships with my staff, and our interaction was still very formal. Both Kolbakov and Grishin were clearly puzzled at being summoned to speak with me in person. They were polite but wary.

When I showed them the President's letter however, they relaxed – clearly wholly unfazed. Yes, it was true some things hadn't been done as required – but it wasn't their fault. Others were to blame. In any case, they both assured me, they would accept the inevitable reprimands without question. In my meeting with Kolbakov, he added: "When I receive your letter, I'll add it to my collection."

For an instant I bristled at his flippancy. Would he speak like this to a Russian manager? But something in his manner told me it wasn't disrespect, that he just wanted me to understand.

"Collection?" I said.

"I have many. In this company they come regularly."

It turned out that my predecessor had for months been under fire for recruitment failures and had regularly passed the pain down to Kolbakov. Why hadn't they just sorted the problem?

"It's impossible," Kolbakov said. "Our senior management never agree about who we should hire. They change their opinions before we complete anything. So, we never finish."

Routine reprimands it seemed, whether written or face-to-face, made surprisingly little impression on my Russian colleagues, who accepted them with a shrug. They were a piece of theatre, culturally expected, but through overuse, no longer effective. The one sanction which could produce real anxiety was the threat of an entry in an individual's Labour Book. The Labour Book was a Soviet legacy – an official document which was something of a cross between an employment passport and a resume. It documented a person's career history, recording both success and failure, reward and punishment. Everybody had one, and a black mark in a Labour Book could have a catastrophic effect on an individual's career and life. Without a positive, or at least neutral, Labour Book it was difficult to find work in the official economy.

Another legacy of communism was the extremely hierarchical nature of Russian companies, which is surprising only if you expect Soviet myths of equality and comradeship to flourish in real life. The dictatorial nature of the Soviet state ensured a top-down, command and control management style that persists in the workplace today. Battalions of senior and middle managers who spent their formative years in Soviet organisations now set the norms. The great irony of Russian business – and perhaps of all bureaucracies – is that despite the interminable processes and regulations, there is little true, effective, control of performance. Behind official facades things are often shambolic.

This is also one of the paradoxes of Russian society generally. The very emphasis on compliance so often fails to ensure people behave as required. It's apparent in Russian public life – in the unending series of corruption scandals – and in the day-to-day experiences of ordinary citizens, whenever they have to deal with some official body. Similarly, anyone with a job is aware of a contrast between what's supposed to happen and what actually does. On a personal level, before Moscow I'd never had a job so enmeshed in minutely defined regulations. There seemed a policy for everything – together with a set of extremely detailed procedures. Yet here lay the conundrum. When people knew what to do, were told clearly, and in great detail – why didn't they do it? Why was so much of what happened in our company a mess? Staff were for the most part intelligent and well educated. They were no lazier, or less skilled than their equivalents in the West. And they had this exceptionally detailed guidance on how to act. Why then were there are so many problems? Why did nothing work properly?

Then eureka! I came across a magazine article on neuroeconomics, a discipline which focuses on how human attitudes and behaviour affect the operation of markets, which offered an answer. The writer described how modern psychological experiments confirm ideas expounded in 1759 by Adam Smith, in his *Theory of Moral Sentiments*. Smith argued that far from being motivated purely by self-interest, humans, as social creatures, develop an innate moral code centred on fairness, trust and reciprocity, which guides them to behave in ways beneficial to society as a whole. Although unwritten, this code acts through conscience and sympathy, and is so ingrained in the human psyche that attempts to replace it, or to superimpose more formal rules, become counterproductive. The article cited experiments with both human volunteers and monkeys, where groups of each were studied in situations in which trust and generosity were expected from individuals, for the benefit of the group as a whole. In one study the researchers noted that both people and primates were willing to forego rewards in order to punish group members seen to be acting selfishly. Another study involved two child-care centres in California, which adopted contrasting ways of dealing with parents who showed up late to collect their children. One centre started fining parents $3 each time they were late; the other simply reminded them that lateness caused inconvenience to staff. The researchers found that the centre imposing the fines had by far the greatest number of latecomers, and concluded that in some way, paying a penalty replaced the need to behave well. Rules and punishments, they theorised, actually work against basic human impulses towards good behaviour. In the business world, it's a clue to why economies with only moderate regulation seem to thrive best. Self-regulation is more in tune with man's innate moral code than over-regulation.

It's reasonable to speculate that in Russia the development of this kind of moral code was undermined by 70 years of communism. The conditions were all wrong. Soviet society was conducive to neither self-regulation nor trust. Personal initiative was discouraged, and the communists erected a vast architecture of controls to police the behaviour of a population they didn't trust. These remain largely intact today and continue to influence Russians' attitudes and instincts. I once heard a Canadian oil-industry executive grumble about the reliability of his Russian subordinates. "They're not like us," he told me. "They don't think the same – they've no God."

He was commenting less on their atheism, I think, than lamenting the absence of a spirit of cooperation, trust and generosity that he believed more prevalent in Western society.

7

My new apartment in Bolshaya Bronnaya was in a pre-revolutionary block, set back a little from the street in a small courtyard. At one time, in line with the Soviet practice of housing occupational groups close together, it had been home to professionals from the Russian film world, and Yulia told me a director still lived in the building.

Now that I was at last settled, I was determined to begin exploring the city. What I'd seen so far had been by chance – while flat hunting or coming and going to work. First however, now that I was out of hotels, I needed to organise myself for shopping. In my immediate area were several small shops and street-kiosks that sold food, drink and limited household items, and directly across from my apartment, on the corner of Pushkin Square that abutted Bolshoi Bronnai, a *Yarmarka* (temporary market) appeared a couple of times a week. This was little more than ten or twelve canvas-roofed stalls, but with fruit and vegetables, pickles, fish and meat of reliable quality and reasonable prices, it was popular with neighbourhood Russians. The problem with small shops, kiosks and stalls, however, was that you had to speak. Basics like tomatoes or cheese could be bought by pointing and saying "*kilo pajalsta.*" And other articles on open display were manageable with gestures. But packaged goods without pictorial labelling were awkward. You can mime toothpaste or deodorant, but toilet rolls? Of course, I could have used a dictionary and made a list, but this was troublesome, and assumed I knew what I wanted ahead of seeing it. I needed a supermarket.

Moscow has no shortage of large, modern supermarkets, but most are in malls or shopping centres in suburban areas. In the historic centre, self-service shopping is smaller scale, and focused on mid-size *gastronomes* – self-service grocers which also carry a limited range of household wares. The nearest to my apartment was *Eleksevski* on Tverskai Street, just off the eastern edge of Pushkin Square. This became my primary destination for food, drink and cleaning products until my wife joined me during my second year in Moscow. (After her arrival Nikolai would drive her out to one of the retail complexes on the city's periphery, to do our weekly shopping in *Auchan*, a French-owned hypermarket.)

Necessity sent me to *Eleksevski*, but on my first visit I discovered it was no ordinary gastronome. The decor inside was gorgeously extravagant, and I was captivated by its period elegance and charm. According to my guidebook, the shop was over a century old, a relic of Imperial Russia, and a celebrated tourist attraction. The 18th century building in which it's housed had originally been the palatial home of a Russian aristocrat. But in 1898 Grigory Eliseev, a St. Petersburg merchant, acquired it and by restructuring the interior converted it into a grand shop. The ground floor and first floor were merged to create a magnificent high-ceilinged hall, which is still the main retail space today. It's hung with chandeliers, and around the interior walls Eliseev incorporated sumptuous neo-baroque ornamentation – elaborate wedding-cake plasterwork, intricately carved pillars, decorative paneling – that give the shopping experience echoes of a visit to a museum or a grand country-house. Grigory Eliseev himself looks down on the splendour he created from an oil painting above a doorway that leads into the shop's alcohol section.

English visitors typically compare *Eleksevski* with Harrods Food Hall. Both sell expensive food attractively displayed, and aspire to exclusiveness, but for charm and ambience the London store cannot compete with *Eleksevski's* decoration and style. During the Soviet years the shop was renamed *Gastronome No. 1*, although ordinary Muscovites never stopped using the old name. It survived as a high-end delicatessen, supplying scarce luxury produce to the communist elite. Even in the 1930s, as famine ravaged much of the USSR, it continued to stock exotic imported foods, and was famously the only place in Russia where a pineapple could be bought.

In 2003, working from Eliseev's original blueprints, the shop underwent an expensive restoration to reverse the wear, tear and decay of the previous century. At the same time, departing from its traditional counter service, checkout desks were installed to facilitate the self-service format that it operated during my years in Moscow. As a place for the weekly shopping *Eleksevski* had limitations, but with occasional excursions to *Sedmoi Kontinent* at the bottom of Arbat I just about managed to buy everything I needed. Its stock was an eclectic mix of imported delicacies and mundane necessities. Fine wines and exotic fruits. Locally packaged bags of cheap, coarse oatmeal. Expensive foreign cheeses. Fancy cakes, pastries and confectionery. Jars of pickled cabbage. Grey plastic bottles of disinfectant. Its quirkiest offering however was of questionable taste and underlined the shop's status as both neighbourhood grocery and attraction for well-heeled tourists. In the drinks section you could buy – complete with its own luxury presentation case – a full-size glass model of a Kalashnikov rifle, filled with premium vodka.

As I scouted other shopping options in the vicinity I also came across a curious dairy in Dmitrovka Street which was clearly stuck in a time-warp. The sign simply said *MOLOKO* (milk), but its business model shouted a relic from Soviet times. Buying anything was a convoluted and time-consuming process, designed presumably for job creation rather than customer satisfaction. The shop had four counters, each manned by a stout lady in a white coat. The first dispensed only butter, the second only cheese, the third milk, and the fourth yoghurt and kefir. There was a cashier's desk beside the entrance, and a stand-alone freezer containing choc-ices and white frozen lollies. Items from each counter had to be requested and processed separately. So, customers wanting, for example, a bottle of milk, a packet of butter, a slab of cheese and two yoghurts had to approach each counter in turn and state their requirements. Each counter-assistant would then hand them a ticket, on which she scribbled their order. They'd then move on to the next counter and do the same again, and eventually, armed with four tickets, queue at the cashier's desk to pay – and receive in return four separate receipts. To collect their purchases, they'd revisit each of the four counters, hand over the relevant receipt, and be given the items they'd paid for. Nine transactions to get a modest basket of shopping!

On my first visit, before I understood the procedure, and assumed it similar to a corner shop in Glasgow, I took a choc-ice from the freezer and crossed to the cashier to pay. The latter rose indignantly and waved a finger in admonition. When I spoke however, she realised I was an ignorant foreigner and not deliberately trying to short-circuit the system. She gestured towards the yoghurt counter, which apparently had control of the freezer. There I obtained the ticket necessary to approach the cashier again – this time legitimately.

The *MOLOKO* experience was quaint and ridiculous. But it touched on two truths about modern Russia – the continuing pervasiveness of crippling bureaucracy, even in the most trivial of circumstances, and once again the widespread lack of trust. In small shops the latter means paying for the items before you get your hands on them. In supermarkets there are banks of lockers at the entrance doors, where customers must deposit their bags before starting to shop. Some have a human alternative – banks of old women who take custody of shoppers' bags on arrival, and like cloakroom attendants, issue numbered tags for later retrieval. If a shop's particularly progressive they might seal your bag in clear plastic and allow you to carry it around with you, as if it were airport-packaged duty-free. Whatever the method, the thinking is clear: shoplifting is the norm; nobody can be trusted. In clothes shops, shoe shops, and even the classier department stores, the assumption's the same. Security men hover menacingly, monitoring your every move, and if the shop's quiet it can seem as if you have a personal guard following you around.

***

Russians expect the worst of other people. They trust neither individuals nor institutions. And expect to be cheated, misled and taken advantage of – by employers, banks, police, business, government bureaucracies, foreigners and all other Russians. Wariness and suspicion are endemic. It's not only a Soviet legacy – but stems also from the economic collapse of the 1990s. For decades the message from Soviet media was *trust no one*. Be on the lookout for spies and saboteurs, and be especially watchful of foreigners. Stalin's purges, with their informers, betrayals and denunciations taught ordinary Russians that even close family could not be trusted. Then in the new Russia, economic mismanagement and the government's failure to meet ordinary people's expectations left millions feeling betrayed. Pensioners who had worked all their lives under the old Soviet system, saw the new state abandon them to an impoverished retirement. And the bank collapses of the 1990s meant countless others lost all their savings.

Today the Russian government acknowledges the issue of trust is a severe restraint on economic development. A blight on investment, and a deterrent to the initiative and risk-taking on which growth depends. Yet, despite its seriousness, foreign observers often find slivers of amusement in the frustrations it creates. On a business trip to London with a Russian colleague, I had an unwelcome glimpse when, to my dismay, my companion, Andrei, insisted we visit our company's London office at the other side of the city. I protested – it was a time-consuming distraction from the meetings we had scheduled. There was nobody there that we had to see, even as a courtesy.

"Do you have a friend in the office?" I asked.

"No, I know nobody. But it's necessary for the approvals."

"Approvals?"

"We must have our visit certified."

"*Certified?*"

"It's very important."

He fumbled in his briefcase and produced a document in Russian.

"Look!"

It was a two-page form with our names already entered at the top. There were other sections below, for signatures and official stamps. It would confirm we'd actually showed up in London on the dates specified.

"Nobody told me about this," I said. "We've got boarding passes. Hotel bills. You've a UK immigration stamp on your passport. Why do we need this too?"

He shrugged. "It's normal. If we don't get certification, we'll have problems in Moscow."

As we headed to the London office I grumbled about unnecessary bureaucracy, but Andrei was unimpressed. It was simply a fact of Russian life. Something he'd always lived with. It had to be endured and navigated as necessary.

"Don't you ever question this kind of stuff?" I said.

"It's like the weather. You just accept it."

There was a hint of defensiveness in his tone – indignation even. Russians will complain at length about their country, but don't like foreigners doing so.

Predictably, our visit to the office did not go smoothly. One of the employees authorised to complete the form was present, but not the other two. We would need to return the next day.

"Can't we leave it with you?" I suggested. "The other guys can sign, and we'll pick it up tomorrow evening."

But the functionary shook his head. That wasn't possible. Each signatory had to *see* us.

Later that evening, as we relaxed with some beers, Andrei loosened up and his unquestioning acceptance of bureaucracy faltered.

"Yes," he admitted, "it can be ridiculous – but there are reasons. Do you know about Mr. Maximov?"

Maximov, he explained, had been sent on a two-week management seminar in Paris – but never attended a class. He'd checked out of his hotel, taken a train to Nice, and spent ten days sunning himself on the beach. Nobody knew. His deception was only discovered by accident – weeks later – when someone in Accounts queried an item on his company credit card.

"What happened?"

"The President was very angry," Andrei said. "He fired Maximov and ordered HR to make some stronger controls. Now we've got this form."

"But three signatures?" I said. "*And* official stamps? It's overkill."

Andrei, however, saw it differently. Bureaucracy wasn't pointless. When people can't be trusted, bureaucratic demands are logical. Three signatures? Because you can't trust a lone person to act honestly. And stamps? Because signatures can be forged – it's more difficult to tamper with stamps.

***

Within days of my arrival in Moscow any lingering adolescent aversion to Russia had vanished. Passing glimpses of the city's sights and curiosities had caught my interest, and I determined to embrace the opportunity to explore. I was aware of my luck in seeing the Russian capital at a dramatic turning-point in its history. A new era of change was underway, although the old Soviet world had not yet disappeared. Indeed, as I'd witnessed, in some areas of life it seemed stubbornly indestructible. Living and working there I could simply have let the city wash over me, passively experiencing whatever naturally came my way. But I recognised that some planning and effort would yield much more, and I resolved to become an active tourist at weekends.

There are of course many Moscows, with their own milieux, landmarks and peculiarities. There's Sex and Drugs Moscow, *Nouveau Riche* Moscow, Literary Moscow, and a succession of historical Moscows spanning eras from the medieval tyrants to the Romanov Tzars, and latterly Stalin and his successors. Few visitors are blank canvases; we come with preconceptions, prejudices and enthusiasms, and if fortunate not only find the version of the city we seek but are granted unexpected revelations from the other Moscows inextricably interwoven with our own. My interests were twofold. As a bookish type I was drawn to Literary Moscow, and I spent many a weekend visiting the homes of great Russian writers and the sites associated with their works. But I was also intrigued by the Soviet city, which a decade and a half after the fall of communism was still largely intact. New, modern developments were underway, financed by a booming oil market, but their scale, in the central areas anyway, had yet to significantly change its physical face. Soviet Moscow was an amalgam – of communist building and the surviving heritage of many centuries. The latter made up the bulk of the city, and the decay which resulted from neglect of this pre-revolutionary fabric was a major element in Soviet Moscow's dreary reputation. My weekend wandering around the city was informed as much by histories of the Stalin years, which I soaked up for recreational reading, as by conventional guidebooks. There was a ghoulish fascination in walking the same streets and entering the same buildings as victims and perpetrators of the Great Terror.

***

From the launchpad of my new apartment, my exploration of the city started in the immediate neighbourhood, and I quickly became familiar with the area around Bolshaya Bronnaya. It had, I discovered, strong Jewish associations, and for a period during the Soviet era was at the heart of the city's Jewish cultural life. Yet it was never a predominately Jewish district. Ghettos like those which developed in other European cities were not a feature of Moscow. Even the Kiti Gorad area near Red Square, where historically much of the city's Jewish population lived, never became a wholly Jewish enclave. On Bolshaya Bronnaya the main evidence of the Jewish connection now is the swanky synagogue at the end of the street. It's unusual and attractive, a modern structure of concrete and glass grafted onto the remains of a much older building. A synagogue was first erected here in 1883, and a section of the original façade can now be seen from the street, encased behind a new glass frontage. In the 1930s Stalin's regime executed the rabbi and then used the building for trade union meetings. When communism collapsed, it was returned to the Jewish community, and a refurbishment was completed the year before I arrived in Moscow. Today, gatherings of Hasidic Jews are a familiar sight in the nearby streets.

Security at the synagogue was tight. High metal fencing and uniformed guards protected worshipers, and body searches were required before entry. Their necessity became apparent one January morning, when Nikolai, in a state of some excitement, arrived to take me to work. Our daily route took us past the synagogue, and he slowed as we approached. The radio news, he told me, had reported a serious incident. Several police patrol cars were parked in front, and a group of officers sealed-off access, but there was nothing to see. We would later learn that a neo-Nazi in his twenties had forced his way in and stabbed nine of the congregation. Luckily no one died.

The Bolshaya Bronnaya synagogue is one of six in the city, serving Moscow's estimated 250,000 Jewish residents. During the twentieth century this number fluctuated greatly, depending on political circumstances. The Jewish experience in Russia has never been easy. For centuries they were persecuted under the Tzars, suffered restrictions on where they could live and jobs they could take, and were periodically attacked in violent pogroms. For a time during the Revolution and Civil War, their fortunes seemed to change, and many became senior communist figures, fuelling anti-Semitic taunts which continue today – that Bolshevism was a Jewish plot to take revenge on Russia. But when the Revolution started to consume its own under Stalin, they once again became a target. And for the rest of the Soviet era the Jewish experience was tumultuous and at times tragic. Even now Russian nationalists point to a disproportionate number of Jews in the ranks of the oligarchs who became rich through the privatisation of state assets, and more than once I heard colleagues grumbling about them stealing money from the people then running away to Israel. At work however, I also got to know one Jewish Muscovite, who would become one of my most interesting and informative contacts in the city.

In Malaya Bronnaya Street, just around the corner from my apartment and the synagogue, was another building with important Jewish connections – the *Moscow Drama Theatre*. Today it's a repertory theatre staging Russian drama and variety acts, but from 1921 until 1948 it was the home of the government sponsored, *Moscow State Yiddish Theatre*. Its history is as dramatic and intriguing as anything that appeared on stage – a fascinating mix of creativity, innovation, politics, prejudice and murder. The repertoire over the years ranged from original plays by Jewish writers, to adaptations drawn from Jewish folklore, and Yiddish translations of Shakespeare. In the early years the painter Marc Chagal contributed murals, set designs and scenery, and one drama, *Tevye the Milkman* by Sholom Aleichem, would decades later become famous worldwide in its Broadway incarnation, *Fiddler on the Roof*. Although critically celebrated for the quality and originality of its productions, the *Yiddish Theatre* was a dangerous place to work. In its early days it was allowed considerable creative freedom, but increasingly the authorities took an interest, and demanded performances aligned with whatever political climate prevailed at the time. The company was frequently censured for errors in content, style and presentation, and latterly productions which strayed too far from social realism risked condemnation. During the 1930s, one playwright whose work displeased a Jewish member of the politburo was arrested and executed. The theatre's driving force for much of its existence was actor and director Solomon Mikhoels, but when Stalin, after the war, launched a campaign of repression against Soviet Jews, Mikhoels became a target. Because of his high-profile and international reputation, Stalin hesitated at holding the usual show trial and public execution, so instead had him murdered. During a visit to Minsk in 1948, Mikhoels was abducted by state security officials, taken to a dacha and killed. His body was then dumped on a road and run over by a truck, to make his death look like a traffic accident. Following the murder most of Mikhoels' leading associates were also executed, and the theatre itself closed. Although it's now more than half a century since the building housed Mikhoels' company, most ordinary Muscovites still refer to it as the Jewish Theatre.

8

It's almost inevitable that a new HR director in any organisation will find at his door a procession of employees with pent-up grievances. With requests that for good reason were denied by the previous regime. Morrison had his holday pay grumble, and my first encounter with Gregory Berkovich was similar. When he asked Valeria for an appointment, he was circumspect and would only say that he wished to discuss a confidential matter.

"Who is he?" I asked her.

"A very strange man. Officially he's an expat like you – except he's American. But really, he's *pretending* to be American. And his name's not Gregory. It's Grigori – and he's Russian." Valeria deliberately elongated the *Greeg-oh-ori* to underline its Russianness.

"Pretending?"

"Yes, he says he's American. But he's Russian and very rude. When I spoke in Russian he refused to answer. And told me: *speak English please* – as if he couldn't understand. Why does he behave like this?"

"What's his job?"

"Something in the commercial team. But I think not so senior."

Valeria's indignation and her open lack of deference confirmed he couldn't be very senior. When he arrived in my office, he was older than I'd expected. A thin, spry man in his early sixties. His dapper appearance – well-cut business suit, white shirt, bright necktie – spoke of energy and self-confidence, and after the usual pleasantries he got to the point immediately and without awkwardness. He was subsidising the company, he told me. It was unfair and unprofessional and he needed the matter resolved.

"In what way are you subsidising the company?"

"Because of the housing allowance," he said. "They pay me $3000 but my apartment costs $3800. *And then* they deduct tax from the $3000. So, every month I'm down $1190."

His English was fluent and accurate, but his accent unmistakably Russian. Valeria had been correct – he wasn't a native speaker.

"Have you raised this before?" I asked.

"Three times already. First with Rusalka – she refused. Then I complained to HR. But these people won't listen. They ignore me – and claim some technicality to avoid paying. My contract's very clear. But you're also an expat so maybe you'll understand better."

"It does sound strange," I said. "But I don't know the details. I'll investigate and we'll talk again when I've more information."

This promise was enough to send him off satisfied – for the moment.

When I asked Grishin for a briefing he cursed under his breath at the mention of Berkovich's name and sighed theatrically. "Mr. Berkovich's case's very simple" he said with weary patience. "We've explained to him many times. *Many times.* He's entitled to claim *up to* $4000 a month but must supply invoices. Mr. Berkovich's invoices say only $3000 – so that's how much the company reimburses."

"He told me he pays $3,800."

"That's also what he told us. But he gives no proof, and I think there's something very *unusual* about his arrangement."

He shot me a look that suggested *unusual* meant dodgy.

For a moment he was silent, clearly considering how much to say, but then went on to explain.

"Mr. Berkovich's not like the other foreigners. But of course, he's not a real foreigner."

Grishin pointed out that he wasn't dependent, like us other expats, on the company finding him an apartment and negotiating a lease. He'd been allowed to do it all himself – which was at the root of the problem. Grishin wasn't alleging direct dishonesty (largely because Berkovich's apartment was in a decent block where $3800 wasn't unreasonable). But that something wasn't quite right. He suspected he was helping his landlord under-declare tax due on rental income, and that he was getting something in return. Clearly however, Berkovich believed he could convince the company to pay the full figure.

"What about his own tax? He's also complaining about that."

"The housing allowance is a financial benefit – like salary – so the company must deduct tax. It's the law. We do the same with all expats. With you it's invisible, because we pay your landlord direct. Also, your contract says the *full cost* of housing is for the company's expense, so we cover your tax. But Mr. Berkovich's contract is different. It only says how much he's entitled to – and nothing about the full cost. It's very clear – but he continues to argue."

"I guess I'll have to disappoint him then. Why is his contract different?"

"I don't know. He negotiated personally with Mr Kolmakov – the Head of the Commercial Department. Maybe it was a mistake. Or maybe Mr. Kolmakov didn't think he should have a normal expat contract. Because he's not a foreigner."

"That seems a bit unfair. Surely he *is* an expat."

Grishin shrugged. "Russian staff don't believe Mr. Berkovich's an expat. It's true he has an American passport. But everybody knows he's just an old-style Soviet Jew!"

I was taken aback by this remark – my first encounter with a strain of open, unapologetic prejudice common in today's Russia.

I would discover that Grishin's casual racism was typical of many ordinary Russians, who routinely, and without embarrassment, voice sentiments that would shock respectable society in the West. Not only was anti-Semitism endemic, but there was widespread prejudice against most ethnic minorities. Moscow was a cosmopolitan city even in Tzarist times, but now, more than ever, the Soviet Union's legacy of a not-always-comfortable assortment of races and religions has produced suspicions and tensions. The ethnic mix was visible in the streets – from the dark hair and sallow skin of natives of the Caucasus, to the Asian features of Kazakhs and Uzbeks from the USSR's eastern edge. Russian newspapers are depressingly full of accounts of race crimes, often perpetrated by fascists, skinheads or ultranationalist groups. But an unreported tide of low-level, everyday intolerance, apparent in throwaway remarks and unprompted abuse, shows its prevalence in wider Russian society. Moscow is a city in which high-profile public figures, such as State Duma deputies, openly make anti-Jewish comments with impunity, and policemen stop Philipino maids in the street and confiscate their money, just because they look foreign.

Racial and religious bigotry is also evident in many areas of intellectual life, particularly in nationalist circles. Moscow is allegedly the world centre for Holocaust denial literature. In contrast to the West, the Holocaust is not taught in Russian schools, and there's little general awareness or understanding of its scale and nature. The efforts of nationalist historians, however, have ensured many historical facts that were downplayed or ignored during the Soviet decades, are now common currency among ordinary Russians. More than once I was told by Russian colleagues that the Bolshevik revolution, and even the USSR itself, were foreign causes – championed by outsiders and not ethnic Russians. Real Russians, whether aristocrats or peasants, along with the Orthodox Church, opposed the communists and suffered oppression. Did I know how many senior Bolsheviks were foreigners? Then I'd be reminded that Stalin and Beria were Georgians, Felix Dzerzhinsky Polish, and Trotsky a Jew. Occasionally, for good measure, it might be added that Jakob Yurovsky, the man who claimed to have personally pulled the trigger to execute the Tzar and his family, was also Jewish.

It's wrong to conclude that an open display of a darker side of human nature is evidence Russians are inherently more bigoted than Westerners. It seemed to me they were just less inhibited in expressing prejudices. At work an uncomfortable episode occurred during my first few months. We were recruiting an HR Administrator, and Valeria handed me for review a pile of CVs newly translated into English. I followed my usual process and separated them into three groups: yes, no and maybe – and asked her to arrange interviews with the *yes* group. She left with the paperwork, only to reappear frowning a few minutes later.

She held up two CVs: "Do you know these aren't Russian?"

"Is there a problem?"

I imagined some work-permit or residency issues.

"I'm just letting you know they're not Russians."

I looked again at the CVs.

"But it says they're Russian!" I said. "Look!"

Their nationalities were clearly shown on the documents.

"Of course that's what it *says*. And maybe *now* they are – but not originally. Their names tell different."

"In what way?"

"Gelashvilli's a Georgian name. And Mordkovich – *Vich* at the end shows he's Jewish. Or maybe his father was Jewish."

I shrugged. "So what? Does it mean we can't hire them?"

"No, no – you can hire them. I'm only telling you for information. I thought you should know."

I left the conversation there, uneasy with what seemed an unsubtle invitation to screen out candidates who weren't ethnic Russians. Maybe it was what her previous bosses demanded? Looking back, I think it was simply a comment. But not wholly innocent.

***

A couple of weeks after Grishin's remarks, I asked Valeria about Berkovich. I'd heard others complain about him.

"What's the problem? Is it because he's Jewish people don't like him?"

"No, that's not the reason. It's because he's …" She paused. "I don't know the word in English…He thinks he's more special than other people. Wait…"

She flicked through the pages of the Russian-English dictionary she kept on her desk. "*Arrogant*! They don't like him because he's *arrogant*. I think you're interested to know more about him?"

"What can you tell me?"

Valeria offered some basic, common-knowledge facts, and later my own reading filled in more background. Berkovich was a returnee, one of thousands of Russian exiles who had drifted back home when the USSR ended. Since few Russians could travel during Soviet times, the émigré community in the West had for decades consisted mainly of descendants of those who fled the Revolution or Civil War, with a tiny sprinkling of more recent defectors and expelled dissidents. The only significant exceptions were the Jews. Between the end of WWII and the 1990s, intermittent bouts of Soviet anti-Semitism alternated with periods when the Kremlin permitted large numbers of Jews to emigrate. The peak era for exit visas was the early-mid 1970s, and it was then that Berkovich left for the West. Like most Jewish emigrants, initially he was officially bound for Israel, but ended up settling in the USA. Now more than thirty years later he had reappeared in Moscow.

As I got to know him, I discovered more of his story. We never became close friends, but we settled into an amiable acquaintanceship. As colleagues we had something in common – our status as outsiders. That we *were* both outsiders was of course a matter of perception. Undeniably I was one. But in the eyes of my Russian colleagues, despite their refusal to acknowledge him as an expat, so was Grigori Berkovich. He may have been born Russian, but as a Jewish absconder, a long-term exile, and an American passport holder he was no longer one of them. Ironically, Berkovich himself, now proud of his US citizenship, would have agreed. It was clear to me that the arrogance Valeria detected was really self-confidence – and satisfaction at having succeeded in the wider world. Yet despite the factors that set him apart, I was the only one who failed to see him as an outsider. He seemed to me as typical a Russian as any other in the company.

He never won his battle about housing allowance, and eventually dropped the matter. But he'd regularly appear in my office, to grumble about HR's handling of some trivial complaint (about his lease car or vacation schedule or business expenses, etc.), but also to gossip in English. His instinctive understanding of Russian bureaucracy meant he never held me personally responsible for the failures of my department. I was nominally Head of HR, but he recognised my limited influence on monetary matters. The System had its own rules and processes, and the HR Department's Russian staff applied then with rigid determination.

Surprisingly, I came to enjoy his conversation, and just as Valeria helped me understand modern Moscow, Berkovich, two generations older, travelled, cynical and – importantly – with personal experience of Soviet life, became something of a window onto the city's past. He was highly opinionated, waspish in his dismissal of his Russian colleagues, and scathing about life in the new Russia. (More than once I wondered why he'd bothered coming back.) But he also had a sense of humour, a penchant for idiosyncratic comment, and a fund of Soviet-era stories and jokes.

"Did you know", he told me one day, "that in Stalin's time you could be shot or jailed just for telling jokes? Yes, it's true. They sent over 200,000 people to the gulag just for that. The wrong type of jokes of course. They didn't need to be directly political – but just suggest things weren't as good as the regime pretended. There's even a joke about telling jokes. Have you heard about the White Sea Canal?"

I had – it was a project of Stalin's which used huge numbers of political prisoners as slave labour to construct a shipping route from the Baltic to the Arctic.

"So – *who built the White Sea Canal? The left bank was built by those who told jokes, and the right bank by those who listened.*"

Hardly rollicking stuff. And typical of many Soviet jokes, which I found either lame or incomprehensible. Berkovich himself acknowledged as much, lamenting that as the ways of the Soviet world faded into history, younger audiences struggled to get the jokes. Sometimes he'd laboriously explain them to me, in the process draining them of the humour which had helped earlier Russian generations cope with the madness of their circumstances. But I was nevertheless grateful, as the subject matter itself intrigued me – the staples of Soviet life: queuing, bureaucracy, snooping on the neighbours, and the inevitable gulf between propaganda and reality.

Amongst these lessons in social history Berkovich told me a few gems, including my favourite Soviet joke:

There were three political prisoners in Siberia sharing their stories: "I was arrested," says the first, "because I got to work five minutes late every day – and they accused me of sabotage."

"I was arrested," says the second, "because I got to work five minutes early every day – and they accused me of spying."

"I was arrested," the third says, "because I got to work exactly on time every day – and they accused me of owning a Western watch."

"You see the paranoia," Berkovich added unnecessarily. "The ordinary man couldn't win. A joke, yes – but profound."

Apart from the jokes, I enjoyed Berkovich's idiosyncratic commentary on Russian life, even when he did no more than echo commonplace opinions. To my mind he was a rare specimen – the closest I'd get to encountering authentic Soviet Man. Paradoxically my opinion was based on his long US exile. As he'd left Russia during the High-Soviet era, he was untouched, I reasoned, by the gradual erosion of Soviet norms and values, by the adjustments and psychological recalibration forced on other Russians as the USSR crumbled around them. He hadn't lived the changes himself, so his mental Russia must surely be frozen in time. This may have been fanciful, but in retrospect I see it contained more than a little truth, and that his perspective on life differed from other Russians I knew.

"When the Soviet Union died," he once mused to me, "it was like a family business that declined then finally went bust. I'm an economist you know – and it's a classic pattern in Western economies. An enterprise succeeds for a few generations then collapses. First there's a founder with a good idea, and the energy to create something new. Then the sons take over and consolidate what the old man started. But by the next generation the family has lost interest in the business itself, and just want to spend their inheritance. Soon the fortune's gone and it's all over. It's a natural cycle – and exactly what happened to our revolution. All the early idealism and energy gone for nothing. Russia's tragedy is that our socialist enterprise never delivered the kind of good life that successful businesses give their owners for a time."

I listened to this with scepticism, unsure whether it was facile nonsense, or a shrewd verdict on the Soviet experience. I'm still, even at this distance, undecided.

"What's our legacy?" he went on. "The system's been destroyed. But Russia's still full of Soviet people – and will take generations to change. Bureaucracy's everywhere. You've seen it – here in our company and in life outside. It was needed in the past because communism depends on people working against human nature. All the controls and rules, audits and inspections – made sure individuals' instincts were squashed down to the demands of the state. Many people thought things would be different when the system collapsed." He paused and chuckled. "But now the controls are needed even more – because everybody's stealing something from somebody else. Russia's drowning in corruption."

He said this with obvious satisfaction.

Berkovich's relish in spotting absurdities, his complaining, and his snootiness towards his Russian colleagues, naturally made him unpopular. His expat contract meant his salary was higher than his local counterparts, yet he fuelled resentment by loudly and unnecessarily declaring he could make just as much back in the USA. I saw, as I got to know him better, a complex personality that was neurotic and insecure, but also a comical mix of egotism, prickliness and discontent. If he wasn't in Moscow for the money, my colleagues would mutter, then why was he here at all? Nostalgia? Maybe – but it was clear that deeper impulses were at play.

I never heard him speak fondly of Soviet life, yet something drove him to reconnect with his past. He had deep personal roots in the city certainly – his extended family had remained throughout the Soviet years. And a human desire to reunite with old friends must have been a factor, together with curiosity about how his homeland had changed during his absence. He also had the pride of the exile – and the urge to show folks back home how well he'd done abroad. He'd returned to Moscow an internationally marketable professional, capable of a career in the USA. A genuine accomplishment. But it clearly wasn't enough. Berkovich wasn't a man at peace and seemed intent on proving something to himself. I often wondered if all the petty conflicts, the grumbling, and the spats with HR, were necessary to bolster his sense of separateness. To feed some kind of self-validation and exorcise old pains.

9

When Valeria told me I was to attend a local conference on *HR Challenges in the New Century* I was dismayed.

"Who decided that?"

"Mr. Ivanov thinks it'll help you understand our environment. You'll go with Grishin and Kolbakov. It's a chance to hear about hot problems."

Hot problems?

"It would be more helpful" I said, "if Ivanov would bother to have a meeting with me."

Valeria said nothing.

But it was a sensible idea, which I should have willingly embraced. The conference prospectus however was intimidating – entirely in Russian, indicating a purely domestic event at which I could not expect the convenience of simultaneous interpretation. In modern Moscow there are hundreds of conferences every week, addressing the needs of an international business audience. Many provide a translation service – at least into English. This would not be one of them.

"But how will I understand?" I remonstrated. "I can't possibly go! It'll be a waste of time."

Valeria was unimpressed. She looked at me with disdain, as if I were a schoolboy pitching to skip lessons.

"You'll take your own translator of course! Sit at the back and he'll whisper everything to you."

I didn't mention that besides the language issue, the agenda itself was less than enticing: *Implications of Pensions Reform*, *Trends in Performance Evaluation*, and such-like. Standard HR stuff, but hardly a promise of a riveting experience.

"Where is it?"

She mentioned a prestigious business institute in central Moscow, of which at the time I'd never heard.

"It's very famous!" she said.

The conference took place in its main lecture theatre, where the heavy, formal decor declared its Soviet origins – dark wood panelling, marble pillars framing the stage, hammer and sickle motifs in the cornicing. And a two-pronged flagpole-holder behind the lectern, displaying both the white, blue, and red flag of the Russian Federation, and another with a complicated motif that was presumably the institute's own crest. The room was almost full, but we found space at the back, and I managed to secure an empty seat to the side of Grishin and Kolbakov, where Dmitri's commentary would not disturb the others.

The event itself confounded my expectations. Instead of a tedious slog, it was stimulating and thought-provoking. The speakers intelligent and articulate. The highlight was a lecture by a professor of Social Policy on the nation's demographic crisis, which drew my attention for the first time to a critical issue facing modern Russia – population decline.

"It's easy to imagine" the professor said in his opening remarks, "when we're choking in traffic, or squashed like sardines on the metro, that if there's a demographic crisis in our country today it's overpopulation. Moscow's burgeoning around us! But Moscow isn't Russia – and in most of the country the opposite's true. We're rapidly losing our people."

Over huge areas of the Russian landmass, he told us, physical evidence of decline was unmistakable. He spoke of empty countryside and dying villages, of ruined industry and abandoned cities. He cited well-known examples: Soviet-era population centres that became causes célèbre – cities in the far east of Siberia, and on the edge of the Arctic circle, now left to rot back into the land. These were places TV film crews repeatedly selected for evocative footage of post-communist decay. But he cautioned against thinking such scenes were simply about population *movement* – a retreat of settlers back to the Russian heartland. Or that Russia's rural depopulation was part of the worldwide drift from the land to the city. For sure, the collapse of collective farming had contributed, but what was happening was a genuine and enormous *loss* of population.

Like all academics the professor relished his statistics.

"In the last twenty years," he said "eleven thousand villages have disappeared from the map. Scarcely believable! Another thirteen thousand that officially exist have no inhabitants. At the same time, we've lost *two hundred and ninety* cities! *What's happening to our country?*"

"Is that true?" I whispered to Dmitri while the professor paused for breath. "So many ghost towns?"

"Probably."

The professor continued with more figures which – in one version or another – I heard quoted time and again during my years in Moscow. The demographic challenge was a staple of Russian newspaper columns and TV news shows. The key point was a population decline of around 700,000 a year. From 148 million in the early 1990s, to 142 million a decade later. On current trends, the professor warned, it would be less than 100 million by 2050.

"1991 was our high-water mark," he said. "Never again will there be as many Russians. It's tragic – and threatens the nation and the state."

An HR conference, he conceded, wasn't the place to discuss national security. But the strategic implications of depopulation worried the Kremlin, as swathes of territory, especially in the Far East, was left unoccupied and undefended. (A frightening prospect for European Russians, who for centuries have feared invasion from the east.) But it was the business consequences that concerned the professor. Population decline meant a reduced skills base, labour shortages, falling demand, economic stagnation and social disruption. Effective HR management however could help mitigate the crisis.

"We're shrinking faster than every other European country," he continued. "*Why?* Put simply – more Russians are dying than being born. The birth rate's down and the death rate's up. Abortions, fertility problems, and social attitudes have cut births. Just like Westerners, middle class Russians delay starting families until they finish their education and progress their careers. At the bottom of society, poverty, insecurity and poor housing are equally powerful deterrents."

The mortality rate was even more troubling.

"*We die earlier than all other Europeans,*" the professor said. "Life expectancy for a Russian man's fifty-seven. In Sweden it's 78. Heart attacks and cancers are the main killers – like most Western countries. But they strike earlier here. Germans start having heart attacks at seventy-five, Russians at fifty-five."

The professor's thesis was that economic and social dislocation following the Soviet collapse directly impacted birth and death rates. Low wages, employment insecurity, poor working conditions, inadequate health provision, all played their part.

"Life's harsh for working people. They're stressed and exhausted, so they drink and smoke themselves to death. Labour shotages are on the way," he warned. "So, we can't afford to neglect our human resources. In particular, we must get more of our young men working. Five million of them – out of a population of 20 million – are excluded from the labour market because they're in prison, are alcoholics or drug addicts."

A poor managerial culture in Russian companies burned workers out, or casually discarded them.

"How many companies show any interest in their welfare? Or recognise that treating people well makes them more productive? It's no accident the post of Personnel or HR Manager wasn't even officially recognised here until the year 2000."

The professor paused, and very deliberately sipped from a glass of water resting on the lectern. "*So – what's to be done?*"

His solution was a shopping list of reforms most mainstream European social democrats would endorse. From employers: improved pay and conditions, more supportive management, and increased investment in staff retention and training. From the government: better health provision, crackdowns on alcohol and cigarettes, improved education and social provision.

At the end of the conference, I offered Dmitri a lift, and in the car asked his opinion of the demography lecture. He'd been forced to pay closer attention than anyone else in the room. Aware Nikolai had little English, he was willing to talk openly.

"It was interesting," he said, "but one-sided. Those old communists love to criticise. But ignore all the Soviet problems."

"The professor's an old communist?"

"Can't you tell? The stuff about working conditions and dying of stress. Maybe it's true – but it was also true in the Soviet Union. My father worked on the railways and my uncle in a shirt factory. They had job security – of a kind. If they kept on the right side of the party snitches and said the right things. Did you notice the professor said nothing about *freedom* in the workplace? These academics idealise Soviet times – because they had it good then. They were respected – in secure jobs with privileges. Now they've to fight in the market like ordinary workers, and they don't like it. That talk about alcoholism – what's new? Everybody was drunk in the Soviet Union because life was so boring. And dying young? You were *expected* to die early then. It was a patriotic duty. The communists didn't want old people. They were *building socialism*" – he said it with a sarcastic edge – "so only the productive mattered. If you stayed around too long you were a burden."

Soviet workers, Dmitri argued, were burned-out by 60 and ready to drop dead. Especially manual workers. They weren't supposed to actually retire. They weren't needed or wanted. "People knew it. So they just died."

This surely contained a truth. When societies place no value on the elderly, it must affect their will to live.

Dmitri's analysis was as acute as the professor's, and he relished sharing it. His openness surprised me. Russians are unpredictable in what they'll reveal. Many clam up in the presence of foreigners, conditioned by decades of Soviet propaganda that portrayed us as spies and saboteurs. Others are simply reticent to air difficult issues in front of strangers. Yet there are some who will grumble openly to foreigners, while hesitating to confide in fellow Russians. A reminder that denunciation and betrayal of friends and neighbours was an inescapable fact of Soviet life.

"The government *is* trying to reverse population decline," Dmitri went on, "Giving women special payments to have more kids. And encouraging Russians abroad to come home. But the money's too low."

The maternity payments offered for second children were modest, an incentive only for poor families. At the same time, a Kremlin immigration initiative sought to lure back to Russia ethnic Russians left behind in places like Kazakhstan, Uzbekistan, and the Ukraine after communism collapsed. The target was a million migrants, but again Dmitri was sceptical.

"A few may come. But the resettlement compensation's not enough for life in Moscow or St. Petersburg. And nobody wants to live in a small, dying town in the countryside."

10

Almost five months after my arrival in Moscow I finally got my meeting with Mr. Ivanov, our President. The call came unexpectedly.

"Marina says Mr. Ivanov invites you to his office at 10 o'clock," Valeria told me.

"Today? That's less than an hour. You'd better ask Dmitri to meet me up there."

I hastily began to marshal my thoughts. After waiting so long, issues which had seemed important early on were no longer at the front of my mind. In the absence of any direction from above, I had simply got on with the job as I thought fit. The HR team had its own long-standing patterns of activity anyway and needed little input from me on routine matters. I regularly signed documents, offered advice, and endorsed decisions as necessary – but had embarked on no significant new initiatives.

Ivanov was frequently away from the office on overseas business trips. He would make time intermittently to chair our Weekly Management Meetings, but despite his occasional presence I had yet to have a conversation with him about his expectations for HR. He showed little appetite for mundane, everyday business, and typically rushed briskly and impatiently through our meetings, his eye clearly on the clock. His main focus was on high-level financial matters, and anything else struggled to keep his attention. In almost direct contrast, his deputy Mr Pryadkin ran the meetings in his absence, with such pedantic attention to detail that the substance of issues often got lost in a morass of minutiae. An old-style Soviet manager, he was more comfortable hiding in the undergrowth than taking decisions or pursuing clarity. Either way, I had yet to discover what the company wanted of its HR function – and more importantly – of its HR Manager. Maybe I would now get some indication.

The Presidential Suite was at the top of the building, accessed by its own separate lift. Visitors arriving on the floor were confronted by a glass security wall, behind which two armed guards were permanently stationed. Dmitri was waiting beside the glass entry door.

"What do we do?" I said.

"Hold our passes against the card reader and press the bell."

This summoned a guard, who checked our names against a printed list before opening the door. He spoke briefly with Dmitri, at the same time shaking his head.

"What did he say?" I asked.

"That *you* are welcome, but I can't come in. The President wants to use his own translator. I'm not required."

He said this with some relief, but as he withdrew raised an eyebrow and added: "Good luck!"

It was a touch of wry humour. Ivanov did not have a good reputation amongst his Russian staff. He was autocratic and difficult to work with, and although respected as an astute businessman, his short temper and bullying manner inspired fear and dislike. On several occasions I saw him erupt in anger when someone in a meeting failed to answer a question satisfactorily. Apart from his closest associates, most employees therefore went to great lengths to avoid dealing with him in person.

Like many of the oligarchs who rose to the heights of Russian business post communism, Ivanov was not a typical Soviet manager. He was a youngish man who would just have entered his twenties when the USSR collapsed. When he left university, instead of following the usual bureaucratic path to a job in some state industry, he had immediately started his own business. Reputedly his first venture had been trading furs in the provinces, after which he went on to cobble together various unrelated enterprises into a significant company.

To thrive in the New Russia, education and intelligence were not enough, and besides energy and entrepreneurial talent, Ivanov must also have possessed fair measures of guile, aggression and ruthlessness. These were not on regular display – at least to me – but I fancied the elaborate security hinted at something dark and guilty about our President. As well as the uniformed guards at his office door, a contingent of armed, plain-clothed bodyguards (reputedly ex FSB men) protected him wherever he went – even within the building. When he visited a meeting room, or the Executive Dining Room, one or two would station themselves outside, and when he travelled it was in a bulletproof Mercedes with darkened windows, tailed always by an armoured Land Cruiser carrying reinforcements. A mini motorcade – almost like a real president.

Watching all this, I often thought: *Who's after you? What have you done?*

Yet my melodramatic assumption was not necessarily correct, as it's common for Russian businessmen, fearful of being kidnapped for ransom, to have heavy security. During the wild 1990s kidnapping, sometimes spilling over into murder, was a regular occurrence in Moscow, and remains a genuine, if lesser, threat today.

Ivanov's translator was already in his office when I arrived. Borisov supported the President alone, and never took on work for the rest of the organisation. He was known to handle his most sensitive and confidential material, and I wondered if his presence meant something delicate would be discussed. I was also braced for a characteristically dogmatic performance from Ivanov – to receive an emphatic set of non-negotiable commands. However, the conversation began reasonably enough.

"You must have settled in," Borisov said, translating Ivanov. "So, what do you think of our company? Is it as you expected?"

My response was diplomatic and positive, and I added that I'd arrived with an open mind and no particular expectations.

"Now you've had time to see how we work" Borisov went on, "what needs to change?"

I'd gradually been drawn into the activities of the wider organisation beyond HR, engaging with Russian managers and staff in other departments, and had identified a host of flaws common in badly run companies everywhere. But I was unsure what to tell the President. A full account might seem overly critical and trigger a defensiveness that resulted in opposition to any improvements. How would he react to hearing we were hugely over-staffed? That most employees were under-skilled for their jobs, routinely avoided risks and shirked responsibility? That his managers bullied their subordinates? And that almost everybody claimed credit for the work of others, while avoiding blame for their own errors?

I decided to focus on two indisputable Soviet legacies that blighted the company: policies and systems were hopelessly convoluted and wasteful; and employees fixated on processes rather than results.

The President nodded solemnly at these.

"Yes, yes! That's true." he said via Borisov. "But is it all?"

"No – there are many other issues. Behavioural and structural. But these two are key. If we tackle them first, I think we'll solve the others more easily."

Surprisingly, Ivanov didn't ask for more detail. Generalities were enough for the moment.

"OK," he said. "Now you must prepare an improvement plan."

He spoke for a moment directly to Borisov, who in turn addressed me.

"Mr. Ivanov wants to talk about a very sensitive matter," Borisov said. "He believes many of our Russian staff are lazy and not so competent. He would like your opinion."

It was an awkward question and I hesitated to answer too bluntly.

"It's true in most companies," I said. "So probably we have some employees like that here."

The time lags inherent in face-to-face translation grant moments of thinking time, and as Borisov spoke I tried to read Ivanov's reaction. A frown told me that the President had hoped for something meatier.

"In particular, Mr. Ivanov wonders if you have identified any of these people."

"Not yet," I said, evading the invitation to snitch. "I can see there are issues in general. But -" And I explained that for a foreigner, language and cultural factors made accurate judgements at the individual level a problem.

"*However*," I continued, "it's not difficult to find out. We could run an assessment exercise to identify strengths and weaknesses. It's normal practice in Western companies. A diagnostic test of some kind."

The President at once seemed more attentive. He nodded his head again – but this time vigorously. I'd unwittingly pressed the correct button. The reference to Western practice had maybe done the trick.

"That's exactly what Mr. Ivanov is looking for," Borisov said. "International standards! It's why you are here. You must help the company implement *International Standards*."

The phrase would become a mantra for the rest of my time in Moscow. Repeatedly invoked as a key focus for the HR department.

As the President closed our meeting his final remarks underlined the point.

"Your plan should be based on international standards," Borisov translated. "And should *start* with an assessment of all our employees."

I left the audience with mixed feelings. The President's general expectations were clear – at a high level. But critically short on detail. What exactly were *International Standards*? And who set them? However, I interpreted the aspiration as a push for modernisation and simplification – with which I wholeheartedly agreed. At the same time, I reproached myself for mentioning staff assessment. *What have I started here?* I asked myself with dismay. This would surely freak everybody out.

11

Eager for ideas for my weekend exploration, I asked Valeria for suggestions.

"Go to Ismailova Market," she said. "Foreigners love it. You won't be disappointed."

It was good advice. Of all the places I went to during my four years in Moscow, Ismailova Market was the one that best repaid repeated visits, and I returned regularly to look, rummage and buy. The journey itself was an education. The market is a thirty-five-minute metro ride on the Arbatsko-Pokroyskaya (dark blue) line from central Moscow to the city's northeastern suburbs. The first time I had difficulty finding my bearings. My guidebook advised disembarking at *Ismailovsky Park Station*, but this was nowhere to be found on the metro map displayed on the train. It turned out that the book, published in the early 2000s, was out-of-date, and the name had been changed in 2005 to *Partisanskaya*, in commemoration of the partisans who fought the Nazis in World War II.

The station itself is a curiosity, and worth a visit in its own right. At a distance of sixty years, its new name is of course a political gesture – a reminder to contemporary Russians of their history – designed to foster patriotism and national solidarity. The statues which decorate the station reinforce the theme – larger-than-life size bronzes depicting guerrilla fighters. At the top of the stairway leading to the tracks is a tableau of three figures dressed as irregulars. They are idealised, depicted in heroic poses, and deliberately selected to represent diversity – age and youth, male and female. The central figure, a robust elderly man, stands on a rock with his right arm raised in warning, while his left cradles a machine gun. At his side a boy crouches, rifle in hand, staring vigilantly ahead. On the other flank a grim-faced babushka stands erect and defiant, also clutching a machine gun. Their faces, steadfast and resolute, speak of courage and determination, encapsulating the virtues the authorities want to celebrate in those who defended their homeland. On the station platforms themselves, similar figures guard the marble columns that support the roof: a bearded old man in a peasant's coat, holding a stick; a youth in a peasant's blouse with a rifle slung over his shoulder.

Partisanskaya Station was opened during the war and is unique in Moscow for its three-track rail line. Officially this extra track was built to handle crowds travelling to a nearby stadium – which was never completed due to the hostilities. It's widely believed however that it was really an escape route from central Moscow for Stalin and the Soviet leadership. As the Germans were expected to invade from the West, the government planned to relocate east if the city fell. Although never officially admitted, a network of secret underground lines was constructed connecting the Kremlin with various railroads leading east. The fact Stalin's wartime bunker is also in the Ismailova area underscores the planning. According to the official metro system guide, only two of the station's tracks are used now. But this is incorrect. On several visits to the market, I saw all three in action.

Ismailova Market is really a group of separate markets that converge at the edges. One offers clothes and accessories – much of it fake designer stuff. It's a ramshackle arrangement of narrow lanes running between rows of stalls, and makeshift shops built of wood and canvas. The ground underfoot is muddy, but a rickety roof protects the merchandise. The dark, cramped spaces, and the fact that bargaining is expected, gives the area an Asian feel. And the majority of the stallholders are not Russians, but immigrants from the Caucasus. On sale are the same cheap, mass-produced clothes and shoes found in street-markets worldwide, although better-quality leather and fur items are also available. Many of these are not much different from articles selling for three or four times the price in the city's fancy malls.

Another market sells food, but the most interesting one is the elaborate souvenir and antiques market housed within the *Ismailovo Kremlin*, a purpose-built wooden replica of a medieval fortress. This is primarily targeted at tourists and contains several small museums and minor attractions. The Russian Vodka Museum and the *Kolobok* café are both worth visits. The former shows the history of vodka production in Russia, with a series of exhibits on the manufacturing process, and features a huge display of antique bottles and advertising material illustrating vodka's central role in Russian life over the years. The entry fee includes the cost of a shot, administered just before you exit. There's also the opportunity to buy a personalised bottle of vodka, with your face on the label. A fairground style head-through-the-hole photographic booth transfers your image on to a specially designed label decorated with gold medals. It's then stuck on a half-litre bottle of a decent, standard vodka.

The *Kolobok* is a tiny café, whose interior walls are painted with scenes from the famous Russian folk tale of the same name. A kolobok is a round bread roll, and the story tells of an old couple who bake one with their last remaining flour, only for it to come alive and run away. It's a Russian version of *The Gingerbread Man,* and the roll's further adventures feature its efforts at avoiding animals wanting to eat it. The Kolobok story is a common motif in Russian folk art, and illustrations can be found on many items on sale in the market itself. When my wife later joined me in Moscow, she bought an expensive hand-painted set of nesting dolls decorated with scenes from the tale. The large outer doll shows the old man with the kolobok, the next doll inside is his wife, struggling to restrain the roll as it pulls to escape, while the remaining ones have a fox and other animals snapping at its heels. Nestling at the very heart of the set, the smallest doll, no bigger than a pebble and painted bread-yellow, is the kolobok itself.

The market area is on two levels. The ground level features souvenirs of all kinds, and the upper one a mix of bric-a-brac, antiques, flea-market junk and original artwork. There's so much on offer, so much variety, that it's impossible to do justice to Ismailova in one visit. During my Moscow years I returned again and again, and almost always discovered something new and interesting – buying a haphazard jumble of objects to clutter my house. But the market's much more than a grand rummage sale; it opens a window on Russia's 20th century history, with evocative reminders of the past in its eclectic collection of artefacts. It lacks the coherence of a museum display, but in many ways tells as much. The relics on sale – prized or neglected, expensively priced or available for a few roubles – give their own verdicts on history. Sometimes what they reveal is so obvious it seems clichéd – like the bronze bust of Stalin I spotted on an antiques stall during my first visit. Too big and heavy for a mantelpiece, it had presumably once rested on a plinth in some public building, but now collected dust alongside an assortment of old cameras, china ornaments, a wind-up record player and a couple of battered concertinas. On other occasions over the next few years, I saw the same bust sporting a wartime tin-hat and a sailor's beret. On my final tour of the market, just before I left Moscow, it was still there on the same stall, unsold, keeping company with a motley collection of other displaced objects. So much for the glory of the USSR. Other mementos of once-prominent Soviet personalities were common at Ismailova, although most were on a smaller scale, intended from the start as souvenirs: porcelain figurines, metal statuettes, plates and mugs decorated with portraits of Stalin, Marshal Zhukov and Felix Dzerzhinsky. Unsurprisingly, Lenin memorabilia is the most plentiful – and the most tacky. The reputations of Stalin and the others rose and fell during the communist period, but Lenin's remained constant throughout, and in Soviet souvenir shops during the 1970s and 80s his likeness was a staple for *Intourist* visitors seeking something 'authentic' to take home from their Russian holiday. My mother had a plastic-and-tin Lenin relief, purchased in the summer of 1979 from the Rossiya Hotel's gift shop.

The quality of Late-Soviet Lenin merchandise was variable, and like tourist-tat the world over has not worn well. The same is less true of mementos of other Soviet leaders. These were generally better made, older products from a time when the heroes in question still shone brightly, and there was propaganda value in well-crafted representations. Their relegation to market stalls marked their current disfavour, but as negative political associations fade they will doubtless become fashionable again as art-works or historical relics. Indeed, there were signs of this already happening. Stalin's portrait might be banished from the walls of public buildings, but his image decorated the face of a range of metal pocket-watches. Carefully displayed alongside old clocks and watches, at first glance they seemed genuine Stalin-era mementoes. (A recently discovered, mint-condition cache? Had it suddenly become unsaleable on the dictator's death, and languished unseen for years?)

"Is this real?" I asked a stall holder.

"Yes real. Very good time!" He wound the handle and held the watch to my ear to prove it actually ticked.

"But is it old? Original?"

He shrugged. "Maybe!"

Maybe? Maybe meant no – and that a factory somewhere was churning them out as we spoke. It was a straw in the wind, not necessarily of Stalin's rehabilitation, but of his irrelevance. Soviet kitsch was now a retro fashion statement. The monster was becoming a trendy curiosity. The same was true of other souvenirs appearing on the stalls. During the four years I visited, Felix Dzerzhinsky statuettes became suspiciously plentiful. Cast in black metal – but without the patina of the genuinely old.

Ismailova of course was not about high-end *objets d'art*. Those found their way to antique and fine art showrooms in central Moscow. The market dealt in everyday objects from the past: old household articles, ornaments, faded artwork, and all kinds of curiosities that were yet to metamorphose from junk into collectables, or even treasures. Military relics were particularly plentiful: everything from uniforms, badges and decorations, to gas masks, army boots and firearms. There were soldiers' tunics with Red Army insignia still intact, sailors' striped vests and berets, officers' caps, Nazi tin-helmets, and hanging perennially on the side of one stall, a white camouflage suit of the kind worn by troops who fight on skis. There were defused hand-grenades, and brass shells in many sizes, including some huge ones for heavy artillery.

You could buy an old Kalashnikov (decommissioned presumably – although it would be unwise to take this as certain), pistols in their original leather holsters, daggers, gunsights and all kinds of paraphernalia for warfare. Most were old, with claims to being historical – WWII artefacts predominated. But there were also newish items, less likely to have combat credentials. Many had probably been stolen from some military arsenal or sold-off by serving soldiers needing cash.

English-speaking expatriates were regular customers at the stalls selling CDs and DVDs. For less than the price of two legal discs, they could have 15 – 20 good-quality pirated copies of recently released Hollywood movies. Amongst the contingent of specialist vendors that catered for hobbyists likes coin and stamp collectors, I found the dealers in Soviet propaganda posters the most interesting. Some stocked only reproductions, focusing on examples with the greatest tourist appeal – the most obviously iconic or decorative. But a few were genuine experts and bought and sold vintage posters from throughout the Soviet period. Rare, original posters are expensive today, and a topic for serious academic study.

Several stalls offered handcrafts from different parts of the former Soviet Union – brightly coloured glazed pottery from Uzbekistan, including tiny porcelain figurines of characters in ethnic dress. Cheap but nice. Russian folk-art was plentiful – at fractions of the costs in the fancy tourist shops in the city centre. Wood carvings of all kinds of animals. Hand-decorated lacquer boxes featuring traditional designs. I once bought two carved figurines of bears – both walking upright – and dressed in archaic human costumes that talented artists had meticulously painted on their wooden bodies. One stands clutching a large salmon, the other strides forward, staff in hand.

My wife became interested in matruskaya, the iconic nesting dolls that have become a symbol of Russia and started a small collection. Her first purchases were run-of-the mill machine-printed dolls of the kind on sale at every tourist outlet, but increasingly she bought selectively, favouring hand-painted pieces illustrated by individual artists. She also spent time talking with stall holders, many of whom were experts on the dolls, and happy to share their knowledge with interested customers. These artist-created dolls are a relatively new phenomenon. In Soviet times the state controlled all matruskaya production and enforced common standards of decoration which precluded any personal expression. Most dolls were relatively plain, featuring women ornamented with the same recurring motifs: flowers, aprons and scarves. Soviet dolls are not easy to get now. Conventional souvenir shops offer only modern versions, and for older examples it's necessary to scour flea markets or the shelves of specialist dealers. Although matruskaya are considered traditionally Russian, they originated in Japan, and their association with Russia is relatively recent. They started to be made in the late 1890s, when local craftsmen in the town of Sergiev Posad, 50 km north of Moscow, copied a doll brought by a visiting Japanese merchant. In Tzarist times the city and surrounding area was Russia's major woodworking and toy manufacturing centre, and the matruskaya provided a remarkably successful addition to their catalogue. Production today differs little from a century ago. Wooden blanks are cut from birch wood, or for the finest dolls, the wood of linden trees, then supplied to a variety of outlets for decoration. Cheap dolls have their designs applied by factory printing, often in Soviet-era factories that are still in operation.

With doll-makers now free to express themselves as they wish, a whole subculture has emerged of independent artists and designers devoted to Matruskaya. One striking development is that modern illustrators paint not just single characters, but whole scenes on each doll. These are often elaborately detailed and range from folk tales to copies of classical paintings. At the lower end of the market there are images from pop culture, including portraits of rock stars, footballers and politicians – as well as some ingeniously bawdy creations that would never have been tolerated under the Soviets. In Ismailova market several artists had their own stalls, where they took commissions to paint portraits on dolls to order. Tourists who feel artistic can also buy wooden blanks in various shapes and sizes, to decorate themselves.

On my first visit I spotted near the market entrance, a stall selling framed photographs. Not tourist views, but self-consciously arty shots – taken in monochrome – each signed and dated on the back by the artist. They were all from the early 1990s and captured a series of quirky Moscow scenes from the immediate post-Soviet years. The old lady in charge of the display proudly told me in English that the photographer was her son.

"He has a good eye," I said – and meant it.

I decided to buy some, and selected as my first a scene at a bus shelter. A group of babushkas are sitting in a row, waiting, their shopping bags resting in front of them. Beside them, on the shelter's advertising panel, there's a head-and-shoulders portrait of a fashion-model publicising a magazine. The contrast is neither subtle nor original: glamour and modernity versus shabbiness and age. The model bites her nails and casts seductive eyes at the viewer; the old women, in their lumpy winter coats, cast their eyes in the direction of the next bus. Yet it's an interesting image, and if the photographer intends any comment, it's affectionate. My second choice was another street scene – a carefully composed shot of an old Lada parked outside a scruffy shop. The faded sign, which simply says *Magazin* (shop), tells us it's a Soviet relic. It's winter and the road's a smear of dirty snow. A scrawny dog skulks past on the pavement, completing a fine portrait of neglect and decay.

When I pointed to my third choice the stall-holder nodded her head enthusiastically.

"*Yes! Yes!*" she said. "That one's special. Historical. You'll never see that now."

It was a shot of Red Square, a close-up of a group of stray dogs in the foreground – St Basil's Cathedral and the Kremlin walls in the distance. A scene that spoke of civic neglect at what had once been the heart of the Soviet empire.

"I like it too," I said. "Maybe the most. Why won't you see it now?"

"Our government will not allow it. Dogs in Red Square? That was when things were difficult in Russia. Now they'll move them."

I was drawn to these three pictures because they marked changing times. They were images from the early Yeltsin era. And I didn't quarrel with the old lady, although I knew she was wrong about the dogs being banished. I often spotted strays wandering in the Square, asleep against the parapet walls of St Basil's Cathedral, or sniffing one another on the pavement outside the GUM department store – with neither a guardsman nor a policeman in pursuit.

12

Stray dogs are indeed a visible problem throughout the city, and Muscovites regard them with ambivalence. Official estimates put the number at over 50,000, and they are unmissable in parks, squares, patches of waste ground, the courtyards of apartment blocks, outside metro stations, and in the areas around food kiosks. Two mangy specimens inhabited the yard behind my flat, routinely scavenging through the debris that fell from our rubbish skip and sleeping next to the ducting where our hot water supply-pipe entered the building. Although I never personally witnessed anything worse than snarling, or an occasional half-hearted fight, strays are officially regarded as a serious nuisance, a health hazard and a danger to the public. Reported dog attacks on Muscovites number around sixty a day, and a third are serious enough to require hospitalisation. The threat of rabies means that 90% of victims also need painful inoculations.

During Soviet times homeless dogs were usually shot, but pressure from animal rights groups ended this policy in 2002, and their numbers have since grown unchecked. Instead of execution the authorities initiated a project to prevent them breeding. Fifteen huge holding pens with a total capacity of 30,000 dogs were built, and a neutering programme begun. Critics complained that the $64m cost was ridiculously over the top, and that the money would have been better spent improving life for the city's human inhabitants – pointing out that London for example, manages the problem with a single shelter with capacity for 700 dogs.

While many Russians view the dogs with disgust, others are sympathetic, even protective, and go out of their way to contribute to their welfare. Despite some scary statistics, strays are generally docile and cause little real trouble. Most are not hungry, and are rarely seen fighting over scarps or stealing food, as legions of well-wishers ensure they are fed. During my time in the city a high-profile group of American expat wives ran a charity to help them. Incidents of cruelty however often provoke public outrage, and the press regularly reports on punishments meted out by the courts to individuals who mistreat strays. In the entrance hall of Mendeleyevskaya metro station there's a bronze statue of a dog called Boy that once lived in the station for three years and became a pet of metro workers. Reputedly it's the world's first monument to a homeless dog, and its inscription reads: *Dedicated to humane attitudes to stray animals*. It was erected by station officials after Boy was stabbed to death in one of the station's passageways, by a fashion model whose pet he had attacked. Following the killing the model was committed to a mental hospital.

Yet despite sentimentality towards stray dogs, there's little general concern about animal rights or welfare in Russia. Campaigns of the kind regularly seen in the West are rare, although not unknown. It's not that Russians are unkind, just that with daily life a struggle for millions, they have more pressing personal matters to worry about. It's also true that social mores lag decades behind Europe or the USA. Just as Russian attitudes to race or sexuality scandalise Western liberal opinion, so the treatment of animals routinely shocks enlightened visitors who encounter them in situations that would elsewhere attract accusations of cruelty, exploitation or simply tastelessness. In Manezhnaya Square, on a prime pitch between the statue of Marshall Zhukov and the archway leading into Red Square, photographers regularly badger tourists to have their pictures taken with their cute props – monkeys dressed in human clothes. A common enough sight in the West a generation ago, and certainly mild on any scale of abuse. Is it cruel at all? Or even demeaning? Is it merely Western sentimentality to project human values on to animals – including, ludicrously, a human sense of shame? For the average Russian such questions simply don't arise. Their response is straightforward: performing monkeys are amusing entertainment. End of debate. Only cranks complain. Enjoy the show!

Similarly, just outside the entrance to Ismailova market, on a cramped, muddy lot behind iron railings, there's a wooden shack, a couple of big logs with a ladder set across them, and a wooden see-saw. It's a tiny showground, where a group of four bears perform for market customers. Their act is rudimentary. They stand on two legs, clamber over the ladder, take turns on the seesaw, and allow their keeper to hug them. Occasionally, the keeper tugs on the chains attached to their collars, and they launch briefly into a dance of sorts. It's a cue for the keeper to rattle his collecting plate and hold it through the railings, entreating visitors taking photographs to contribute towards the bears' upkeep. Cruel? Degrading? I thought not. The bears looked healthy and happy. I never once saw them beaten. In any case they were big and strong, easily capable of tearing a man apart had they wished.

At least the railings around the bears' enclosure kept them separate from the public, but other Moscow animal shows had no such safeguards, and in defiance of common sense and all normal health and safety precautions, exposed visitors to ridiculous risks.

My strongest memory of a visit to Gorky Park in 2007 is of the big cats – leopards, panthers and even a sleepy tiger – being casually allowed to mingle with the public, as if they were poodles. On a patch of open grass opposite the park's fairground-stalls half a dozen animal-handlers displayed their charges and invited visitors to pay a few roubles for a photo-shoot.

"He is not dangerous!" a man with a leopard on a lead told me in English. "Come – you can touch him."

The animal seemed docile enough, but I demurred and backed away. Like the others lolling around the area, it must surely have been heavily sedated. But what quantity of drugs can make a wild animal safe? Safe enough to lie for hours in the sun uncaged? For toddlers to stroke its fur and shout in its ears? No wonder Russia's called the *land of the avoidable accident*.

Equally scary were the animals at the *Nikulin Circus* on Tsvetnoy Boulevard. Dating from the 1880s, the venue is an indoor amphitheatre rather than a canvas big-top. Internally it's a sophisticated, purpose-built space, with a customary show-ring and tiered seating, giving it the feel of a traditional circus. During performances dangerous animals were contained within cages in the ring, but remarkably, in the building's entrance hall, near the snack bar, souvenir shop, and public toilets, there was a roped-off area where children could pose for photographs with tigers and other animals. Again – no safety precautions. Presumably, like their Gorki park counterparts, the handlers relied on drugs. In the case of the circus, concerned Muscovites protested, and along with animal welfare activists and child safety campaigners, called for the photographic sessions to be banned. The circus proprietors however routinely denied there was any real danger – or that any of the animals were ever drugged.

Against this background, I witnessed a couple of small protests on behalf of animal welfare close to my apartment. The first was a demonstration that took place on the corner in Pushkin Square. A group of young activists – men and women – had assembled outside the Benetton store and, taking advantage of the warm summer weather began removing their clothes to publicise their cause. Standing naked, they then proceeded to cover themselves in body paint, while posing for press photographs. A curious traffic cop looked on, but did not interfere, and a spokesman announced that their purpose was to draw consumers' attention to the use of Australian wool in Benetton products. This, they claimed, is obtained by a cruel process called mulesing, which involves shearing the skin from lambs without the use of anaesthetic. Having made this point the protestors quickly dressed again and disappeared.

Some weeks later, just across the road from Benetton, at the *Café Pushkin* corner of Tverskoi Boulevard, an animal-rights activist handed me a leaflet. It advised that to draw attention to the torture and murder of animals, a demonstration would be held on the same spot the following morning. All Muscovites were invited to attend. It was a Saturday, and hoping for a repeat of the Benetton performance, I strolled over to the boulevard at the time specified on the leaflet. Despite the general invite I found no protesting crowd – but a group of no more than six or seven protesters who held up placards for the inspection of a single reporter and his photographer. I sidled over and listened while their leader, a tall, severe lady in black clothes, made a very brief speech. As far as I understood her Russian, the protest that day was to take the form of a funeral for a murdered animal. She gestured dramatically towards the ground, where a hole had already been scraped in the boulevard's earthen path. Another lady then opened a plastic bag and produced a fur coat which she slowly and ceremonially placed in the hole. It did indeed look a sorry sight – more moth-eaten though, than tortured. The reporter made some notes, the photographer took a couple of shots, the coat was returned to the bag, earth kicked back in the hole, and everyone went on their way.

***

The companionship of a shared language saw John Morrison and Norman regularly drift into my office mid-morning to swap company gossip over coffee, and mourn the trials of daily life. It soon became a habit, and as the new boy in town I found these experienced Moscow hands educational. Their personalities were very different, but they had key assets in common – Russian wives – who provided insights into local society denied to other foreigners. Morrison was discoursing on the latest febrile rumour passed on by his wife – that the government was covering up an accident at a nuclear power plant just outside Moscow, and that radiation was polluting the city (completely untrue) – when a disconsolate Norman joined us.

"You don't look too happy," Morrison said. "Something up?"

"Too right! Ina just called. Real bad news. There's a problem with the house."

"Your new house?"

"Yep. About as bad as it gets – seems the deal's off."

"What happened?"

"The local mayor's being an asshole. You know how it works – buy off officials to get things done. Our builder got approval for twelve houses – in exchange he was to give one to the mayor. But the mayor's reneged on the deal, and suddenly wants two. He's sticking – won't negotiate. At two the development's uneconomic, so the builder's pulling the plug."

"Can't you do anything?"

"No – nothing. It's between the builder and the mayor. And whatever other shadowy figures are in the background. We're just collateral damage. The only positive thing is we're getting our deposit back. It means we've wasted a year. And prices have gone up."

"Is there a Plan B?"

"Maybe. A long shot we passed on a while ago. But Ina won't be keen."

He broke off and we sat in silence for a few moments.

"I really thought we'd something going here," he said. "It's my own fault. I should've bought years ago when I had the chance."

"Hindsight's great," Morrison said. "The Moscow property market's a hellish rollercoaster. I nearly got burned a few times. Luckily, Olga got a title through her mother, so in the end we didn't need to bother."

Norman nodded sadly: "No such luck for Ina – she's from out of town. We'll need to sort something ourselves."

"What about Plan B?" I asked. "Can you share it?"

"Not yet," Norman said. "It's complicated – needs more thought."

Later that day Norman phoned me.

"About Plan B as you call it, I didn't want to speak in front of John. There *is* an opportunity, but it's tricky. What are you doing tonight? Fancy a beer and I'll show you? Ina's on an audit in Kaluga until Thursday."

My interest in Moscow property had waned since my own accommodation was settled, but I recognised Norman wanted to talk away his disappointment. So, after work we took the metro to Christy Prudy – the stop nearest the flat he currently rented.

Christy Prudy (literally Fresh Ponds) is one of central Moscow's prime residential districts. On the Boulevard ring, it's an attractive mix of good quality 19th century houses and apartments, clustered around a small lake, from which it takes its name. Public gardens border the lake, and a floating restaurant is moored at the water's edge. The overall ambience is quirky and attractive.

"That's it over there," Norman said, after we'd walked for about ten minutes along the boulevard. "Pretty close to where we're living at the moment."

He pointed to a handsome four-storey Victorian building on the other side of the street. Its ornate stucco walls were painted pastel green, and the entire ground floor was occupied by a branch of a commercial bank.

"The flat's on the top level – at the far end. That's the entrance at the left – down a passage to the back. I guess the door on the street used to be the way in, but it's the bank's now. Three bedrooms, a living room and a real big kitchen. Being on top's a bonus. It means you own the air space. That's important here – in case you ever want to build up."

"It looks brilliant," I said. "And what a location!"

"A lot needs done inside. It's real shabby – never been refurbished since it was built. It's the only reason we can afford it. The problem is – it's co-ownership. That's why we gave up before. There were three guys involved – but one wouldn't play ball."

Norman explained that the property, originally designed for a single family, had for the past eighty years been used as a communal apartment.

In the housing privatisations of the nineties, ownership generally passed to residents based on their Soviet-era registration papers, which specified where citizens could officially live – down to the precise address. (Permission to live in Moscow itself was tightly controlled, and highly prized.) Anyone legally resident in a property usually became its owner or part-owner – creating huge complications in cases of multi-ownership. Sometimes a tenant would buy out the others in a straightforward deal, but newspapers of the era reported innumerable frauds. Crooked tenants cheating others out of their shares. People made homeless after signing away their rights when drunk. Violent evictions. Locks changed. Death threats. And chancers who agreed to sell, took the money, blew it, then refused to move out.

"I guess when John said his wife got title somewhere," I said. "It's where her parents lived."

"Exactly! I don't know their details, but I'll bet it's where they were officially registered. Good luck to them," Norman said. "They're Muscovites of course. Ina's folks are provincials and couldn't even live here in Soviet times. They got title to a shack in some god forsaken village near Tomsk. It's worthless – so no inheritance for us."

"Are the same three guys still living here?"

"As far as we know. Last time two of the owners agreed to sell, but the third guy wouldn't budge. We tried to negotiate but he got real slippery. I don't know if he wanted a better deal, or just wanted to stay. In the end we walked away when we got the chance to build in Orlovka. We'll try another throw of the dice here – the location itself's worth it. Places like this are getting scarcer. Basically, only three kinds of folk can live inside the Garden Ring now. Foreigners like us, with employers paying the high rents. Rich Russians, who can afford the best and live anywhere they want. And the legacy types – like the guys here – who were in situ when the USSR collapsed. They're cashing in and moving away, so there's less and less ordinary people."

Norman pointed to the top far corner of the block.

"See that window – that's the bad guy's room. Legally he also owns a third share of the bathroom and the kitchen."

"Couldn't you buy out the other two – and just move in? Then get him out later on. Make life difficult for him?"

"We thought about that – very creatively. All the things we could do. But it's too risky – financially and personally. Anything could happen. Suppose he's violent, or has druggies or whores visiting? What if he *did* sell up – but not to us. To somebody real bad? Like the local mafia. Buying a place's expensive enough without risking all your savings. Back in the nineties you'd have got it real cheap. Property prices were low and I had the cash to buy something outright. But now we'll need a mortgage."

"Why didn't you?"

"Loads of reasons. Caution, foolishness. I wasn't married then – and didn't know how long I'd stick around in Moscow. I didn't see the boom in house prices coming. But mainly I got distracted by business – and even tried to dip my toes in the commercial property market."

Prior to joining our company Norman had worked, under the radar of officialdom, in an assortment of small Moscow businesses. Nothing criminal: a mail order bookshop, a shoe importer and an electrical goods retailer. Legitimate concerns that found a foreign accountant useful for dollar transactions and overseas transfers. Except that they rarely kept complete books, or met their taxes in full, and inevitably paid staff with brown envelopes of undeclared cash.

"They were all more lucrative than my job now," he said. "And that was years ago. But just like back home – you need a provable income to get a housing loan so I had to go legit."

He was in the same position as growing numbers of middle-class Muscovites who look to that Western staple – the mortgage – to bridge the gap between savings and the cost of a property. This conversation was the first time I'd heard him mention commercial property.

"I'd a notion to set up on my own," he said. "A consultancy serving businesses too small to do their own in-house accounting. Low level stuff. Payroll, invoice processing, that kind of thing. The plan was to hire half a dozen school-leavers to do the routine stuff. I'd oversee everything to make sure it was done right. But I couldn't get a deal on an office. There was a perfect place just off Triumfalnaya Square, across from the *American Bar & Grill*. One floor in an office block. The whole place had been empty for years. I managed to find the owner and tried to get a deal. We haggled for months but I couldn't get a result. He wanted some ridiculous rent and wouldn't move. Crazy – because he'd nothing coming in. Looking back, he'd either no intention of leasing it, or changed his mind during negotiations. It's a great site so maybe he'd other hopes and didn't want the inconvenience of tenants. Or maybe he was planning some speculation. Who knows? I wondered if he was the real owner – or just a front for somebody. The mafia? Maybe he just didn't have proper legal title. It used to be a government building, so you have to wonder how got it in the first place.

Anyway, it's a few years ago and it's still empty today. Nothing surprises me because Moscow's the world capital for crooked property deals."

This was undoubtedly true of the two decades that followed the collapse of communism. Scandals surrounding the privatisation of high-profile state businesses and assets made international news, but more troubling for ordinary Russians was widespread criminality in the domestic property market. Innumerable householders were wrongfully dispossessed, lives were destroyed, and insecurity and anxiety blighted Russian society. Experts in the subject identify three broad approaches crooks used to dishonestly acquire domestic properties – with hundreds of variations within each. The first involved initially getting access to a home semi-legitimately. Predators offered vulnerable householders generous personal loans, and when they struggled with repayments, demanded living space in the debtor's home as compensation. Then they registered themselves as residents at that address, acquiring as a result legal title to a share in the property. This could then be sold on at a huge profit or used as a springboard for a complete takeover of the home.

A second type of scam used fraudulent documents, and generally occured when householders moved, or exchanged apartments. In these circumstances two transactions were required: de-registration from the first property, and registration at the second. As the two procedures took place at different times, swindlers used the time-lag to steal titles from their victims. Typically, owners were asked to sign away their rights in return for a promise of similar ones in another property. But when the time came to register the second home, they discovered the promissory document was fraudulent, and they'd lost everything. Such a scam supplies the plot for A D Miller's *Snowdrops,* a novel about contemporary Moscow which was shortlisted for the 2011 Man Booker Prize.

The third method involved bureaucratic criminality, with crooked notaries, judges and registrars destroying, falsifying and forging records to steal properties directly from the state, or from the relatives of householders who have died.

"Aren't you worried you'll be scammed too?"

"Yes – there's a risk. It's why Ina's not keen to buy here in the centre. Too many dodgy characters involved with these old properties. But if we don't do something we'll never own a home. There's crookedness everywhere – witness our Orlovka debacle."

"And if you can't get this one?"

"Dead man's shoes maybe. It's risky and messy – but a lot of people do it. You find an old person with an apartment who's hard up – preferably someone with no family – and do a deal. Get it all drawn up legally. They get to stay where they are, and you pay them every month for as long as they live. Like a pension. When they die the apartment's yours."

"Suppose they live for years?"

"That's the risk. But lots of folk take it. It's a common arrangement. Some do it in good faith – others, well... You hear stories about unscrupulous buyers getting impatient. And previously healthy pensioners suddenly getting ill, or dying in mysterious accidents. I'm not sure it's a world Ina and I want to be part of."

13

"*Paeachally!*" I said and clicked my seatbelt shut.

Nikolai turned his head and chortled appreciatively.

"*Paeachally!*" he repeated – then pointed to the sky and made a whooshing noise: "*Gagarin!*"

I had simply said *Let's Go*. Practising an expression I'd acquired in that day's Russian lesson about the language of travel. Unwittingly however I'd used what for Russians is a famous phrase: Yuri Gagarin's final words to his controllers, before blasting off to become the first man in space. Associations like these help lodge things in the memory, and Nikolai's remark ensured I remembered *Let's Go* while other more elaborate expressions slipped away.

The company paid for my Russian lessons, and in the early days I made conscientious efforts to acquire some fluency. My teacher was an academic lady in her late fifties called Katya Bagmanova, who taught English at Moscow State University, and supplemented her official salary moonlighting as a Russian language tutor for embassies and companies with foreign staff. Three times a week she came to the office and drilled me in Russian for an hour. *Drilled* is the correct word, for her approach was strict, rigid and heavily biased towards rote learning. Her dry, serious manner testified to her knowledge and professionalism, but did nothing to encourage or inspire. As I wearily rehearsed grammatical constructions and memorised lists of vocabulary, I fancied I'd just been unlucky in our HR department's choice of teacher. But later on, I recognised that Katya's style was the norm for Russian language teaching – old fashioned, grammar-based and boring. The textbooks reflected this. In contrast to the amazing range of colourful, creatively designed materials available to foreign students of English, Russian language learners are confronted with a limited selection of drab manuals which make no attempt to stimulate interest. It's not that Russian publications in general are inherently dull. The stock in Moscow's bookshops shows a vibrant contemporary publishing industry which turns out high-quality, imaginative and often lavishly illustrated books of all kinds. And at prices so reasonable they put Western publishers to shame. But textbooks for foreign learners of Russian are a different proposition. Most have a Soviet air, and are purposeful, earnest, and demanding. They seem to say learning's not supposed to be fun. It's a privilege and a serious business – so knuckle down and don't expect any fancy theatrics to sweeten the pill. Many textbooks in use today *are* of course simply reprints of old Soviet publications. Demand is not big enough to encourage investment in new, innovative titles. In a world that wants to learn English, ELT publishing has become a phenomenon, generating financial returns that permit the development of ever more attractive products. But there's no equivalent mass-market for Russian. Indeed, the disintegration of the Soviet empire has increasingly marginalised the language, as newly independent states forsake it for their own.

I submitted to Katya's instruction without demur for over a year, and although I often found it painful, gradually saw results. More and more of life's background chatter became intelligible: snatches of strangers' street conversations, exchanges between Metro passengers, shoppers gossiping at checkout desks. Banal, mundane – but in a way a reassuring. It brought me a sense of connection, and I felt I was waking up to the world around me. As the months passed her teaching became less prescriptive, and grammar gave way to Russian conversation, which I reinforced by practicing on Nikolai as we sat stuck in traffic. Yet despite the progress, I thought something was missing. I'd improve more quickly with the help of the kind of modern, interactive resources commonplace in English language training.

"Have you any DVDs or CD ROMs I can use?" I asked Katya.

She grimaced and shook her head.

"Nothing?"

"No. But you can watch television. Maybe that'll help."

I'd already tried watching Russian TV, but the speed of natural speech defeated me. I needed something I could stop and rewind. I also wanted an accompanying text – so I could look up difficult words in a dictionary.

"Maybe you could buy a film," Katya suggested. "There are many famous Russian films on DVD."

This was a good idea. With a Russian Classic on DVD, plus a printed version from a bookshop, I could prepare my own bespoke language-training kit. A play would be ideal. A settled text – with clearly delineated dialogue.

Chekhov?

Yes, I decided, Chekhov. As a student I'd actually studied *The Cherry Orchard* in English translation.

In the *Dom Knigi* (House of Books), across the road from the Moscow City Government building on Tverskai Street, I bought a paperback Russian language copy of *Three Plays* by Chekhov. It contained *Uncle Vanya, Three Sisters,* and *The Cherry Orchard.* But surprisingly it was weeks before I managed to acquire a film version of any of these titles. Finding Russian or Western DVDs was usually easy in Moscow. Official video stores carried wide stocks of Hollywood blockbusters, as well as all kinds of more esoteric titles. However, the vast bulk of the city's DVD trade was in cheap pirated copies sold by illegal traders, in underpasses, metro stations and on street corners. Periodically the authorities half-heartedly clamped down on the pirates, largely to appease US lobbying about intellectual property rights, but there was little serious attempt at eradicating the industry. The occasional disappearance of a supplier was more likely a result of a failure to buy-off the local cops, than any official crackdown. For all the Hollywood outrage at the scale of Russia's movie piracy, the reality was that most Russians could not afford DVDs at official prices – it was a cheap pirated copy or nothing.

In my hunt for Chekhov, I searched my familiar DVD outlets in central Moscow – legal and illegal – but with no success. I even rummaged through the offerings of the fly-by-night street vendors, who were normally best avoided – impromptu pavement stalls consisting of a shaky trestle table and a cardboard boxful of discs. From experience I'd learned their wares were often dodgy – the picture quality might be good, but the audio unreliable.

"Is it in English?"

"Yes, Yes, English!" I'd be told, only to later discover a soundtrack in Turkish, Armenian or Hindustani.

The big studios supplying the legal marketplace generally issued DVDs with multi-lingual soundtracks. But pirating's easier when only one language-track is copied, so dealers at the bottom of the market habitually peddled substandard versions. I therefore usually bought only from kiosks equipped with TVs and DVD players (of which there were a surprisingly large number) that allowed customers to preview the quality of their products.

After my initial enthusiasm I'd given up looking for a filmed Chekhov, when I spotted by chance, in the window of a kiosk next to Smolenskaya Metro station, a disc entitled in Russian: *The Stories of Anton Chekhov*. The packaging proclaimed it part of a *Russian Classics Collection,* and it turned out to be a set of Soviet-era movies and TV shows based on Russian literature. A photograph of the writer fronted the box, and an array of smaller figures in Victorian dress – movie stills depicting characters from his works – encircled him. It wasn't clear what the disc actually contained, but at only 120 roubles (an illegal copy of course) – I took a gamble. Later, when I clicked through the menu, I found no *Three Sisters* and no *Cherry Orchard,* but there was *Uncle Vanya*. The rest of the disc contained not plays, but TV dramatisations of his short stories, including the famous *Lady with the Little Dog*. The *Vanya* proved to be a good quality Mosfilm production from the 1970s, and I resolved to make it the basis of my Russian self-help program. After a couple of heavy sessions with pencil and dictionary, translating the play's early scenes, I sat down, DVD remote-control in hand, to undergo the full interactive experience.

In this production, the play's action was prefaced by a montage of period photographs from the era in which *Vanya's* set – the 1890s. Mosfilm used them as a framing device, to remind its Soviet audience of what life was like in pre-revolutionary Russia. There were shots of the Tsar, of royal pomp and splendour, of the Russian aristocracy at play – at the races, hunting stags. Juxtaposed with these were photographs of workers and peasants. Careworn faces, pathetic children, hard work, and casually disregarded dead bodies.

The play itself is about a group of middle-class intellectuals marooned on a country estate, where they examine their lives, reveal regrets, and confront their fears and failures. There's an ecological theme, and some sideways disapproval of Russia's new capitalism, but Chekhov is not overtly political. His interest is in human fallibility, in wasted lives, lost ideals and frustrated longing. The DVD's introductory montage however adds a political dimension, inviting us to reflect on the sickness of the society that produced such flawed, ineffectual, unhappy characters. Whether Chekhov himself would have endorsed such an explicit interpretation is debatable. Like so much of his work *Vanya* is enigmatic. Is it a critique of pre-communist Russia – or simply a description of the human condition?

As I ran the disc, the text of the play in hand, I quickly discovered this version of *Vanya* an unsatisfactory tool for language learning. Rather than a straight recording of a stage performance, I'd acquired a film *adaptation,* and the action on screen didn't match the text in front of me. I'd failed to anticipate the filmmaker's art – the extent to which visuals might replace Chekhov's lines. Yet I was glad I'd tried to use it, for I'd stumbled across something unexpected and satisfying. Watching Mosfilm harness a Russian classic in the service of contemporary ideology was intriguing, an illuminating insight into the Soviet relationship with the past.

With my DIY Russian tutorial a failure, I resorted to supplementing Katya's lessons with a more conventional product – an Oxford University Press audio pack I sent for from the UK.

14

With six Russians and two foreigners on the company's management team, our weekly meetings would have been impossible without simultaneous translation. Two of the Russians spoke fluent, elegant English, but the others had only rudimentary proficiency. As these included the President, it was unquestionable that every Russian would speak only Russian. Equally, Norman and I could fully understand only in English, so everyone listened on headphones while the conversation flipped between languages – like UN delegates. We made our contributions into microphones fixed to the table in front of us, and an interpreter sitting in a soundproof booth outside our meeting room, steered us between the two languages.

When Dmitri, our usual interpreter, broke a foot chopping logs at his dacha, Pavel Gubarev, a melancholy man in his mid-twenties, was drafted in from an agency as a temporary replacement. Day-to-day we could muddle through without an interpreter, with various other employees translating bits and pieces as their language skills allowed. But in management meetings a professional was essential. The first time Pavel performed it was clear his style was very different from Dmitri's. The latter was direct, literal and fearless. When the President barked an insult or delivered some savage put-down, Dmitri from his soundproof booth provided a correspondingly abrasive equivalent in English. It's commonly held that the best male interpreters are uncompromisingly frank, never shying away from rough language or brutal sentiments, while their female counterparts, though no less accurate, are inclined where possible to choose softer, more diplomatic translations. It's something I noticed myself and concluded that women interpreters are indeed more tactful. (I wondered if they were routinely asked just to translate stuff that was already sanitised. Had their customers an old-fashioned, gentlemanly aversion to swearing in front of women? But I quickly rejected the theory as absurd – squeamishness about giving offence is never a concern in the macho, rough-and-tumble world of Russian business.)

In their restraint and prissiness, Pavel's translations had a feminine feel. He toned down caustic remarks, dodged the most brutal unpleasantness, and never directly translated swearing. In formal management meetings bad language was rare anyway; the tone was set by the President who was harsh and critical, but never foul-mouthed. In his absence however, and in side-meetings and follow-up discussions, the discourse markedly coarsened, and anything might be said. Here Pavel's discretion was noticeable. Where Dmitri would have cheerfully translated that Lossky was a *fucking useless moron,* Pavel settled for Lossky being *worryingly misinformed.* Not quite equivalent – but close enough to pass muster. In avoiding profanities, his English at times had a quaint, almost archaic air, with hints of Edwardian slang of the kind found in PG Wodehouse. I enjoyed this quirkiness and came to appreciate the artistry of his performance. Although my Russian was poor, I could recognise a good number of swear words and terms of abuse, and in the month or so that Pavel assisted us, I entertained myself in meetings that were otherwise dreary slogs, by guessing how he would deal with these. Surprisingly, my Russian colleagues appeared oblivious to his penchant for euphemism. Surely, they must have noticed that when they swore in Russian the English version was diluted? But nobody quibbled; it didn't seem to matter. It was enough that they'd blown off steam in Russian.

After one of our meetings Pavel approached me and asked if his English was OK. I thought it near perfect. But since his style was so different from Dmitri's, I was curious where he'd learned.

"In the university in Tashkent," he told me. "And from TV and books."

"Tashkent?"

"I was born there. But my parents are Russian. *Were* Russian."

Pavel's story was a cameo from the Russian diaspora. From the neglected world of people marooned in some newly liberated independent state when the USSR disintegrated.

"My father was an army officer. Originally from Moscow. But he was posted to Uzbekistan in 1978. My parents were very happy about it, because life in Tashkent was much nicer. Moscow in Soviet times wasn't so comfortable, but in Tashkent there was sunshine and good food. And the political atmosphere was more relaxed. Do you know what people used to call Tashkent? – *Bread City*! It was famous in the USSR. There was always food – because of the climate and the good agriculture. Even in Stalin's time – when Russia had famines – in Tashkent you could eat and survive. Of course, that was long before my parents arrived there."

Pavel had been born in the early 1980s, and he was raised in Tashkent's Russian community. When the Soviet Union collapsed the Army offered the family a move back to Russia. As Pavel told it, they had the right to an apartment in central Moscow – and there was one actually earmarked and available. But to their enduring regret, his father made the catastrophic error of electing to remain in Uzbekistan.

"I guess he became lazy. Or maybe just scared that after years away he couldn't cope back home. It was easier to stay-on. So, he joined the Uzbek army and we became citizens."

"Is he still in the army?"

"No. He retired. Now he sells tobacco in a small shop. He knows he made a crazy decision. But it's too late. For all of us."

I mentioned official efforts to attract exiles back home, but Pavel was dismissive.

"It's impossible," he said. "Where would we live? Selling my father's house in Tashkent will buy nothing in Moscow now. He's too old to find work – or to start a business."

"But you work."

"Yes, but it's not stable. It's temporary. I live with my aunt – my father's sister. I can't afford anywhere else here. I'm unofficial and that's a big problem."

Although ethnically and culturally Russian, as an Uzbek citizen Pavel was legally a foreigner, with no residence or employment rights.

"I work for the agency," he said, "because I don't have the correct papers for a permanent job."

"Can't you apply for citizenship?"

"Yes, I'm entitled – because of my father. But it's a complicated process. Very bureaucratic, and the bribes are expensive. Maybe I'll never save enough. Moscow's a hard, cold city. It sucks the life out of people like me."

In this touch of self-pity, I glimpsed a deeper, more intense character behind the measured facade of his working identity. As we talked his tone hardened.

"What about Tashkent?" I said. "Why not go back? Settle?"

"Look at my face Mr. Strachan," Pavel said. "Do I look Asian? Chinese?"

I shook my head, wondering what nerve I'd struck.

"In Uzbekistan today we Russians are nothing." He became more heated. "A dictator controls the country and only local people get good jobs – Asians. There are no opportunities for Russians. Or for anybody who isn't Muslim. Everybody wants to leave, but it's not easy. The discrimination's sly. They can't persecute us openly. The government understands if they attack us directly Russia will destroy them. But they don't want us, and life's difficult."

"You speak Uzbek?"

"A little only. I can understand more. At home we spoke only Russian – the same at school. At university I studied English because it was the language of the future. But Uzbek – no."

Might things now have been different, I reflected, if before the world turned upside down Pavel and his fellow Russians had engaged more sympathetically with the local population? Or even bothered to learn their language? But I resisted commenting and let him continue with his post-colonial angst.

"You know Mr. Strachan, nationalism's very strong in Uzbekistan. They hate Russians and want the country for themselves. I can understand that. But look at Moscow – it's full of Uzbeks and other foreigners, but I'm Russian and can't have a life here. How am I to understand *that*?"

It sounded like a cue for a political complaint, and I expected a Russian nationalist diatribe on immigration. Pavel however launched instead into a reflection on nationalism itself. He was thoughtful and articulate, if unoriginal, and his theory contained two contradictory propositions – which he failed to reconcile. The first was that nationalism is for losers. It rested, he argued, on a pooling of resources – like communism. But in this case cultural resources. It attracted people who, as individuals, were incapable of making their own marks in life. Successful people didn't need it. But to those with no hope of personal achievement nationalism offered common ownership of a culture – allowing them to puff their chests in pride at sharing in the collective achievements of a nation.

Pavel's second premise was that opposition to immigration is not always racist prejudice. It could be a rational response to a threat – especially for the non-religious.

"A threat to their culture," Pavel said. "Even to their *immortality*."

"What? Seriously?"

"Yes! If you don't believe in God or an afterlife, what is there after you've gone? What do you leave behind? Famous people – like artists or big-time politicians – have names and reputations. Achievements for the history books. But ordinary people? We're anonymous. Invisible."

But, he argued, because we've been here – living and working, learning and passing on knowledge – we've influenced our times and helped created our culture. As long as that culture survives something of those who made it lives on. For most people that's their only legacy.

"You can be a small fish in a big river, Mr. Strachan," he said, "but if the river keeps flowing…you get the idea!"

"I understand but -"

"Then what happens when foreigners arrive?" Pavel said.

He answered his own question – they diluted and distorted cultures that were one people's unique contribution to the world. Not deliberately. Just by being around and thinking differently. By telling different stories and honouring different ideas. Inevitably it meant the native culture died or changed beyond recognition.

"Does that matter?" I asked.

"Not to me – and I think maybe not to you. But to many people it does."

I refrained from asking Pavel the obvious question – about the impact of Russia on Uzbek culture. But on a visit back to Scotland, with his words in my mind, I asked a Scottish nationalist acquaintance about his party's policy of opening Scotland up to increased immigration.

"The population's declining," he said. "We need migrants to grow the economy. The more the better. We're not one of those racist movements that hate foreigners. Everybody's welcome."

"So, the point of independence is purely economic? Scotland's just a patch of land to be exploited economically?"

"No, I'm not saying that. Of course, it's a lot more. It's about people…and managing our own affairs."

"Why must we manage our own affairs? What's the point of an independent Scotland if our culture's threatened by a flood of incomers – doesn't that matter?"

I was being deliberately provocative. Interested to hear him square economics with a wider meaning of Scotland.

"Surely Scotland's about culture and traditions as much as economics?" I added. "A shared heritage we've developed over centuries. Something unique."

"All that's true. But you can have both. Nationalism doesn't need to be defensive."

It was a fair response – but not necessarily the only insight into nationalism's motivations. I would have liked to hear him debate with a Pavel.

"Have you heard about Bread City?" I asked Valeria after my discussion with Pavel.

"Of course – it's Tashkent. I've never been there but think it's very nice. A good place to live."

15

During my early days in Moscow, when strangers stopped me in the street wanting directions the encounters would end quickly. My flustered incomprehension might draw apologetic chuckles when they realised I was a clueless foreigner, but more often prompted a brusque dismissal. However, as my Russian improved, I began to take satisfaction in responding helpfully. *Yes – the Moscow Conservatory? Go to the corner of the boulevard there and turn left. Then straight along Nikitskaya Street – maybe three hundred metres – until you see it on your right!*

Strangely, as if by some psychic correlation, the better my Russian became the more I seemed to get stopped. It happened surprisingly often. Moscow is full of visiting provincials, as well as residents from the city's peripheral housing estates who routinely get lost when they venture into the centre. Many Russians struggle to read maps – a legacy apparently of Soviet times when, except for soldiers and spies, they were generally forbidden and unavailable.

"Valeria," I asked, searching for an explanation for being frequently stopped, "how Russian do I look?"

"What do you mean?"

"If you'd never met me before – and if I didn't speak – would you think I'm Russian?"

"Now yes – but when you arrived at first you looked like a foreigner."

"How? What's different now?"

She thought for a moment and then shook her head. "I don't know. It's not easy to explain."

"My clothes are the same. I've had this shirt since I came. And the suit. Maybe my hair?"

She glanced at me appraisingly. "No, it's not different."

On this I knew she was wrong. From the start, getting a haircut in Moscow had been a problem. I could find no barber anywhere near my apartment, and I balked at paying upwards of $60 in a hotel salon. My Russian colleagues advised visiting a big supermarket, as these usually had barber shops on the premises. But most were out in the suburbs, so every few weeks Nikolai would fight his way through the traffic on the Third Ring Road to keep me groomed. But then I discovered a unisex salon near the Mendeleyevskaya metro station – a ten-minute train journey – and I became a regular for the rest of my time in the city. It was an unpretentious place which shared its entrance with a hardware shop, and the two middle-aged ladies who ran it spoke no English. But it was clean, efficient and cheap. I communicated my requirements by pointing at the styling photographs on the walls. From amongst the pictures of male models sporting ridiculous bouffants, coloured quiffs, floppy aristocratic styles, and retro feather cuts, I selected a nondescript short-back-and-sides, which was the closest to my usual look. In truth, it didn't matter. I soon recognised the pictures were purely decorative, and never once saw a customer leave with anything different from me – the standard product of the Russian hairstyling sausage machine – short, clumsy and without a parting.

"My shoes then?"

Like my hair, I knew these had changed. Before I left Scotland a friend who'd holidayed in Moscow related an experience at a museum pay-desk. The cashier had leaned over and inspected his shoes, then charged him the higher tourist rate, rather than the discounted price for Moscow residents. His smart English brogues were the giveaway, and he took it as an indication that all Russians were identifiable by scruffy Soviet-style footwear. But as I'd discover, he was badly mistaken. The average male Muscovite wore shoes that were distinctly more fashionable than his British counterparts. It was the conservatism of his footwear that had exposed my friend at the museum. The vogue in Moscow was for slim, pointy-toed, retro-style winkle-pickers – the kind favoured by rock stars, and ubiquitous in the West in the 1960s. Most were Italian-made and seriously ill-suited for Moscow's crumbling pavements and winter snows. But fashion of course trumped practicality, and like so much of the extravagant clothing on sale in the city, their popularity was surely a belated reaction to decades of Soviet austerity. Since the men's sections in shoe shops offered little else at reasonable prices, I too began wearing them. One nice touch I discovered was a fur-lined variant which to the naked eye looked no bulkier than the classic, streamlined models, but kept the feet warm in colder weather.

Valeria however was dismissive of shoes being a part in my transformation.

"No, no – they're not important. Nobody sees them. I think maybe you've changed inside yourself. Your soul – your *spirit* – is now more Russian."

Soul? Spirit? This was deeper than conversations with Valeria usually went.

"How's my spirit more Russian?"

I could see her struggling to answer – not with finding words in English, but in defining what she meant. After a pause she said: "Maybe you're more sad."

So, there it was. Confirmation that my acclimatisation was complete. All the adjectives I associated with Russians' public demeanour – depressing, unsmiling, dour – applied equally to me. When I contemplated my Russification however, I recognised what Valeria couldn't have known – that my apparently new-found melancholy wasn't new at all, but just in-bred West-of-Scotland despondency resurfacing.

Negativity and pessimism lie at the core of the Scottish character. We have a talent for gloom and resentment. Glasgow isn't known as the *city of the imagined insult* for nothing, and undercurrents of aggression and antagonism are deeply ingrained in the culture. From my first days in Moscow, I was struck by echoes of home – by bleak faces, a preference for scowls over smiles, and a familiar air of downtrodden umbrage. Both Glasgow and Moscow are characterised by public incivility, rudeness and low-level hostility. On the streets everyone's in conflict with everyone else. Passers-by bump or elbow aside other passers-by. Shoppers let doors slam in the faces of other shoppers. Service in shops and restaurants is grudging or slapdash. Day-to-day life can feel hard going. And there are the drunks – morose drunks, obstreperous drunks, unsteady drunks, embarrassing drunks, lunging drunks. Plentiful drunks.

As my Russian improved however I also began to understand that in one area at least, what I took for deliberate discourtesy was really awkwardness. When Russians speak to strangers, they can sound uneasy and abrupt. Decades of calling each other *comrade,* or *citizen,* has left them confused about how to address even their fellow-countrymen today, and Russia has yet to settle on a consensus for modern norms. There have been attempts to revive pre-revolutionary polite forms such as *gospodin* (Mr.) or *barin* (sir) for men, and *gospozha* (Mrs.) or *barynya* (madam) for women. And although these are heard occasionally, they have not generally caught on. Communist salutations were intended to level out social differences, and many Russians continue the custom by referring to each other as *man, woman, boy* or *girl*. Critics argue that such socially neutral forms – which deny the respect for people as individuals that was inherent in the old, pre-revolutionary salutations – has led to a coarsening of discourse and a degradation of social relationships. Currently, amidst the confusion, different forms of address are favoured according to age, with older people naturally clinging to Soviet ones, while the young struggle to find comfortable modern replacements for *comrade*. Similarly, the old are more likely, when speaking with strangers, to use diminutives such as *synok* (sonny) or *dochka* (little girl, pet), and for those with more years on the clock, *mother* or *father*. Some Russian commentators view this positively, arguing that it demonstrates the emotional depth of Russian – as opposed, for example, to the coldness of polite English usage.

***

Similarities between Moscow and Glasgow should not be exaggerated. Beyond just size, there's more different than alike about the two cities. Yet in some important areas of life there are genuinely striking affinities – in the physical environment, and especially, in the values and behaviour of the people. My point of comparison was the city I knew best: the 1970s Glasgow of memory. It was echoes of that Glasgow, that I would hear repeatedly in Moscow.

In my early, flat-hunting Moscow days, when the city's golden domes and historic buildings took second place in my attention to residential housing, the stone-built Victorian tenement-blocks inside the Garden Ring struck a not-always-welcome note of familiarity. As I trudged up stairways accessed directly from the street, to view apartments in varying states of refurbishment, I found musty, lived-in smells, dingy lighting and an air of general neglect which seemed transplanted straight from Scotland. Communal passageways garnished with cigarette butts; abandoned bottles propped against walls. More than once I spotted an empty beer-can wedged into the ornate iron balustrades that supported stair bannisters. Occasionally a pool of drying vomit, or from the rear of the close, a whiff of urine, indicated a desperate drunk had ducked in from the street the night before. The flats themselves, with their high Victorian ceilings and wedding-cake cornicing, were internally remarkably similar to Glasgow's of the same era. And outside, the scruffy streets, uneven, crumbling pavements, pot-holes, dirt and litter underlined the connection.

Tenement living in Britain is largely a Scottish phenomenon. English cities expanded with back-to-back terraces of low-rise housing, while Scotland preferred the European model of tenement flats. As a result, the central areas of Scottish cities today continue to have a more European feel than their English counterparts. Unsurprisingly, when the BBC for example filmed Alan Bennett's Cold War drama, *An Englishman Abroad*, in 1983, they travelled north of the border for location shooting, and used Glasgow and Dundee for exterior scenes set in 1950s Moscow. The film tells the story of a strange encounter in Moscow between visiting English actress Coral Browne, and Soviet spy and defector Guy Burgess, and has been acclaimed as one of the greatest productions in television history. It was lauded for the quality of the acting, its masterly script exploring themes of loyalty, betrayal, sacrifice and regret, and for the seeming authenticity of the setting. Visually it *looks like* Moscow – and critics enthused about its evocation of the grim, depressing ugliness of the Soviet-era city.

Paradoxically, it wasn't a tenement which provided one of the film's key images, but a shot of Glasgow's *Moss Heights Flats*, a post-war high-rise in the city's Cardonald district, which served as the location for Burgess's Moscow apartment. A forlorn, dismal, and forbidding tower-block, it became a motif for the new Russian life that was his reward for treachery and defection. Many years after I first saw the film I discovered the real-life provenance of this building and enjoyed an ironic reflection that my parents' certainty of a special bond between Scotland and Russia had been correct after all: Glasgow's Stalinist municipal planners had produced a structure that in spirit and style fitted nicely into the Soviet world.

Beyond the film's visual portrait however is another truth, for Glasgow's post-war redevelopment experience was, at a macro level, very similar to Moscow's. As bulldozers tore apart central areas of both cities, residents were decanted to newly built housing schemes on the outskirts, miles away from their original communities. In Moscow this migration was coupled with massive additional post-war growth, resulting in a city that today has a historic centre inhabited by the rich, foreigners, and a dwindling population of native Muscovites – while the majority of ordinary citizens are exiled to huge peripheral estates which are like larger versions of Glasgow's Easterhouse or Castlemilk. High-rise ghettos of social problems, disaffection, and alienation.

Comparisons like these would not have gladdened my mother's heart. Yet my observations on the spirit and character of the Russian people would surely have troubled her even more. Her reference points were political and romantic: a conviction that all Russians love Burns' poetry, that Celts are genetically more communally minded than the English (allegedly making Scotland more receptive to socialism), and that Russians and Scots alike disdain petty nationalism and embrace an international outlook. Idealistic stuff – and shades of the old Comintern. My own perceptions were much darker. I saw two nations united in negatives. By a common lack of sunshine that depresses the spirits and feeds a love of strong drink, as well as a predisposition to bad health and violence. By an addiction to melancholy and maudlin sentimentality.

Alcohol and smoking of course featured greatly – with the former responsible for the many tawdry vignettes of bad behaviour I routinely witnessed in Moscow, and which brought to mind identical scenes in Glasgow. Drunks, publicly urinating against trees in the afternoon sunshine in Tsvetnoi Boulevard, might have been Glaswegians caught short in Kelvingrove Park. The red-faced man I saw breakfasting on a can of lager every morning, as he waited at a bus-stop in Pushkin Square, had innumerable clones in Glasgow. The late-night brawls, the vomit on the pavements, the sullen, edgy drunks in buses or metro carriages, were all echoes of home.

Like Scotland, Russia also nurtures a tradition of woeful service in shops and restaurants. Both Glaswegians and Muscovites seem to refuse on principle to deliver a satisfactory customer experience and eating out in Moscow can easily feel like being in Scotland. There are of course exceptions – friendly, efficient shop assistants and waitresses – and in the more expensive establishments there's usually little to complain about. But the norm sits somewhere on a spectrum ranging from the simply comical, through the slapdash and indifferent, to the surly and positively hostile.

In Russia such shortcomings may be teething problems, as society painfully adjusts to the expectations of a consumer economy. Or maybe not. My experience was that the worst service was usually provided by men, and I came across an article in the *Moscow Times* which showed I was not alone in this. Written by a visiting American academic, it chronicled his dismal attempts at shopping in Moscow, where it seemed that in every establishment he entered, the men behind the counters were offhand, rude and unhelpful. As a retired language professor who spoke Russian like a native, and easily passed for a local, he concluded the source of their behaviour was not a dislike of foreigners, but the innate aggression of Russian men. The women, he declared, were generally warm, polite and friendly, but the men – unless in the company of close friends – were abrupt, snarling and antagonistic. It was a trait he'd first noticed as a student in Russia in the mid-1960s and discovered unchanged four decades later. He cited two reasons. The first was historical: the massive casualties of World War II left the country with a shortage of men, causing mothers and other female relatives to spoil and indulge young boys so much, that they created generations of self-centred, male egotists. Secondly, he argued, Russian mothers see it as their duty to actively encourage rude and aggressive behaviour in their sons, to prepare them for survival in the harsh, confrontational, man's-world of Russian society. It's an upbringing that ensures Russian men generally have little respect for women, and as the professor pointed out, a clue to why around 80% of all Russian marriages end in divorce. The feminisation that in recent decades has transformed Western societies, has yet to touch Russia, and a macho culture, akin to what once flourished in Glasgow and the industrial West of Scotland, continues to prevail.

In Scotland, the war cannot be blamed for the perennially lousy service culture. But vestiges of the old macho spirit remain, and undoubtedly contribute to the shortcomings. These are typically less about competence than attitude. Self-conscious notions of masculinity and the dignity of labour, forged in the lost world of heavy industry, mean Scottish men have an aversion to service jobs, which are seen as women's work. Service equates to servility, and many men assert their pride and independence by performing their duties grudgingly and with bad grace. Spilling the soup, under-heating the pies, or losing the laundry become revolutionary acts. Big Alec might be a waiter or hotel porter on minimum wage. But he's as good as you are – and don't you forget it!

***

Scottish poet Hugh MacDiarmid wrote of shunning the middle ground, in preference for a life lived "*whaur extremes meet.*"

It's a phrase that articulates a fundamental Scottish characteristic – the impulse to live on the edge, and a fondness for excess rather than moderation. And it seems to me to apply equally to the Russians. At the deepest levels of character and temperament the two nations are very alike – emotionally drawn to the wilder, self-destructive edges of experience. Both of course share an obvious penchant for drinking to oblivion, but the affinity goes deeper. While the English national character is anchored on temperate good sense and a spirit of compromise, both the Scots and the Russians are attracted to radicalism – even fanaticism. At times in each nation's history, extreme philosophies – Scottish Calvinism and Russian Communism, doctrines characterised by dour authoritarianism – seemed to offer the ultimate answers on how life should be lived, and profoundly affected the national psyches. The English spirit of *live-and-let-live,* with its toleration of eccentricity and dissent, does not sit naturally with the Scots or the Russians. Calvinism in Scotland, like Marxism, elevated communal values above the interests of the individual, and demanded conformity in thought and action. Just as Soviet ideology was enforced in all areas of everyday life, the Scottish Church controlled its population at the parish level, where Kirk Sessions, overseen by stern ministers and sanctimonious elders, meted out punishments to those accussed of moral lapses or wrong thinking. Luckily for the Scots, penalties were milder than in communist Russia – shamings in church and humiliating public penances, rather than deportation to the gulags or bullets in the head.

Interestingly, in day-to-day life both Communism and Presbyterianism relied heavily on a universal type to ensure obedience – local busybodies, who snooped on friends and neighbours, and readily informed on suspect behaviour and beliefs. Decades of this kind of suffocating scrutiny (centuries in the case of Scotland) must surely have contributed to the somber, guarded dispositions of Scots and Russians alike.

Culturally, the absence of a relaxed middle ground leads to a curious juxtaposition of opposites. Academics point to it as a persistent theme in Scottish literature – a dichotomy most famously expressed in Stevenson's *Jekyll & Hyde.* (It's tempting to see it also in the titles of Russian classics – *War & Peace, Crime & Punishment* – but this, I think, is a stretch too far.) In ordinary Scottish life it was once present in the contrast between episodes of wild, drunken disorder, and a formal adherence to grim Presbyterianism. Today it's also apparent in the public behaviour of both Muscovites and Glaswegians, in whom intense rudeness (at times hardening into menace) often coexists with genuine warmth and friendliness. Moods can change quickly, and swing unnervingly between both extremes. Russians can be intense, anxious, thoughtful and emotional in private, but commonly shield themselves with faces that become dour, expressionless masks in public.

A final intimation of a metaphysical affinity between Scotland and Russia was revealed to me in a grocer's on New Arbat, when I stumbled on a display of bottles of Barr's *Irn Bru* – a Scottish soft drink that has become the nation's favourite hangover cure. It's a local Scottish product unavailable in most of England, which I'd never seen on sale anywhere abroad. But here in the heart of Moscow, by some appropriate miracle, it sat proudly on the drinks shelves close to their selection of vodkas.

16

Norman and I had exited the Oxotni Riad metro station at the bottom of Tverskai Street, and were walking up towards Pushkin Square when he reminded me I'd once said I wished to see more of Moscow than just the usual tourist stuff.

"Here's a chance now," he said. "Let's go along here."

He turned left, leading us off Tverskai and into Nikitsky Perleluk, a quiet side-street of old houses and 19th century apartment blocks.

"Do you know the story of that place?" he said, and pointed at a handsome, rambling blue and white pre-revolutionary mansion visible behind the brick wall of a tree-shaded garden.

I knew nothing about it.

"It looks empty," he said. "But it used to be the Tunisian Embassy, and for a time was all over the newspapers and TV. A girlfriend I had in the early days knew about it and brought me here. Supposedly it's haunted. But not with ancient ghosts – like you get in old castles or graveyards. People started seeing things in the 1990s."

One night the ambassador's wife was on her way to the bathroom when she met a naked girl running along the corridor. She was very pretty – with blonde hair done up in traditional Russian braids – and looked about 14 or 15. She didn't speak, but her face was contorted, as if screaming in terror, and although she seemed real, she suddenly vanished through a wall. The next morning the wife told the ambassador, who thought she must have had a nightmare. However, other people in different parts of the embassy also started seeing similar things. Young girls, all about the same age, terrified and running naked. The girls themselves were always silent, but at other times in the night scary noises could be heard all over the embassy. Crying and moaning and female voices pleading for mercy. What gave the story credibility was that the witnesses weren't janitors with a taste for vodka, but senior diplomats not given to fantasy, like the Military Attaché and the embassy's Head of Security.

"Naturally it scared the shit out of the embassy staff," Norman said. "And loads stopped turning up for work."

The appearance of these phenomena coincided with activity by the Moscow City Water Department, who'd sent a team to repair the building's hot water supply. Parts of the garden were dug up for access to pipes, and workmen who opened a section of ducting found human remains. A forensic examination showed they were the bodies of six teenage girls.

"Each had a bullet hole in the back of her skull," Norman said.

When the remains were removed the disturbances in the house stopped; no more ghosts were reported.

"Have you heard of Laverenty Beria?" he said.

"The secret police chief?"

"Yes. That was his house. The bodies were allegedly girls he raped and murdered. He'd drive around Moscow, and whenever he saw a girl he fancied in the street his bodyguards bundled her into his car. He was notorious for also raping wives and daughters of colleagues. And actresses, servants, anything in skirts."

Beria's name is familiar to everyone with even the skimpiest knowledge of the Stalin era. He was one of the regime's key players, a historical figure of genuine substance, and reputedly a monster of evil and depravity. There's a mountain of published material about him, and our visit to his house prompted me to read more about his life and crimes. I discovered that Norman's story covered just some of the grisly allegations about Beria. There were countless other tales of sadistic violence and sexual misconduct extending over decades. Of political scheming underpinned by cruel force. During other renovations on the house, collections of human bones were uncovered in cellars and behind walls, and black marks were found scorched on walls and floors, by the blowtorch Beria used to personally torture victims. A heavy metal door concealed a fully equipped torture chamber.

Beyond the gothic horror however, historians acknowledge that Beria was an effective politician and administrator, and the ablest of all Stalin's senior henchmen. He was also a man of genuine intellect and culture, with a wide range of knowledge and interests, and a capacity for charm as well as ruthlessness. At one time he'd been a top-level footballer, and his accomplishments as an amateur musician inspired an incident in Martin Cruz Smith's novel, *Stalin's Ghost* (2007), in which a modern-day Russian official tries to impress guests with a treasured artefact – an old 78 rpm gramophone record, a one-off recording, in which Beria plays dance music on the piano to accompany Stalin singing a folksong.

Physically Beria was not imposing, and his appearance perfectly fitted his unsavoury reputation. Photographs show a man with fast-receding hair and curiously staring eyes. When I first saw one, he seemed strangely familiar. Then I recognized his remarkable similarity to the late British actor Donald Pleasence, in one his more sinister film roles.

From his appointment as head of the Soviet secret police, the NKVD, in 1938, until near the end of Stalin's life, when the old dictator seemed to turn against him, Beria was one of Stalin's most trusted and reliable political operatives. Tellingly, it was to Beria that he delegated responsibility for acquiring a Soviet atomic bomb. During the Cold War, with paranoia about communist expansionism growing, Western journalists paid increasing attention to Beria's reputation in Moscow and began to portray him as a power behind the throne. As a result, he appeared twice on the front cover of *Time* magazine. The first occasion was in March 1948, when the legend below his cover image read: *Communism's Beria – the cop at the keyhole is king.* The accompanying article argued that the *"police state mentality"* which characterised communist regimes made it as *"easy to kill on the party's orders as drink a glass of water."* His second appearance was in July 1955, when the magazine announced his fall with the legend: *Beria: enemy of the people,* and the magazine ran a cover story entitled *Russia: Purge of the Purger.*

One of the best and most readable accounts of Beria's career is in Simon Sebag Montefiore's *Stalin: The Court of the Red Tsar* (2003), a history of the dictator's closest circle based on material from newly available Soviet sources, including Stalin's own archive. Montefiore's Beria is a fascinating, if repulsive figure, in whom, unlike the other one-dimensional butchers who carried out Stalin's orders, depravity clearly coexisted with exceptional talent. Disentangling fact from the invention of political rivals is difficult when examining his reputation. But when Montefiore tackled him again for a BBC documentary in 2005, his focus was a claim allegedly made by Beria himself – that he murdered Stalin.

Who Killed Stalin? used witness testimony, as well as actors in dramatic reconstructions, to depict the events of Stalin's last days, and to investigate conspiracy theories surrounding his death. The official cause was a brain haemorrhage – which has long been suspected a cover-up by the Soviet authorities. Various curious details about his death – including its convenient timing – made conspiracy theories plausible. His bodyguards reportedly behaved unusually on the night his final illness struck and were tardy in seeking medical help when it became obvious something was seriously wrong. In addition, a number of those close to him, including members of his family and most of the Politburo, had strong motives at that time for wishing him dead. Most feared the dictator was turning against them, and preemptive action in the interests of self-preservation would have been understandable. The most memorable part of the film however is the sequence of authentic interviews with surviving relatives of Stalin's henchmen, in which they are asked to speculate on the identity of the likely murderer. The same answer is given by each of them: Beria.

In the end however Montefiore concludes, disappointingly, that Stalin indeed died of natural causes, and that the suspicious behaviour of those involved was simply fear-induced paralysis. None of the players was bold enough to enter Stalin's private quarters, even in a crisis, or take responsibility for summoning a doctor, so any possibility of saving him was missed through inaction.

Beria's own end was not long in coming. When Stalin died, he was initially euphoric, imagining himself as his successor. But his Politburo colleagues, fearful for their own safety should he inherit, had him arrested, tried in secret and executed. Like so much high-level Soviet intrigue, the facts are obscure. Officially, Beria was arrested in June 1953, accused of conspiring with Britain and other foreign powers to restore capitalism, and after a trial finally executed in December. According to rumour however, he was shot immediately after his arrest, his captors fearing something might go wrong if they kept him alive. A trial was then staged using a double – to throw a cloak of legality around what had already been done.

17

Mornings at work began with what became a little ritual. Just before nine o'clock Valeria brought in coffee and a typed schedule in English of my appointments for the day. She would wait, fidgeting in front of my desk, while I scanned it for surprises. Most meetings were routine events I'd initiated myself, but occasionally there was some obligation from the company's senior management, or an unexpected approach from elsewhere.

"What's this?" I asked one day, indicating the slot immediately after lunch.

"It's your meeting with Mr. Morozov."

"*Mr. Who?*"

"Mr. Morozov. He's new and wants to meet you – he started a few weeks after you came."

Her tone was disapproving, and our visitor obviously unwelcome. However, it was unavoidable that I saw him. Heads of HR must be available to employees, and I guessed I would hear a catalogue of queries and complaints.

"Do I need a translator?"

"No. Mr. Morozov speaks quite good English."

"I should see him."

"If you wish."

Just after lunch she opened my door, and I heard her address the visitor in the outer reception area with frosty politeness: "Mr. Strachan has agreed. You can come in please."

A dark-haired man in his mid-forties offered me his hand. "Ivan Morozov – very pleased to meet you."

I studied him briefly as he positioned himself in a chair. He was crisply dressed in a dark blue suit and white shirt – very much the new man keen to make a good impression. I guessed he'd later settle into crumpled workaday comfort. For now, though, there was something about his clothes that did not look Russian. His jacket fitted too well around the shoulders, and his tie was too carefully knotted.

"Thanks for seeing me," he said. "Just wanted to say hello and introduce myself. I heard you were here. I've not long arrived."

There was no hint of a Russian accent – his voice was pure London. When she'd said he spoke good English, Valeria hadn't hinted that he spoke *only* English.

"You don't sound Russian."

"It's not surprising – I'm not. I know, I know – the name! I get it all the time. Everybody here thinks I'm Russian – they *consider* me Russian. And assume I speak it. My grandfather was Russian, but I was born in Harlow. It's annoying at times. Instead of treating me like other foreigners they make it plain they think I *should* speak Russian. Some of them anyway. They'll pretend to misunderstand me. Or forget – deliberately – that I can't understand them. Then press on mercilessly in Russian. They're making some kind of point of course – but I'm not sure what it is."

Valeria's attitude, I guessed, was symptomatic of what he was encountering.

A feature of expatriate life is the acceleration of relationships. Compatriots thrown together in foreign lands form friendships more quickly than back home. Life stories are exchanged earlier, driven no doubt by some psychological need to fix new

161

acquaintances in context. The normal process of gradual self-revelation is short circuited. In addition, an HR professional has licence to ask personal questions, and I soon had Ivan talking about his background.

His grandfather, he told me, was Russian – but had settled in England after the revolution.

"I got to that age when you start reflecting on your life," he said. "I suppose like people who are adopted at birth – and want to track down their natural parents. It's not the same, but there are parallels. I got curious about my family's roots, and I took this job when the chance came up. I'll look around here and dig a bit into the past."

"Is Moscow – is Russia – what you expected?"

"I *had* no firm expectations. I learned all the usual stuff about Russia from TV. What it was like before – and after – the wall came down. But if anything, now I'm here it all seems more normal than I imagined."

Was he hoping to discover some long-lost relatives? I mentioned the actress Helen Mirren – I had read an article in the *Daily Mail* about her attempts to trace her grandfather's Russian family. She had believed them all lost, killed during the revolution, or in Stalin's labour camps. But it turned out that many had survived, and in visits to Moscow, and to the family's home village near Smolensk, she was united with living representatives from several generations.

"I read that story," Ivan said. "There *are* similarities – but overall, there's a lot more that's different in our circumstances. Helen Mirren had something to go on – documents, old letters, family recollections – that kind of thing. Unfortunately, I've nothing. No idea where to even start searching. There's nothing on paper, and my father rarely spoke about *his* father. The occasional remark, not much more."

"Is your father still alive?"

"He died eight years ago. I realise now I should have talked to him when I had the chance. You know what I mean – talked to him *seriously* about his family – his roots, that kind of thing. He never volunteered anything. But I should have made an effort to draw information out of him." He shrugged. "Now it's too late."

He was quiet for some minutes, then continued pensively.

"My father was a very strange man. The only time he mentioned his Russian heritage was to taunt my mother. Her background was Greek, you see. He'd get all pompous and put her down by saying things like: *I am Russian! Heir to a great, world-class, civilisation! The Greeks have only a village culture!* His silence was partly my fault," Ivan went on. "I never gave him any encouragement. For most of my life I just wasn't curious. Anyway, officially he wasn't even Russian. My grandfather was Russian, but my father was born in Greece. Our family story is very tangled."

Ivan's grandfather had fled Russia a year after the revolution, travelling south until he reached Athens. This much Ivan knew. A single man in his 20s, his grandfather had settled long enough to marry a local girl and have a son – Ivan's father. Within a few years however they'd all upped sticks and moved to London.

"As a child my father spoke Greek at home," he said. "It was his first language – because of my grandmother. I have no idea if my grandfather ever talked to him in Russian. Or told him about life in Russia. But I suspect he didn't."

"Why did he flee Russia?"

"Why did anybody? To escape the Bolsheviks. But there was also something restless in his character. Something unstable. He couldn't settle anywhere. Even in London. One day he announced he was going to Greece on business – and just never came back. My father was a teenager at the time, but he went to Greece looking for him – and found no trace. Nobody knows what became of him."

"And your mother?"

"She's still alive. She was a lot younger than my father. Her parents were from London's Greek community. That's how she met my father. I've a huge family on her side – in England and in Greece."

Ivan spoke warmly of his Greek relatives, of childhood holidays in the Greek sunshine, and family gatherings in London. Of Greek cousins, uncles and aunts.

"So, you see, my story's unbalanced. The family I know about – the one I grew up with – is Greek. But I've a Russian name, and that half of me's a mystery."

"What do you hope to find?" I asked. "Relatives? A story?"

"Maybe nothing. I've no idea where to start looking. I've nothing to go on. Only my name. Helen Mirren's family were upper class. Landowners and military officers. Mine, I fear, were peasants. There are no ancestral lands to return to. I'm not expecting any emotional reunions. But I'll try. See how it goes."

"Can't you get help? A private detective?"

"I thought of that. Or one of those genealogy companies. There's no shortage of people like me in Moscow – descendants of emigres looking for their roots. So, there *are* organisations doing it. But where do I start personally? I've nothing to go on. Our family's from somewhere in the Moscow region – *I think*. But even that's not certain. I've no paperwork. No other links. Not even intangible stuff. I mean – I don't even have memories, anecdotes, gossip, to work with…I'll need to do some more thinking. Ask around. To be honest, I'm not certain how much is possible. Maybe I should be content just to be here and absorb the culture and environment – that kind of thing. To feel myself Russian – without looking for family history or blood ties or a place of origin."

"Is that enough?"

"We'll see. But I can't help feeling that carrying a Russian name must mean something. It's sexist, I know. But it's your father's side of the family that matters most. The male blood line provides your identity. If it sounds macho and old fashioned maybe that's the Russian in me. Anyway – there's something more pressing to talk about. Do you have a cleaner?"

I shook my head at this change of subject. "Not yet. I've been thinking – but haven't got round to it."

"My landlord's offering to put me in touch with one. But I'm uneasy."

I understood his reluctance to let a stranger into his personal space. But his concern was deeper.

"There's surely security issues," he said. "As a foreigner it's difficult to know who to trust. Most Russians think we're wealthy – and might have something worth stealing! Makes us easy targets – at least more vulnerable than the average man in the street. I'm not saying a cleaner would rob me. I'm sure my landlord would recommend someone trustworthy. But the point is who talks to who. The cleaner tells a friend she works for an Englishman in Yutsenkov Street. The friend's druggie son overhears and passes it on. Then late one night the bad guys come calling. Maybe I'm paranoid – but you get the picture. I'm inclined to stay under the radar and do my own ironing."

When I next saw Ivan I found him very downbeat.

"How's the research going?" I said.

"I've pretty much given up. Getting nowhere. I *did* try a couple of things though. Have you heard of the *Russian Abroad Foundation*? – it's over at Taganskaya."

"No."

"They focus on Russians who fled the Revolution. Part library, part museum. Archives relating to Russian émigrés. Artefacts in glass cases, that kind of thing. An interesting place. Worth a visit. I looked around and talked to a curator – hoping to turn up something."

"Was anything useful personally?"

"Nothing. It's big-league stuff. Lives of important people," Ivan said. "Not anonymous men like my grandfather. You should go though – there's a lot of general historical interest."

The *Russian Abroad Foundation Library* was a symbol of rapprochement between the modern Russian state, and the White Russian diaspora. The Foundation had its origins in the early 1970s, when Alexander Solzhenitsyn, recently exiled to the West, began urging the families of other prominent émigrés to collect and preserve their personal papers in one place. Over the years an archive was built up, and after the collapse of the Soviet Union the Moscow City authorities provided the Foundation with space for a library. Today it's housed in a modern building near Taganksaya Metro station, and contains over 50,000 items, including a collection of published works about Russians overseas, and an assortment of private family records, personal correspondence, and rare manuscripts written by famous exiles. The Revolution saw the flight not only of the old aristocracy, Tzarist politicians and defeated military figures, but also much of the country's creative and intellectual elite. This diversity is reflected in the library's contents. It holds, for example, the private papers of helicopter pioneer Igor Sikorsky, and opera bass Fyodor Chaliapin, as well as key figures in anti-communist émigré circles, such as the Tzar's cousin Grand Duke Nikolai Romanov. Several years after I left Moscow the Foundation, in recognition of his role in its establishment, officially renamed itself *The Alexander Solzhenitsyn Russian Abroad House.*

"Have you done anything else?" I asked Ivan. "What about a detective?"

"No detective – but Gulnara found a genealogy outfit on the internet. They've an office in Marosejka Street."

Gulnara was his secretary.

"I went there," he continued, "and it's just what you'd expect. Scruffy room, boxes of papers everywhere, a couple of PCs and a printer. Loads of old reference books – gazetteers, directories, that kind of stuff. And posters of family trees stuck on the walls – advertising I suppose. A guy called Popov was fluent in English – and seemed knowledgeable in a theoretical way. He gave me a sales pitch about the techniques they use and showed me photocopies of military and parish records – a lot of them handwritten by the priests. He had census documents, and other official papers. Apparently in some parts of the country it's not too difficult to track people down – even for peasant families. The key thing's to find the village they originate from. Often there are more sources than you'd imagine. But Popov admitted it's seriously difficult in some places. Western Russia's a problem – because invasions and warfare means most archives there were destroyed."

"What does it cost?"

"Anything from $100 to a few thousand – depending on what you want done and how complicated it is. But we didn't get that far in my case. Because he dropped a bombshell. Something that never occurred to me before – although it's so bloody obvious now."

I looked at him expectantly.

"He asked if I'm sure Morozov was my grandfather's real surname."

"Oh!"

"And I'm not. It probably *is* genuine – but I've no proof. When you think about it, a young guy fleeing for his life might change it to cover his tracks. So, you see, I think I've hit a brick wall. Time to give up."

"That's a pity."

"Yes, but I'm glad I tried. I'd always have wondered…And I'm glad I came and saw Moscow."

"Do you feel at home here?"

"It's not home – but it *is* special. And it's caught my imagination. Probably because I *want* to feel a bit Russian. But to be honest, Moscow's more mundane – although at the same time more mysterious – than I thought. Don't say anything, but I won't stay here long now. I've seen enough to go back to London satisfied."

***

Not long after my conversations with Ivan, a more public narrative of exile and return caught my attention. Amidst huge publicity, the remains of two celebrated White Russians and their wives were repatriated from the US and Switzerland, for reburial in the cemetery at Moscow's Donskoi Monastery. Civil War General Anton Denikin had fled Russia in 1920, after his forces in southern Russia were defeated by the Red Army, while religious philosopher

Ivan Illyn was exiled in 1922 for criticism of the Bolsheviks. Denikin died in Michigan in 1947, and Illyn near Zurich in 1953, but after years of negotiation, and the active encouragement of the Russian state, their bones were now coming home. TV and press coverage stressed the repatriation's historical significance, and although ostensibly a religious rather than an official occasion, it enjoyed the full support of the Kremlin. It was conceived as a national event – and was reported as such. At the airport a military guard of honour carried the four coffins to waiting hearses. The funeral service in the monastery's cathedral was a solemn Orthodox occasion, with prayers, candles, incense, and elegiac music, and an address by Patriarch Aleksi II, the head of the Russian Orthodox Church. The burial itself took place with full military honours, a tricolor draped over Denikin's coffin, and a canon fired in salute. Accompanying soldiers carried mementos – Denikin's hat and an assortment of Tzarist medals. President Putin himself did not attend, but sent a personal envoy, and amongst the motley collection of other guests representing different elements of Russian society were Moscow's Mayor, Yuri Luzhkov, Culture Minister Alexander Sokolov, and far-right demagogue and leader of the Liberal Democratic Party, Vladimir Zhirinovsky. Rubbing shoulders with these VIPs were monarchists and descendants of the worldwide White Russian community.

Outwith the official cordon a crowd of ordinary mourners looked on, and news clips showed a group in Cossack uniforms, while others displayed icons or portraits of the last Tzar. The general's 86-year-old daughter Marina was in attendance at the graveside, to scatter earth and lay a bouquet of flowers. A resident of France, she had been granted Russian citizenship by President Putin to pave the way for this return.

Observers spoke of the poignancy of the event itself, while at the same time recognising its deliberate symbolism. It was a political gesture – an act of rapprochement by the Russian authorities to anti-Bolshevik émigrés. An attempt to make peace with the country's pre-revolutionary past. It chimed with a quote Putin reportedly made during a visit to a cemetery near Paris, where he stopped in front of a memorial to White Russian soldiers and said: "We are children of the same mother – Russia. And it's time for us all to unite."

Denikin's funeral was also a reminder of the Kremlin's increasing enlistment of Orthodoxy in forging a new post-Soviet national identity. Official invitations described it as a ceremony of 'national reconciliation', and in his address Patriarch Alexi spoke of it symbolising the end of the Civil War, and a return to unity for the Russian people and the Orthodox Church. Some commentators detected an attempt to invoke the Romanovs, and Imperial Russia, as a strand of this new identity. The latter has become a curiously paradoxical project, fusing several impossibly contradictory elements. The rehabilitation of Stalin as an archetype of strong leadership and state power, sits uneasily with a celebration of the Tzar, the Church and Old Russia as exemplars of traditional values and national pride.

When I tested Denikin's name on Valeria, she confessed she'd never heard of him before this recent burst of publicity. A famous figure in émigré circles, he was largely unknown to ordinary Russians. As an enemy of socialism, he was deliberately ignored during the Soviet years. (Official oblivion however did not mean official disregard, and during his exile in the West Stalin's agents made several unsuccessful attempts to assassinate him.) Now however, at the behest of the Kremlin, the Russian press laboured to educate the public – stressing the stance of Denikin (and Illyn) during WWII, when they remained steadfastly opposed to the Nazis. It's a critical message – for relationships between émigrés and the Russian state were for decades overshadowed by the huge number of Whites who sided with Hitler during the war, in the desperate hope of defeating Stalin. For a country that continues to take enormous pride in its victory over Germany, this wartime disloyalty still poisons the perception of émigrés for communists and nationalists alike.

As I watched the Denikin drama play out in the Russian media, I was conscious of witnessing, albeit secondhand, something unique. An event with both contemporary significance and a direct, living connection to world history. Of course, something grander and even more important had taken place in St Petersburg in the 1990s, when Boris Yeltsin had the remains of Tzar Nicholas II and the Imperial Family interred in the crypt of the Cathedral of St. Peter & St. Paul. Again, the intention had been reconciliation, and the Orthodox Church participated in the funeral rites, despite doubts about the authenticity of the bones. Although these had been recovered from a clay pit near Yekaterinburg, where the family's Bolshevik executioners reputedly dumped them, many experts had doubts about their provenance.

The Denikin reburial lacked the tragic dimension of Nicholas II's, yet carried its own resonance. The political implications of what once would have seemed an impossible return from exile, were less interesting than the light it cast on modern Russia's relationship with the past. The heavy media coverage of the funeral captured in photographs and newsreel clips, a series of little vignettes that illuminated different responses to Denikin's repatriation: Ordinary Russians seen by-passing security, to hand soldiers flowers to put on the graves. Once all the VIPs had departed, mourners kissing the wooden crosses placed on each of the four graves. An old woman telling TV reporters that the funeral was an act of repentance, atonement for the crime of the 1917 revolution. Gennady Zyuganov, the leader of the Communist Party grumbling sourly about the ceremony's grandeur, then downplaying its importance by declaring that anyway communists don't make war on the dead. A journalist reporting on the monastery setting – and relishing its irony. (The monks' cells, he reminded us, had been communal apartments during Soviet times, and its crematorium took in the bodies of Bolshevik enemies.) A particular nugget was the attendance at the ceremony of Oscar-winning filmmaker Nikita Mikhalkov, often cited as a living symbol of modern Russia's schizophrenia. Mikhalkov is a monarchist whose aristocratic father not only supported the communists but wrote the Soviet national anthem – including a revised version praising God instead of Stalin. Remarkably, a military band played the Soviet anthem outside the cathedral, drawing what one reporter described as an "audible gasp" from mourners. In the spirit of reconciliation – and possibly mischief making – Mikhalkov used the occasion to call for other high-profile reburials, including the return from the USA of the remains of composer Sergey Rachmaninoff, and despite implacable opposition from the communists, the removal of Lenin's mummified body from its Red Square mausoleum.

If the Denikin funeral was a symbolic attempt at reconciliation with Imperial Russia, it was also plainly a focus on only one side of the country's history. Modern Russia has yet to make serious efforts to come to terms with its Soviet past. Some of Stalin's worst crimes have been acknowledged, and individual historians are free to study the Soviet decades, but no large-scale re-evaluation has been undertaken. There has been no official accounting or exorcism of the Soviet Union's lies, failures, atrocities and betrayals. For a brief period after the fall of communism it seemed this might happen, but in the absence of genuine desire, the moment passed.

18

The best literary walk in Moscow is along the Boulevard Ring from Pushkin Square to the Kropotkinskaya Metro station on Volkhonka Street. It takes about forty minutes and passes through the richest areas in the city for literary associations. The stretch beginning on Tverskoi Boulevard was minutes away from my apartment, so it became part of my life in Moscow, and I walked there almost every day. The statue of Alexander Pushkin that stands looking over traffic at the edge of the Square is a fitting departure point. As Russia's national poet, he has the same iconic status as Shakespeare in England. He's unmissable in Moscow, memorialised in over 150 sites in the central area alone. While his writing embraced many genres, from short stories and fairy tales to historical dramas, he's revered primarily as a poet and his great verse novel, *Eugene Onegin*, is a key text in Russian literature. His continuing popularity with the Russian public is evident in the Pushkin Square Metro station, where selections of his poetry adorn the platform walls. Pushkin's works deal with universal themes: love, tensions between duty and personal happiness, the trials of ordinary people, and conflict between individual aspirations and the expectations of society. His key legacy however was that he pioneered the use of simple, colloquial Russian as a language for literature – in contrast to the flowery, overblown style favoured by his predecessors. His language is the language of Russia today. Yet despite this freshness, my personal attempts at reading him were not successful – his genius lost on me as my Russian never managed to adequately tackle his original texts. English versions inevitably proved the maxim that great poetry is untranslatable. Difficulties in replicating rhyme, rhythm and shades of meaning in a foreign tongue, can mean translated poetry – from any language – seems limp and banal.

A hundred yards or so down the Boulevard is the statue of another poet – Sergei Yesenin. Before my Moscow adventure I'd never heard of him, so initially paid it little attention. It sits in a dark area, with high buildings on either side, and mature lime trees that block out the sun. One autumn evening however, as I passed just before dusk, I was caught by unfamiliar splashes of bright colour, and approached to find the statue decked with floral bouquets. Not just bunches of flowers, but elaborate shop-prepared displays, dressed with lace and ribbons. Although the figure is twice life-size, and stands on top of a granite plinth, someone had draped garlands around his neck and shoulders. Now curious, I researched Yesenin, and found that 8 October was the anniversary of his death. The rest of his story is colourful and dramatic.

The current popularity of both Pushkin and Yesenin is due in part to their romantic reputations. After a career of baiting the Tzarist authorities and calling for liberty, Pushkin died young – in a duel, defending the honour of his wife Natalya Goncharova. Likewise, Yesenin is adored and mythologised today for his rock-star lifestyle of drugs, alcohol, trashed hotel rooms and multiple marriages. The son of peasants, he came to Moscow in 1912 when he was 17, published a series of lyric poems which are still immensely popular, then hanged himself in a St. Petersburg hotel room at the age of 30. When his body was brought back to Moscow for burial, the *Church of the Apostle John* – a beautiful 17th century gem located on the boulevard just behind his statue – was the setting for his funeral ceremony. I found Yesenin's work more accessible than Pushkin's, but I struggled again to do it full justice.

During the Soviet years the authorities viewed Pushkin and Yesenin very differently. Pushkin's difficulties with the Tzar's regime gave him perfect credentials, and his star remained undiminished throughout. Yesenin however fell into disfavour when his initial support for the revolution changed to disillusionment, and his decadent lifestyle further offended communist prudery.

Throughout its history the Boulevard has been a prestigious location. In its early years it was home to aristocrats and the city's wealthiest families, a place for fashionable Muscovites to take the air and stroll in their finery. In *Anna Karenina*, Kitty, Dolly and Natalia walked here in their satin dresses, "escorted by a footman with a gold cockade in his hat." It's no longer the haunt of high society, but popular with bohemian types and intellectuals, and the area near Yesenin's statue was, I noticed, a gathering place for Moscow's young, gay women. Little groups congregated on park-benches, sat under trees chatting and drinking beer from cans, and strolled hand-in-hand along the paths. Strangely though, there seemed no sign of gay men. Was the girls' presence coincidental – or did the Yesenin connection draw them to this spot? Did his messy, flawed, tragic life have the same resonance Judy Garland has for gay men? As I researched his story I reflected on the irony of a gay connection, for Yesenin himself was defiantly heterosexual. Apart from a series of mistresses, over the years he had five wives, one of them the famed American dancer Isadora Duncan. I decided to ask Valeria about him. What was his reputation with her generation?

"Of course I've heard of him!" she said. "We studied his poetry at school."

"Is it good?"

"It's romantic. About life in the countryside and people in our villages."

"But is it any good?"

Valeria was silent for a moment.

"My teacher said it was good. But Robbie, I'm not so interested in poetry. His story's more interesting – that's what everybody remembers."

Hardly enthusiastic praise for a poet loved by millions for his affecting, nostalgic, musical verse. But she had a point. The Yesenin cult is as much about his life as his work. It helps that he's seen as a rebel, and that the communist authorities, suspicious of his individualism and critical of his debauchery, banned his works for decades.

"And now the truth's clear," Valeria went on.

"What truth?"

"About his murder – it was in the film."

Apparently, a year earlier Russian TVs Channel 1 had shown a historical miniseries dramatising Yesenin's life. The facts alone would have been enough for a lurid melodrama, but the filmmaker also contrived a controversial ending – based on the persistent rumour that Yesenin was killed by the KGB's forerunner, the NKVD. Historians familiar with the circumstances of his death are sceptical, and accept the official verdict of suicide as most likely correct. But for a generation of Russians, seeing him murdered on TV will surely change the record.

"Do you believe it?"

"This is Russia," Valeria said. "Anybody can believe what they want about our history."

I was about to ask if my assumptions about the gay girls near his statue were correct, but instead let it rest. A few weeks later however, Morrison spotted a story in the *Moscow Times* that prompted a discussion. We were drinking coffee with Norman, when Morrison held up the newspaper and said: "See who's on the front page – Peter Tatchell!"

"Who's Peter Tatchell?" Norman asked.

"A gay rights campaigner. He's English – you won't have heard of him."

"Yesterday the *Times* said he was in town," Morrison continued. "Now it says he's been arrested. Look at the photo – he's getting led away by a couple of riot police. Big strapping guys. Looks like Peter's enjoying getting his collar felt."

This was untrue. Tatchell's face was expressionless. If there was anything, it was a hint of resignation. Morrison however pressed on, warming to his story.

"He came for some march that was banned. It happened anyway and he's ended up in jail. According to the paper he was barracked by a religious crowd chanting *Moscow's not Sodom!* But there's always a bright side – if you believe the stories about prisons do you think he'll count it a satisfying visit?"

Norman and I said nothing, and Morrison took our silence for reproach.

"Oh come on," he said. "This is Russia. They don't do political correctness. We can say what we like."

He was silent for a moment, then continued in a more serious tone. "Maybe it's not a *New York Times* take on life, but in some ways there's *real* freedom of speech here. You can talk about race or homosexuality without getting crucified. Say most things – even if they're nasty. Back home they'll criticise Russia for lack of democracy – and *talk* about freedom – but if you say anything taboo the same freedom-lovers soon close you down."

It's not easy to be openly gay in today's Russia. Although homosexuality was decriminalised in 1993, it's still widely condemned, and the prospect of gay men parading in the city's streets provokes outrage from politicians and religious leaders. The Orthodox Church formally condemns homosexuality, and the Mayor of Moscow at the time of Tatchell's visit publicly branded gays abnormal, and gay parades satanic. The Kremlin too is anti-gay – but for tactical rather than moral reasons. Their hostility is a calculated swipe at the degenerate West, designed to keep the Church on side, and stifle any Western notions of openness and toleration that could lead to pressure for political reform. Gay nightclubs in Moscow routinely suffer campaigns of intimidation, and when gay public events are permitted, they attract aggressive hostility. A motley collection of opponents, including skinheads and religious representatives – usually old women and Orthodox priests – will typically attend and shower them with rubbish, eggs and rotten fruit. No wonder there were no obvious male homosexuals near the Yesenin statue.

But they do have their haunts in other parts of Moscow, as Morrison pointed out.

"It's strange," I said. "The fuss about gay men – when gay females gather on Tverskoi Boulevard and nobody bothers. But maybe I'm reading it wrong and they're not gay at all?"

"You're not wrong," Morrison said. "They are what they seem. But somehow they're tolerated. I guess they're not threatening. A couple of guys hand-in-hand's another kettle of fish. They need to be careful. But there *are* places – if you want your bum felt in Moscow head for Kitai Gorod Metro Station. Or cruise through Ilinskiye Vorota Park."

***

Set back from the road on the stretch of boulevard between the Pushkin and Yesenin statues, is a sprawling yellow and white mansion that in 1812 was the birthplace of socialist philosopher and writer, Alexander Herzen. Commonly known today as *Herzen House,* it's perhaps the street's most interesting building. Although an important figure in Russian radicalism, Herzen was until recently largely forgotten in the West. His profile revived when dramatist Tom Stoppard made him a central character in a trilogy of plays entitled *The Coast of Utopia,* about 19th century Russian thinkers in exile. The National Theatre in England staged the work to critical acclaim in 2002, and while living in Moscow in 2007 I spotted a review in the local press of a production running at the city's *Russian Academic Youth Theatre.*

With Herzen again briefly in front of his hometown public, I wondered what my Russian colleagues made of him. But his name drew blank looks, and I concluded he was a dusty irrelevance in post-Soviet Russia. Later however, a Russian acquaintance of a literary persuasion was more informative.

"Of course, I know Herzen!" he said. "Some people believe his statue has magical powers." He was referring to the memorial that sits in the mansion's grounds.

It's well known that touching statues of Pushkin or his bride Natalya Goncharova brings luck in love, but Herzen's powers were more worldly.

"If you kiss his statue on the backside," my friend said, "you may win a Nobel Prize for literature – or at least become a successful writer."

From then on, every time I passed the mansion I'd glance towards the statue, hoping to spy some aspiring author caressing the rear of the philosopher's granite frock-coat.

Since 1936 *Herzen House* has officially been the *Maxim Gorky Literature Institute,* a venue for writers to socialise and give public readings of their works. Some have also lodged there, (Boris Pasternak had a small apartment in the 1930s), but more recently it acquired new fame through its association with Mikhail Bulgakov's surreal novel, *The Master and Margarita.* Bulgakov's book is widely regarded a masterpiece of 20th century literature, although it remained unpublished during the author's lifetime and for decades later, due to its political sensitivity. Moving between two settings, 1930s Moscow and Jerusalem at the time of Jesus, it's both a satirical portrait of the contemporary city, and a meditation on themes that were anathema to the Soviet state – religion and spirituality, freedom and truth. As the Moscow sections lampooned various thinly disguised institutions and prominent citizens, they were particularly dangerous for Bulgakov. Some critics argue that when Satan appears (in the figure of the central character, Woland) with a bunch of ludicrous henchmen, he's intended as a direct parody of Stalin.

Bulgakov's Moscow is the city within the garden ring, and many sites in the book are largely unchanged today. Some were given fictitious names, but it's rarely difficult to identify them from descriptions in the text. *Herzen House* became *Griboyedov House,* the home of a literary association called *Massolit,* whose chairman encounters the devil at Patriashy Prudy, and sparks a series of weird events across Moscow. *Massolit* was a satire on the official Soviet literary organization based in the Gorky Institute, and the scenes there culminate in a deliberately started fire which destroys the premises. In real life the mansion remains intact, a must-see destination for those Bulgakov fans who experience central Moscow in the way Joyce enthusiasts see the Dublin of *Ulysses* – as a literary theme-park, of interest mainly as source material for the novel.

For devotees of Bulgakov the most important destination in Moscow however is not on the Boulevard, but a fifteen-minute digression west to the Garden Ring, where an archway between a coffee-shop and a pharmacy on Triumfalnaya Square leads into a small courtyard of tenement flats. The official address is 10 Bolshaya Sadovaya Street, and it's the location of the State Bulgakov Museum. Bulgakov had various homes in Moscow, but remarkably two of them were in this courtyard. The earliest, apartment no. 50, is now the museum. From 1921-24 the writer and his wife shared a room in a communal apartment here. It was not a pleasant experience. The other inhabitants were rowdy and disreputable – some kept piglets and chickens in the shared kitchen – and frequently there were vicious rows. Long after he left Bulgakov remained haunted by memories of life there, and famously put them to use in his work. The apartment became the inspiration for the Strange Flat in *The Master and Margarita*, where weird things started to happen when Woland's entourage took up residence.

As a house museum, Bulgakov's flat is unusual. Most Moscow examples are stuffy affairs, that freeze homes exactly as they were in the days of their famous occupants. They become depositories for their personal belongings, and articles associated with their lives.

Bulgakov's however is less concerned with preserving the interior as he personally knew it, than recreating the feel of Moscow life in general during the 1920s and 30s. There are fewer personal artefacts than normal, although there *are* some – including, in a glass case, a manuscript of *The Master and Margarita*. But the house is filled with furniture and typical domestic items from the time. More ambitiously, it's a culture and arts centre as much as a traditional museum. Visitors can wander freely, inspect the exhibits, and study the various audio-visual displays on offer. In keeping with the overall ambience, these are often on themes related to Moscow in the inter-war years. They also change regularly – providing a reason to visit more than once. I was satisfied with a single tour each of Gorki and Chekhov's houses but returned many times to the Bulgakov Museum. Besides the official offerings, I found the bohemian atmosphere congenial. One room is now a café, and there's also a small theatre which stages excerpts from Bulgakov's works, and readings of new material by contemporary writers and poets. There was even a black house-cat named Behemoth – after the magical cat in *The Master and Margarita* – which was allowed to roam as it liked through the premises.

Tourists typically look around then leave, but for local Bulgakov devotees the museum is a place to congregate, relax and socialise. The regular patrons are mainly young, an interesting mix of student and artistic types, eccentrics, *Margarita* nerds, and serious scholars. They gather inside the house, and out in the courtyard, where more than once I detected a whiff of pot in the air. From the 1970s, when the novel was first available in Russia, and long before the flat became a museum, this was a place of pilgrimage. Visitors came to sit on the steps, discuss the text, and experience the mystery of the site. Some continue to believe it's haunted, and point to parallels between the book and events in real life. During Woland's tenure a number of occupants inexplicably vanished – clearly due to supernatural causes. Similarly, in the 1930s several of the flat's real-life residents also suddenly disappeared. Believers in a paranormal explanation however conveniently forget that it was the height of Stalin's Terror, and citizens were disappearing all over Moscow.

While *The Master and Margarita* has become a literary phenomenon with an enthusiastic international audience, my own response to Bulgakov is ambivalent. Russians love him for the revenge his novel takes on Stalin and the inter-war Soviet elite. Academics and professional critics are grateful that his dense, complicated, multi-layered work provides raw material for unlimited analysis and interpretation. And many younger readers, weaned on Harry Potter and *Lord of the Rings,* are drawn to his fantasy and magic. *The Master and Margarita* it seems, provides something for everyone: comedy, satire, religion, surrealism, the occult, love. I found parts hugely funny, others thought-provoking. Yet overall, its very variety seems a weakness. Its splintered narratives crash off in different directions, at times gripping readers, at others leaving them mystified and unsatisfied. It fails to hang together as a coherent whole.

***

Continuing along the Boulevard Ring, Tverskoi Boulevard gives way to Nikitski Boulevard, the site of what is the finest piece of public art in Moscow: an early 20th century statue of the writer Nikolai Gogol. It stands in the courtyard of the yellow two-storey house in which he lived for the last four years of his life, and where he died in 1852. It's my favourite of all statues in the city – an iconic monument that portrays the writer not as a stately public figure, but a real man – mournful, careworn, and despairing. It's Gogol in the last years of his life – sick and troubled. He's seated, slumped, head bowed, with his body muffled by his cloak, as if it might shield him from the pain of the world. Whether the sculptor intended it or not, the pose carries an echo of Gogol's *The Overcoat*, the most famous short story in Russian literature. Originally the statue was sited a few minutes away, at the top of what is today Gogolovsky Boulevard (the next segment of my walk). But in the 1950s it was moved to its present location, as the Soviet authorities thought it too melancholic for such a high-profile setting. Unlike most public monuments it's a great work of art in itself. Yet the reaction at its unveiling in 1909 was similar to the Soviet response. Instead of acclaim the observers, expecting their heroes to look regal and imposing, greeted it with consternation and silence.

At the spot on Gogolovsky Boulevard where it used to sit, there's now a second Gogol, a conventional portrait erected when the first was removed. This version conveys no sense of sorrow or inner turmoil; the writer stands three metres high, erect and dignified, book-in-hand, on a plinth engraved with an appreciative inscription from the Soviet government. The house on Nikitski Boulevard where he died is now a museum to his memory, and it's preserved largely as it was in the mid-19th century. As the Boulevard was the most direct route from my apartment to the Arbat area, I passed it often, and each time registered a twinge of annoyance at one anachronistic detail – a modern PVC window disfiguring the gable that adjoins the street. *It's a historic monument for goodness sake! The last home of one of Russia's greatest writers!* The site of something truly iconic – the fireplace where a few days before his death, Gogol famously burned the manuscript of the second part of his novel, *Dead Souls*. Couldn't they have fitted an appropriate period window? *Why this cheap, plastic, double-glazed unit?*

In time though, I came to revise my precious verdict. Wouldn't Gogol himself, with his sense of comedy, and fondness for mocking bureaucratic absurdity and incompetence, have relished the window's incongruity? Did it better celebrate his essence than the pious conservation of most house-museums?

***

Standing amongst trees on the central path of Gogolovsky Boulevard – the last lap of my literary walk – is a memorial to the novelist Mikhail Sholokhov. During my second year in Moscow the *Moscow Times* reported its unveiling, and a few days later, on a warm morning in late May, I went to investigate. Sholokhov was an important name during my student days, and to have him unexpectedly resurface brought back many memories.

He has always been a controversial figure. When he died in 1984, he was the most celebrated writer in the Soviet Union, with over sixty million copies of his books sold in Russia alone. *Quiet Flows the Don*, his saga about the Revolution and Civil War, is regarded by many as the greatest Russian novel of the 20th century. A sweeping historical epic, it meshes the private lives of a group of ordinary people during a period of conflict and change, with a depiction of the larger social and political forces sweeping their country. The early parts are a compelling portrait of Don Cossack culture and village life in peacetime, while later sections focus on military struggles, capturing in evocative battle scenes the horror and confusion of war. It brought him international fame –

including the Nobel Prize for Literature – yet throughout his career he attracted scorn and disapproval, becoming after his death a neglected, unfashionable figure in the new Russia. It was no accident that it was more twenty years after he died before the Moscow authorites finally honoured him with a public memorial.

Sholokhov's problem was his close association with communism. He was a Soviet, rather than simply a Russian writer, and unlike his younger contemporary Alexander Solzhenitsyn, remained a loyal communist throughout his career. He accepted official posts and political honours, and he was a high-profile critic of the dissident movement during the Late-Soviet period. His ideology made enemies in both Russia and the West, and the stick used to beat him was the accusation of plagiarism – a claim which dogged much of his career. Detractors alleged he wasn't the real author of *Quiet Flows the Don*. Allegedly, he stole the manuscript from the baggage of a dead White Russian army officer and claimed it as his own. He was therefore scorned as both a Party lackey and a fraud. Solzhenitsyn was a leading critic and repeated the plagiarism slur in a literary article in the 1970s.

The question of authorship remains, after more than eight decades, a fascinating, unsolved literary detective story. With no solid proof of plagiarism, adversaries construct a circumstantial case by combining details of Sholokhov's life, with what they claim is internal evidence in the novel. He was too young and raw they argue, when the novel's first parts were published, to write with such breadth, subtlety, and psychological complexity. Would a hardline communist plausibly create such balanced and sympathetic portraits of White Russian fighters? Or depict Red Army officers as unflatteringly as they appear in the novel? A refusal to idealise the Reds was suspiciously un-Marxist. Similarly, the fate

187

of the novel's central character, Grigory Melekhov, seemed further proof Sholokhov was not the author. At the end Melekhov goes home to his White Russian family – a resolution that's realistic and artistically satisfying – but troubling for critics unwilling to concede a communist writer might put art before ideology. The correct outcome it seems, would have been for Melekhov to join the Red Army.

There was also no physical evidence of Sholokhov's authorship. His personal archives were long lost, so no papers directly linked him with the novel. When a version largely in his handwriting surfaced after his death, doubters claimed it had been cooked up in the 1920s, to rebut early allegations of theft. Latterly however, a computer analysis by Swedish academics compared the novel's word patterns with undisputed writing by Sholokhov and found them statistically too close to be accidental – vindicating him in the eyes of many critics. Yet the dispute continues. When evidence supporting Sholokhov appears, opponents quickly muster rebuttals. It's unlikely there will ever be a conclusive resolution.

My own discovery of Sholokhov was as a student in the 1970s. Although not on any prescribed reading list, he became a talisman for bookish left-wingers in that era of Cold War tensions. In truth, less for his work than the fact he wasn't Alexander Solzhenitsyn. The latter's defection had made him the darling of the Western media, and his novels flooded the bookshops. The Left, naturally, were sick of him – and mustered Sholokhov in response. Here was an alternative modern master: a Great Russian who stood for all the right things. Many of my contemporaries absorbed this new orthodoxy and enthused about *Quiet Flows the Don*. Solzhenitsyn was a reactionary propagandist, and Sholokhov the authentic voice of Russia. A writer who understood the lives of ordinary people. It was a judgment most of us were ill-equipped to make, but it satisfied a need at the time. And now, more than thirty years later, hopefully a wiser man, I stood in front of Sholokhov's new memorial, admired the sculptor's artistry, and determined to re-read *Quiet Flows the Don*.

The memorial is in two parts. A life-sized bronze rowing-boat rests on top of a huge slab of black stone. It slopes down at an angle, with the stern at the highest point. There Sholokhov sits, his jacket draped around his shoulders, oars resting at his sides. He's gazing ahead – as if over a river. Behind him is a complementary structure. A section of grass banking, between the footpath and the iron railings which shield the Boulevard's gardens from the road, is overlaid with panels of granite. They provide a smooth incline, on which there's a collection of stone horses' heads – suggesting a herd swimming in a river. It's not only a statue, but also a fountain, and water flows from the top, lapping the horses' necks, catching the light and producing an effect of life and movement. It's an unusual and attractive monument, both visually interesting and for those familiar with Sholokhov's work, loaded with meaning. Alexander Rukovoshnikov who designed it, pointed out the symbolism to the *Moscow Times*: the horses are swimming in different directions, echoing the confrontations of the Civil War.

I was lucky that morning, soon after the memorial's inauguration, to see it at its best, with the water flowing as intended. When I visited again later in the year the water was off, and the granite slope dry and strewn with leaves and litter. A design fault meant the drain at the bottom of the slope was prone to blockages, and if left running, water cascaded over the edge and flooded the footpath. The failure to align artistry and plumbing was a trifling flaw however, in an otherwise impressive monument.

19

Surprisingly, birthdays are important occasions in Russian life. I would have guessed the opposite, assuming communism's denial of the individual had forever banished such bourgeois observances. But in the New Russia, birthdays are widely and often lavishly celebrated. Aside from parties in private homes and restaurants, there's a tradition of celebrations in the workplace, and whenever an anniversary occurred in our HR department a party was held in a meeting room, everyone contributing to buy food and drink. For convenience these usually took place at lunchtime on Fridays, rather than on the day itself. At that time staff could drink freely, confident no senior manager would look for them.

The drinking was heavy, the mood relaxed, and it was a chance for me to chat informally with my Russian staff and hear them speak off-guard. Gossip and truths normally suppressed, surfaced as the vodka flowed. At a gathering around the time of some Duma elections, a tipsy Kolbakov broke off his conversation with some Russian colleagues and abruptly turned to me. "What do you think of Mr. Putin?" he said in English.

I shrugged non-committedly. "I don't know much about him."

As a foreigner, I was wary of political discussions, and when talk drifted in that direction I avoided contributing. In my ignorance I might have scratched dark sores from Russia's past and caused offence or embarrassment. I wasn't in Moscow as a journalist, so had no obligation to probe the political currents around me. Yet I was not oblivious to them. My time in the city coincided with the high Putin years, and I watched his public performance with curiosity and respect. Although careful to keep my opinions private, I was also keen to hear those of my Russian acquaintances. And happy enough to gently prod a conversation if necessary.

"I've never voted for Mr. Putin," Kolbakov continued. "Never!"

"I didn't know he's up for election."

"He's not. But his party's in the Duma election – and I won't support them."

"Is this an important election?"

"No – it's not important. The Duma doesn't matter. It's just the home of hot air. But I'll still oppose him."

The State Duma is the lower house of Russia's legislature, separate from the Presidency, and largely subservient to its will. A parliamentary assembly that can initiate legislation, with a constitutional right to vet government ministers. But the real power lies with the President, who exercises control over all important matters of state. As Kolbakov indicated, the Duma is essentially a glorified talking shop. Yet it does have political significance, since its actions can influence the national mood. The Kremlin therefore takes care to ensure its supporters occupy a key proportion of Duma seats.

"What's the problem with Mr. Putin?" I said.

"I don't trust him. He's a dictator – and won't allow real freedom in Russia".

He reeled off a series of complaints that echoed criticisms common in the Western press – corruption, incompetence, political repression. In this however, I knew Kolbakov was out of tune with most of his countrymen, for whom the picture is more complicated. While Putin's ruling United Russia party, together with its opponents – an uneasy colletion of liberal reformers, communists, extreme nationalists, and noisy marginal groups – regularly fill the media with squabbles over policy and the condition of Russia, the predominant response to politics from the wider population is indifference. Political engagement – even awareness – is limited, and largely the preserve of the middle classes and the Moscow elite. Kolbakov, and most of those with whom I worked, were members of a big-city, liberal, outward-looking professional class, whose views were unrepresentative of the Russian majority.

It's easy when contemplating modern Russian politics, to fall back on the cliché of a nation getting the rulers it deserves – particularly when the general lack of political involvement stems from apathy rather than fear. Russia today is not the Soviet Union, and citizens are unafraid to express political opinions. Mostly they just can't be bothered. Politics are a distraction from the struggles of day-to-day life, rather than a means of improvement. Dismissing such passivity as laziness or stupidity, however, is inadequate. Those without strong political commitments – the provincial majority, ordinary workers, the poor, the anxious – are neither unenlightened nor negligent, but in all likelihood hold views directly opposite to Kolbakov's. During my years in Moscow, the majority of Russians genuinely supported the established order and Putin, whom they welcomed as a force for stability after the upheavals of the 1990s.

I changed tack with Kolbakov and threw him a question about Putin's public profile.

"What about the sports? He seems a real tough guy."

Kolbakov snorted. "Showing off like a schoolboy? Is that how a serious leader should behave? He's an embarrassment."

I was referring to the Russian media's portrayal of Putin as a man of action. To the photographs that circulated worldwide of him bare-chested on horseback, competing in judo contests or, rifle in-hand, stalking dangerous animals in the wilderness. I understood Kolbakov's distaste, but thought him wrong to interpret the President's macho image as personal vanity or celebrity PR. The key point was that Putin had created a character for himself – he was playing a part. The posturing might provoke ridicule in the West, but his target was not an international audience, or even Russia's wealthy elites and educated middle classes – but the mass of ordinary Russians for whom his displays of masculinity contained important messages. Putin's image was of disciplined masculinity. His activities required not only guts and aggression, but also training, hard work, and above all self-control. The testosterone on display was the soldier's or athlete's – not the wife-beating drunk or the street brawler. Politically of course, this deliberately contrasted him with the drunkenness and shambling personal profile of his predecessor Boris Yeltsin. And signalled a new era in Russia of pride in the state.

If psychologically it drew a line under the 1990s, it also spoke to the concerns of ordinary people. In the anxious society that is modern Russia, a macho strongman as a national father-figure promises security and protection in insecure times. For Russian men he's a role model, who combines strength with self-respect and self-control – challenging the hopelessness of swathes of the male population mired in unemployment, drink and drugs. His PR team carefully balance his public physicality with a softer side – standard heartwarming political props, like visiting hospitals, smiling at babushkas and accepting flowers from children. Unusually for a Russian male, he's also famously teetotal – which gets approval from ordinary women, who contrast his strength, sobriety, and good health with the alcoholism and weakness of their husbands, fathers and sons.

None of this however chimed with Kolbakov, who saw only a bumptious autocrat. Personal dislike prevented a subtler, more balanced assessment.

"What Russia needs," he told me, "Isn't pretending and silly photographs. We'll never change without real democracy – like you have in England."

Later on, I tested Valeria on the same subject. She was from the same generation as Kolbakov, but a few years younger. I repeated his criticisms, without telling her the source. Her response was thoughtful and pragmatic. She had none of Kolbakov's idealism.

"Of course we have some problems," she said. "But they're not so terrible. Anyway, I am not interested in politics. Young people don't care. There are more important things."

"Like what?"

She thought for a moment. "My work – my career. Music or art for example. Some people like movies – and personal life of course. That's the most important thing – personal life."

"There must be something you'd change?"

"Many things – but everybody in the world can say that."

Was Putin a tyrant?

She shook her head and looked at me firmly.

"He's not perfect, but you must understand Robbie, Russia's not like England. We need strong control. Russians won't behave well unless the government forces them. When I was a child life was difficult here. Even in my hometown. It's a quiet place, but there was trouble because the government didn't have good control."

Control, strength, security – unavoidable in any assessment of Russian politics. Time and again I heard that the country was essentially ungovernable, that only a strongman at the helm would prevent chaos. T'was ever thus – Russia it seems prospers best under firm rulers: Ivan the terrible, Peter the Great, Stalin. Putin simply followed in their footsteps – with the support of Valeria and the majority of the population.

It helps of course, when presidential action confirms the hard-man image. Tough talk, anti-Western rhetoric, threats to neighbouring countries, high-profile attacks on dissenting oligarchs, all received public approval. Above all, the war in Chechnya established Putin's reputation for confronting terrorism and promoting law and order. Critics argued that improved stability was an illusion. That massively increased expenditure on security and policing did nothing to make Russia safer – pointing to an annual murder rate in the first decade of this century that was higher than during the wild Yeltsin years. Yet however accurate the statistics, they didn't capture the public mood. Political PR worked: Russians felt safer – and gave Putin credit for it.

***

As a foreigner, the governance of Russia was not my business. I listened to my colleagues, looked around me, and quietly came to my own conclusions. Increasingly, I was out of tune with Western commentators who characterised the Kremlin's philosophy of Managed Democracy as a drive towards autocracy. For opponents like Kolbakov it indeed meant restricting liberty – a failure to trust ordinary Russians with political power. For others, like Valeria, it was a realistic response to the chaos of the 1990s. A recognition that Russia was not yet ready for too much freedom. There's no denying the Kremlin lacked the confidence to tolerate free public debate and manipulated the political process and intimidated the media. Yet it's farcical to portray this as a return to totalitarianism. With the exception of a short period during the Yeltsin years, ordinary Russians today have more freedom of speech – and action – than at any time in their country's history. The state exercises nothing like the hold the communists had over Soviet citizens. There's freedom of movement, of economic activity, thought and opinion. It's possible to grumble, demonstrate, and complain in ways that would have been inconceivable under communism. Terrorists and others who threaten security, will be crushed – but ordinary people need no longer fear the prying attention of authority. Critically, there's now a distinction between what it's acceptable to say in public and in private. For journalists this can be tricky. Over the past two decades, Moscow, has for them, been one of the world's most dangerous cities. A series of high-profile murders of journalists outraged international opinion, with suspicion falling on organs of the state desperate to prevent the press probing political scandals. Paradoxically, this is a sign of greater openness. The state can no longer exert the kind of comprehensive suppression of information and opinion that happened in the past. It now takes bullets to silence inconvenient voices.

20

A feature of our company's pursuit of international standards was the regular appearance in the office of foreign consultants, hired to advise on some conundrum or other. The pattern was always the same. After a period of showy and disruptive analysis that frustrated and angered staff, they would quietly disappear, leaving behind a set of recommendations that were ignored and never mentioned again. It was wasteful and ineffective, but nevertheless evidence of the President's refusal to yield to complacency. He was scratching at a sore – aware of a problem but with no real idea how to fix it. As he contemplated his dysfunctional organisation, with its absurdities, inefficiencies and general incompetence, some imagined model of a well-run Western company must have taunted him. Consultants invariably did no good, but in the absence of real remedies their arrival at least signalled action and kept people on their toes.

My first personal involvement came when I suggested to Ivanov that we could assess the competence of staff. A few days afterwards he announced at a Weekly Management Meeting that he'd ordered me to prepare a programme for staff development – which would begin with an assessment exercise. I would present details of the grand plan to the meeting in two weeks time.

The testing was no surprise, but it was the first I'd heard of either a development programme or a two-week deadline. When Mr. Pryadkin asked who would be assessed, the President turned to him, and with a strange glint in his eye said: "Vladimir Fedorvich – *everybody* will be assessed. All of the company – including everybody in this room."

There was silence as the news sank in. Ivanov seemed to enjoy the discomfort of his managers, but as it became apparent nobody else wanted to speak, he continued.

"I'll take the same tests myself," he declared. "It'll be interesting to see what we discover. Strengths and weaknesses of course. But one thing's certain – no good manager has anything to worry about."

His final comment did nothing to raise the mood in the room.

Within a week I'd put together an outline of a programme, secured Ivanov's approval and had a budget agreed. Things could move quickly when it suited the President. The plan was to assess staff in two phases: senior and middle management first, then in a second round, the rest of the organisation. As the news spread there was widespread consternation, and I was lobbied repeatedly by individuals searching for loopholes. Morrison commented hopefully that of course it applied only to Russians – didn't it? No – it didn't! Various members of the HR department assured me they personally had no fear of an assessment – but in the interests of impartiality and professional etiquette, believed HR should be exempt. To their disappointment, I advised their anxiety was unfounded since external experts rather than HR would run the programme and administer the tests. Only Berkovich seemed genuinely unfazed. With his usual disdain for his Russian colleagues, he looked forward almost gleefully to what testing might expose. "It'll show *officially* what we know to be true," he said with grim satisfaction. "It's not surprising so many people are worried."

Ostensibly the goal was to supply independent, objective data about development needs – for use in planning training courses. And this was largely true. But few believed it, preferring instead the inevitable rumours of pending sackings and demotions.

Three foreign consultancies were invited to tender for the delivery of a psychometric testing programme, and a team duly arrived from London to implement Phase 1. This took place over a torrid three days, in which groups of grumbling, sweating managers were subjected to a battery of tests – Russian language versions of standard assessment tools used worldwide. Straightforward stuff that did not justify the angst engendered. The President, as promised, took part like every other manager. At the end, the completed tests were bundled up and taken to London for collation and analysis, with a confidential report on each individual expected within three weeks. Because of their sensitivity, these were to be delivered in the first instance direct to the President for his review. The wait was a nervous time, rife with speculation about impending changes. I expected a call from Ivanov to discuss the next steps, but he was silent, and in the end the whole matter was a non-event. He sat on the reports for over a month, then quietly announced that having studied them in detail, would take no further action. The results remained confidential, and Phase 2 was cancelled.

Amid the general relief various conspiracy theories surfaced – all mistrustful of Ivanov's motives. The project's closure, it was alleged, was just a ploy, as Ivanov planned to use the results anyway – to pick off people and fire them one by one. Alternatively, it was a financial issue – the scale of the likely training needs had caught Ivanov by surprise, and he preferred to spend money on things he actually cared about. But the favourite theory had it that Ivanov had been shocked by poor results in his own test and concluded that either a) the process was flawed and therefore no results could be trusted, or b) the process was valid – which meant there were other managers better than him. Naturally, either outcome was unacceptable.

Whatever the reason, assessment was now off the table. But it wasn't the end of our flirtation with consultants, and every few months, some new initiative would begin. Since many required no HR input, I was aware of their existence only through office gossip, or the presence of unfamiliar faces in the corridors. Like everyone else I was weary of them, but as Head of HR played the game with resignation and a show of equanimity. I was the obvious starting point for queries about people or organisational matters, and I answered silly questions from consultants with courtesy, and nodded wisely when appropriate. My Russian colleagues were less relaxed, and I saw a complicated mixture of emotions at play. Fear of change – predictably. Annoyance at time wasted. But above all indignation – anger even – at the disparagement implied in the use of outsiders, especially foreigners, to examine what they were doing. At the start of each new project, they were immediately ready to take offence with any consultant who seemed to slight them.

"They speak as if we know nothing," Grishin once complained. "Like anthropologists studying a strange tribe. Are we just waiting to be found? Do we need told how to run a business? Is Russia a desert?"

There's something in the Russian DNA that reacts with special anxiety to the prospect of scrutiny. Latent fears bred in by historical experience. A Government Inspector calls. The KGB investigates. The Party demands answers!

When I once asked Grishin to collect data for some Swiss consultants working on succession planning, he was markedly unenthusiastic.

"All these questions," he grumbled. "But you never know what they're trying to find. So how can we answer?"

"They just want background," I said. "To understand how the company works. Just tell them what you know – the truth as you see it."

He dismissed this naïveté with a look, and continued:

"In the past – in Soviet times – we had many reviews and inspections. It was normal. They were tough. But we always knew what they wanted to find. So, we were prepared. We told them what they expected to hear and they were happy. It was serious, but also a game. Nobody wanted a problem. But now -?"

Grishin's past was the workplace of the 1980s, when both inspectors and management largely went through the motions. As he told it, there was a well-understood ritual of audit and inspection. All actors played their parts according to a script, and it was in nobody's interest for serious faults to be revealed.

"Many forms were completed. A lot of paper. But nothing was a surprise. Of course," he added, "it wasn't always like that. In Stalin's time inspections were very dangerous."

As everyone knew, failure then could get you shot. But Grishin was recalling the Late-Soviet era, now often called the *Soviet Twilight*, and his memories echoed the much-quoted axiom about productivity and reward: citizens pretended to work – and the state pretended to pay them. It's glib, but at the same time astute – and sums up the underachievement, slackness and deception accepted as the norm during the period. Berkovich had a Soviet joke (which

I've also seen in published collections) that's a clever commentary on the post-war evolution from tyranny to stagnation then collapse.

Stalin, Khrushchev and Brezhnev are travelling together in a railway carriage when suddenly the train stops. Stalin sticks his head out the window and shouts: "Shoot the driver!" But the train doesn't start moving. Khrushchev then shouts, "Rehabilitate the driver!" But it still doesn't move. Brezhnev yawns and says, "Comrades, comrades, let's draw the curtains, turn on the gramophone and pretend we're moving."

When Gorbachov later took power, a further line was added, with the new leader proposing: *"Comrades, let's all of us get out and push!"*

Against this background, was it any surprise that those of my Russian colleagues, whose formative working years were during the lethargic Twilight, were spooked by the unpredictability of what a foreign consultant might discover?

***

The fact most consultants were English-speaking, and worked through interpreters, only exacerbated local suspicion. The arrival, therefore, of Ivan Koslov should have been different. Ivan was an expert in organisational design, assigned from the New York office of an international consulting firm to conduct a review of the relationship between the company's Moscow HQ and its overseas branch offices. He was expected to sniff out inefficiencies, propose improvements, and design a strategy for restructuring.

Ivan was in his early forties, had a serious demeanour and dressed soberly – the very picture of the US corporate consultant. He was an American citizen, but as his name suggested, of Russian origin.

"I got sent because I speak Russian," he told me downheartedly, a few days into the project. "I don't think it helps. Maybe the opposite. But at least I get a chance to visit family here."

He was having as hard a time with our Russian staff as any other foreign consultant. I could imagine their chatter. Why's this Russian pretending he's American? What's so special that he knows our business better than us? He speaks Russian, does he? All the more reason to be careful of what we tell him!

Ivan however turned out one of the most interesting individuals I met during my Moscow years. His proposals for organisational improvement made me yawn, but I was intrigued by his recollections of his Moscow childhood, and his thoughts on the world he'd left behind – the world of the Soviet Twilight.

"Whenever I visit my father," he told me, "I see on cable TV the old Soviet shows I watched as a kid. My parents are stuck in the past – so it's what they like. Most are rubbish – like any old TV. But they take me back. Make me think about things. Remind me I used to be Russian."

"Used to be?"

"I'm American now. I *feel* American. My wife's American. And my kids."

He was silent for a moment then went on:

"There are many Russians where I live in New York – but I avoid them. They wallow in the past, as if they've never left. Speak Russian at home, buy Russian food, drink tea from a samovar instead of coffee. It's sad, and not my scene. Mentally – and emotionally – I've moved on."

"What about your roots? They're here surely?"

"Logically, yes. And I'll never deny them – but I've changed with time. I've *become* American. More American than I ever was Russian."

I said I understood, but in truth listened with scepticism. At forty-five he might renounce his heritage. But at sixty would he yearn again for the earth of Mother Russia?

"How come you ended up in America?"

"That's the thing – it was by chance" he said. "I got a scholarship – so I went. I wasn't a dissident. I wasn't forced to leave. And I wasn't running away. I'm not one of those exiles with a grudge – the kind who torture themselves about everything they've lost. When I was at college, most of my class expected life in Russia to go on as normal. But we soon sensed changes – that things would be different. We had to think about what we'd do in the future. I was twenty when the USSR ended, but I'd studied English for nine years. Even before Perestroika my father understood changes were coming. He was far-sighted and wanted his children to be prepared. When I arrived in America, I knew I'd stay forever. I found America exciting. And refreshing – yes refreshing!"

Refreshing, he explained, was the right word, because the contrast with Moscow awakened and energised him. For most Russians the period of Ivan's youth – the 80s – wasn't a scary time, but a boring one. The horror and drama of the Stalin era were in the past – and for Ivan's generation not even a memory. And while drab, life was at least stable and more comfortable. Yet for Ivan and so many of his generation, it felt suffocating. Brezhnev and his geriatric successors presided over a stagnating economy and a stuffy, listless society. Official lies continued as normal, although the difference between propaganda and reality was comic and disheartening rather than sinister. Apathy and detachment shaped the spirit of the age, as ordinary people ignored Marxist dogma and quietly got on with life. As long as you wore the right face in public, you could live an internal life of mental freedom. When ageing Muscovites today look back at this era – sometimes with nostalgia – many recall youthful frustration at what seemed to lie in front of them – more of the same.

"But it's different here now," I said to Ivan. "More like the West. Couldn't you settle in Moscow?"

"I've a life in New York. And a family. Anyway – this is still a difficult place. There are too many hang-ups. Bad things happening under the surface. I don't have patience for the bureaucracy now. The system's changed but not the people. They're still Soviet. Russia won't be free of the past until the last Soviet generation's gone. You know, I was here last year. On an assignment with TNK BP. I guess you know most Russians prefer to work for foreign companies than local ones. They're more relaxed and treat their staff better. But when I started digging, I found some people who were uncomfortable. They missed the rigid structures of a Russian company, and couldn't cope with managers asking their opinions, instead of just telling them what to do."

"What do you consider the last Soviet generation?"

Ivan thought for a moment.

"There's no simple answer. Everybody alive in Russia today's part Soviet. Even kids born after the collapse. They've inherited stuff from parents and teachers. Attitudes, beliefs. There's no hard dividing line. It's a matter of degree. My father's pure Soviet. My brother – a bit."

"And you? How Soviet are you?"

"You're expecting me to say none. Or just a little. Because I'm American. But for sure there's a lot – but buried I guess."

"What about people like Valeria? She's fifteen years younger than you."

"I'd say she's transitional. Sure, she came of age later – but you can't erase the early years. Her schooling. All the Soviet myths and ideology. Something must have stuck. But there's another side too – and it's important. A paradox. The younger you are, the more likely you'll believe new hype that glorifies the Soviet Union. The stuff the Kremlin's using again to stoke up national unity. People of my age are sceptical – but younger generations just accept it. They didn't live through Soviet times and can't instinctively tell the difference between propaganda and truth."

When the Soviet archives began to open up after the fall of communism, the immediate rush, unsurprisingly, was to research the big stories of Russian history – Stalin, the famines, the Gulags, the Cold War. The near-contemporary world was of little interest. Later studies looked at the process of the Soviet collapse itself – the political turmoil, the background economics, the machinations and scheming. But the day-to-day life of the Late-Soviet era attracted little attention. Now however, three decades later, it's distant enough to view with detachment, and historians and cultural commentators are taking a new interest. Ivan's recollections of the period intrigued me. His narrative of stagnation, and personal sense of drift, contrasts with my own memories of the time. Viewed from the West the USSR still seemed a mighty power. In Scotland, the Left, manipulated and allegedly secretly funded by the Kremlin, noisily campaigned against the deployment of American cruise missiles into the UK, and a myriad of protest groups, both creepy and comical, agitated under the slogan Better Red Than Dead – predicting imminent annihilation unless Britain abandoned the drive to rearm. Neither Ivan nor I realised at the time that behind the bluster, and the facade of invincibility, the USSR was in its twilight, disintegrating from within and about to implode.

"How optimistic are you for Russia's future?" I asked.

"We'll be OK, in time."

"*We?*"

Ivan laughed. "You got me. I guess I am still Russian. It's not all bad news here. Along with the crap, some things are changing for the better. And some of the bad things have even been good."

"What do you mean?"

"Things that seemed bad at the time – if you lived here – turned out to be blessings. Like the crash of 1998 – when the banks failed and the economy tanked. In New York I escaped it, but folks here had it hard. Lost savings and jobs. But it's exactly what the country needed. A kind of economic catharsis – that got rid of the worst Soviet practices – as well as many of the managers resisting free market reforms. The same with the oligarchs. Ordinary people hate them. But they're modernising Russian industry. Doing things the state wouldn't. Rationalising. Closing out-of-date plants. Investing in new operations. Westerners, like you, think most companies are still Soviet – and it's true. But it's a matter of degree. If Russian companies are badly run today, imagine what it was like in the past."

21

Moscow is a winter city, at its best when the streets are under snow, rivers and ponds are frozen hard, and the golden domes sparkle in sharp winter sunshine. But not all winters are alike. And in my first two years, nature delivered two extremes: the intense cold of a classic Russian winter, followed a year later by one of record-breaking mildness.

According to the meteorologists, the year I arrived saw the harshest winter in over seven decades. As the days shortened and autumn slipped away, the temperature dropped sharply and brought showers of heavy snow that would lie for months. In some countries, cold weather keeps the inhabitants huddled indoors, their lives largely dormant until the thaws arrive. But Muscovites just wrap-up warm and get on with life. On my kitchen wall in Scotland, I have a painting of a Russian troika – a traditional sleigh pulled by three horses running abreast. It's an idealised scene: a lady in Victorian furs holds the reins; a scarlet rug over her legs gives a bright splash of colour that contrasts with the white landscape. The horses are caught on the gallop, all energy, spirit and zest for life, their hooves throwing up sprays of powdered snow. It's a joyful image that evokes the fun of a traditional Russian winter. And although a very different world from modern Moscow, it hints at the outdoor pleasures Russians still find when it freezes. All over the city there are picture-book scenes – groups of men ice-fishing through holes cut in frozen ponds and lakes; people of all ages skating and sledging. On any evening, scratch ice-hockey games, lit by the street lamps, take place on Patriashy Prudy's frozen pond, and in hundreds of other locations throughout the city. Even Red Square becomes part of the fun, with a public skating rink erected in the centre for a few months every winter. It was there I made my own first attempts, hiring skates at the rink's kiosk and teetering unsteadily around, in the shadow of the Kremlin walls.

When snow falls, Gorky Park transforms itself from a tatty fairground into a picturesque winter playground. The trees are decked with fairy-lights, and the paths sprayed with water – to make them ice over and become skate tracks. A network of these runs amongst the trees, letting Muscovites feel they're skating through a frozen forest. After a few sessions in Red Square, I felt confident enough to try the Park, but my visit was not a success. At the wooden hut that served as a skate-hire depot, the attendant demanded not only a rental fee and a cash deposit, but that I also leave my passport with him. A sensible precaution maybe, for unlike the Red Square rink, the Park covered a large area and had porous boundaries – making it easy to vanish into the distance with the skates. However, in this city of scams, I was reluctant to trust my passport to a stranger, so abandoned the notion and walked around instead.

Deep into my first winter, I took a decision one Friday afternoon that alarmed Valeria. Although our office closed at weekends, I had permission to enter on Saturday mornings for a Russian language lesson. Normally Nikolai would drop me there at 10 o'clock, then drive off. Why hold him? After two hours tuition I'd clear my head with a leisurely stroll home. It was a chance to explore the city, to made sightseeing detours through central Moscow on the way back to my flat. Although the weather had become intensely cold, I was my determined to walk home as usual the following day. But Valeria was shocked.

"No Robbie, you can't!" she said. "You'll die."

"I'll be OK. Other people do it."

"That's different. You're not Russian."

"I've made up my mind," I said firmly, and held up a hand to command silence. "Just tell Nikolai to drop me off and he can go home as usual."

She looked at me and shook her head. "I'll have no boss on Monday. My crazy boss will be dead."

"Thanks for your concern. But don't worry – look Valeria." I motioned her to the window and pointed below. "They're not dead, are they?"

The street was quieter than usual, but the presence of a few human figures was my vindication.

"As you wish," Valeria said. "But I think you'll regret this."

There were however signs it was no ordinary winter's day. The sky was bright and the road clear of snow – there had been no new falls – and even the icy pavements looked no more treacherous than usual. But the car exhausts signalled a difference, the white fumes hung heavier than usual, struggling to rise at all. And the pedestrians seemed equally sluggish. They walked differently – head down, ploughing on, abandoning for once the tiny, deliberate, steps usually adopted to negotiate slippy areas. As if it was enough for now to simply move at all, the effort enormous and painful.

"In any case," I said to Valeria, trying for a knockout, "what about my teacher? Will she be dead?"

"She'll use the Metro and be outside only a few minutes. She's not crazy! If you won't use Nikolai" Valeria said, making a final stand, "I think I must telephone Maria and cancel the lesson. Yes?"

But I did not cancel, and with some trepidation just after noon the next day, my head freshly stocked with Russian verbs, I set out to walk home through the coldest Moscow weather in seventy-five years. Within a few minutes I knew Valeria had been right. My stubborn stupidity had sent me on a painful slog for which I was ill prepared. My breathing in the freezing air was short and difficult. The exposed skin of my face, my nose, burned in the cold. My knitted ski-hat, warm and comfortable on a normal winter's day, was now ludicrously inadequate. My ears, although completely covered, ached in the freezing temperature and I knew I needed one of those fur Cossack hats the politbureau used to wear.

There was no excuse for my folly, because Valeria's warnings had been underscored by days of TV and newspaper coverage of the exceptional cold. There had been official warnings, and human-interest stories about police jailing vagrants to protect them from certain death on the streets. Stray dogs were being given shelter in Metro stations. Everything stressed the weather's lethal intensity. Even a normal Moscow winter sees hundreds of deaths from exposure. The victims are not just the homeless. Drunks are at particular risk. It's all too easy for a reveller in an alcoholic haze to miss his way home and freeze to death on the streets – often hidden from sight in a snow drift that lies undisturbed for months. For centuries this has been an inescapable fact of Moscow life, and in the old days, before the advent of organised snow clearing (with mechanical diggers and trucks carting snow away for disposal at a series of Melting Stations around the city), the spring thaw was classically the time when the city gave up its winter secrets. Just as green shoots forced themselves up through the soil, so dead bodies – *snowdrops* as the locals dub them – emerged from the vanishing layers of snow and ice. It's still the case today, although the numbers are smaller. Murder victims, hapless drunks, suicides and hobos all rise and reveal themselves after their winter concealment.

I trudged painfully across Moskvoretsky Bridge, barely glancing at the frozen river beneath me, concentrating only on each laborious step. No thoughts of any sightseeing – only of the shortest way home. I passed St Basil's Cathedral, and in Red Square made directly for the heated sanctuary of the GUM shopping centre. I'd been walking no more than 15 minutes but felt like an exhausted explorer as I entered with relief through the side door in Llinka Street. GUM offered me a precious 250 metres of indoor progress, to the top of Red Square, before I had to go back outside and make for the underpass at Okhotny Riad Metro station, that leads on to Tverskai Street. What was better I wondered? To force on quickly to the next shelter, and risk my lungs exploding with the cold – or to take longer, keep a careful, steady pace, but subject my nose and ears to additional freezing pain?

When I reached the Central Telegraph Office on Tverskai Street, the McDonalds branch opposite beckoned like an Alpine monastery to a lost traveller. It was a dark, cramped outlet which I normally avoided, but for once it seemed incredibly inviting. No takeaway today. I lingered with my meal at a table, delaying the moment when I must go outside. As I sat, however, I had time to absorb a little vignette which, strangely, stayed in my memory. Its very ordinariness somehow touched me that cold day. At a table beside me were a middle-aged couple, and a youth in military uniform. All three were noticeably uncomfortable amidst the predominantly teenage clientele. The youth fiddled with a paper cup and a half-eaten burger, while the man and woman picked at some food wrapped in aluminium foil – obviously prepared at home. I guessed the youth was on a day's leave from barracks, meeting anxious parents who had travelled some distance. Nobody said much, but the real affection between them shone warmly. For an expat living a privileged existence in the city centre, it was a rare glimpse of ordinary Russian life.

The rest of my journey was a ridiculous, convoluted zigzag, that saw me ducking into every second shop for a few minutes warmth, before slowly pressing on my way. When I finally got home however, my relief was touched by a measure of childish satisfaction. It had been a silly, unnecessary escapade, but part of me felt like a polar explorer who had just conquered a frozen wasteland.

Daytime temperatures that winter hovered between -30 and -32 Celsius, extremely cold even by Moscow standards. At night they went as low as -35. By contrast, in a normal January something around -10 to -14 is expected. Like so many of the city's Victorian buildings, the heating system in my apartment proved wholly inadequate, and I never felt comfortable despite regularly donning an overcoat on top of a fleece to sit and watch TV. When the cold stopped me sleeping at night I would pile on an additional duvet. My windows were not modern double-glazing, but the old-fashioned Russian version, featuring two panes of glass 4-5 inches apart. In a normal winter these kept the windows inside from icing over, but that year the cold penetrated, and I got used to living with sheets of thickening ice on the internal glass.

I'd periodically scrape them, and one day as I worked on my living room window, I spotted at the top of the five-storey block opposite, a man on a window-ledge with an ice-axe, chipping at a wedge of frozen snow. His other hand clutched a rope, anchored somewhere on the roof above him. It was a precarious spot just to stand still, but as he swayed with the movement of his axe, he looked insanely vulnerable. For a moment I wondered about access – had he come over the roof or through one of the windows? Then my attention moved to the rope, and I peered for a sign it was attached to some kind of safety harness. There was none, and it seemed he depended for his life solely on the strength of his grip. Such scenes are common during a Moscow winter. By law, if an icicle falls from a roof or balcony and hits a pedestrian, the owner of the apartment or building is liable. Any icicle bigger than ten centimetres must be removed, and the city authorities enforce the rule by fining those who fail to take action. Occasionally teams of experienced workmen, using basket-cranes or cherry-pickers, can be seen clearing away ice – usually on official buildings. But risky DIY attempts are more common. Throughout the city, men foolishly perch on ledges, stretch out of windows, or crawl on icy roofs eight stories above street level – without any kind of safety equipment. Many have doubtless fortified themselves against the cold with vodka, exemplifying the fatalism and recklessness in the Russian character, and again proving their country the land of the avoidable accident.

My winters in Moscow were never again as severe. The second in particular was unseasonably mild, with the temperature by mid-December fluctuating day-to-day from a few degrees above freezing point to a few below. Occasionally there were light dustings of snow, which rain soon turned to slush, and Muscovites became impatient for the thick, solid, whiteness of the imagination. By the turn of the year the temperature rarely fell below 5 degrees Celsius, and January turned out the warmest in fifty years. Predictably, global warming was mentioned, but professional forecasters blamed a persistent warm-front drifting over from the Atlantic Ocean. As this swept east, temperatures over large parts of the country were affected, and in places like the bleak wastes of Yakutia, transport links were disrupted when the ice-roads on which they depended failed to freeze over. In Moscow the mildness brought other problems, some of them psychological. With the Moscow River and other open water ice-free, sportsmen such as ice skaters and hockey players grumbled at being deprived of their usual facilities. And the bears at Moscow zoo awoke from hibernation two months early. Above all, however, people were miserable. Muscovites generally complained of depression, and I too felt in low spirits because of the weather. Critically, the lack of snow meant a lack of the sunshine – and of the reflected light the city needs to lift the midwinter gloom.

During a particularly miserable spell Valeria raised a topic that causes vigorous debate amongst Russians.

"In this weather," she said, "the holidays this year will be very bad."

"Why do you say that?"

"They're always too long. Unless you've money to go to Egypt, there's nothing to do except eat and watch television. Long holidays are OK in summer. But now? The government needs to find a solution."

Her grumble was about the length of the public holiday over Christmas and New Year, when much of the country closes down for ten or more days. The period is elongated to accommodate both church and state. The official Gregorian Calendar has Christmas on 25 December, but the Orthodox Church retains the old Julien Calendar, which celebrates it on 7 January. Likewise, the Julien 1st of January (the date of the Old New Year) corresponds to the 14th on the Gregorian calendar. Russians therefore have a choice of two Christmases, and two New Year's Days – and the full period is officially a holiday. Many of the ultra-devout celebrate both, but secular Russians increasingly demand a reform of public holidays to reflect the needs of contemporary society.

22

In Scotland, when Christmas and Hogmanay are out of the way, the local press has for decades turned its attention to the next seasonal page filler – the Burns Supper story. These appear in the lead-up to the anniversary of the poet's birth on 25 January, and like the suppers themselves, with their ritual toasts and speeches, conform to a classic, unchanging formula: a Burns Club or St. Andrews Society in some foreign location is in crisis. A last-minute mishap has prevented the delivery of the haggis customarily served at dinner. With the event under threat an international appeal is made for assistance, and from somewhere in deepest Scotland, a 'family butcher' emerges to save the day. (It's always a 'family butcher' – photogenic in his white apron and hygienic hat – never a supermarket chain or meat canning factory.) He rustles up a suitable pudding, there's a compulsory dash to the airport with all the drama of transporting a human organ for transplant, and the day is saved for relieved Burns enthusiasts in Rio or Almaty.

To heighten their readers' patriotic glow, some newspapers list the famous places hosting celebrations – with the indisputable star the Kremlin Burns Supper. Its inclusion is particularly compelling, implying an appeal beyond just expatriate Scots. Here are serious, powerful Russians, men with their fingers on the nuclear trigger, convening to honour the bard. I've always been sceptical about this Kremlin connection. If it existed at all, it was Burns enthusiasts exaggerating a minor event into something more significant. (Did it really take place in the Kremlin itself – in one of the historic buildings used by the elite of the Russian state? Or just some corner of the huge conference and banqueting complex that sits within the Kremlin grounds, and can be hired on a commercial basis?) Likewise, I've read countless times of how Kremlin Burns Suppers are televised nationwide in Russia but have yet to meet anyone who has ever actually seen a broadcast.

Burns Supper stories are parochial, self-congratulatory, and at times simply invented – but they have a long pedigree. And when I spot one, I invariably recall a fierce teenage squabble with my mother about the Kremlin event.

"Look!" she said, pointing with pride at a newspaper photograph of a kilted figure at an airport departure gate. "He's off to Moscow for the Burns Supper!"

"So what?"

"You won't get that in England or America. The Russians have always loved Burns."

I made a face. Unimpressed that some luminary of the tartan music scene was on his way the Soviet Union. The Scottish entertainers she admired were corny and embarrassing. As was her reverence for Burns.

I sniggered. "Maybe he'll end up in Siberia – freezing without his trousers. Anyway, all this Russian stuff's bullshit. What about the Florida story yesterday? You were happy enough going on about that."

The previous day's newspaper had reported the emergency dispatch by jet of a haggis to Miami.

She reddened. "Just watch your tongue!"

My scorn had touched a nerve.

"But you did!" I said. "How come the Moscow dinner's a bigger deal than the Florida one?"

"It's not the same thing," she said dismissively. "The American one's just some Scots folk holding their own meal. The Russian one's official."

Several decades later, living in Moscow, I recognised that – bizarrely as I saw it – there was some truth in her claims. The tartan cheerleaders that I fancied inflated Burns' importance to boost their own cultural credentials were not complete fantasists after all. Burns' fame in Russia is genuine. His poetry has been taught in schools for decades, and I discovered both Valeria and Nicolai, from different generations of Russians, recalled reading him in class. There's no better demonstration of the truth of Russian regard, than the fact that the Soviet Union was the first country in the world to commemorate Burns with a postage stamp – on the 160th anniversary of his death in 1956.

Most Russians know Burns' poetry through the translations of Samuel Marshak (1887-1964), a celebrated Soviet-era literary figure who produced Russian versions of various English language greats, including Shakespeare, Kipling and William Blake. Although he was himself a respected poet as well as a translator, Marshak is renowned in Russia today primarily as the author of a collection of children's books which have remained popular through several generations and are still in print. A browse through any Moscow bookshop reveals shiny new editions of Marshak titles for children – as I discovered when I searched their shelves in vain for copies of his Burns translations.

Ironically, it was my mother who set me in pursuit of Marshak, triggering an interest when she produced from a drawer a curiosity I'd never seen – a facsimile, she told me, of a manuscript the

Russian had personally presented to the Irvine Burns Club, the world's premier Burns association, during a trip to Scotland in the 1950s.

"Now you're living in Moscow" she said, "you might be interested in this."

It was a poem in Scots dialect which Marshak had composed in Burns' honour, entitled:

To Robert Burns
On the 200th anniversary of his Birth
25 January 1959.

The twelve verses of Marshak's poem are an excellent pastiche which captures Burns' style, mimicking his favourite stanza form and echoing his rhythms. They also demonstrate a skilled use of dialect that would do credit to a native Scots speaker, never mind a foreigner. His tribute was never published, but it remains in the club's archives. My mother must have had her copy for decades, but never mentioned it before my Russian adventure. She knew nothing about Marshak himself, beyond the fact he was Russian and an admirer of Burns – credentials enough for her to cherish her copy.

When I set out to find a Marshak edition of Burns in Moscow, it proved surprisingly difficult. The city's bookshops are excellent, and typically carry respectable selections of foreign authors both in Russian translation, and their original languages. Editions of English poets are commonplace; there's no shortage of Coleridge, Byron, Hardy – even Christine Rossetti. But strangely no Burns. Was it something to do with him being taught in schools? Maybe there's no market for stuff that's force-fed in childhood? In a sign of changed times however, I discovered during my search, mixed in with the standard highbrow fare, countless translations of pop culture that would have been inconceivable in Soviet-era bookshops. Burns was absent, but weirdly I found propped alongside Baudelaire, a Russian version of songs by the Backstreet Boys. Further along the rows Elvis Presley rubbed up against Alexander Pope. The biggest stock of such gems was in the huge *Moscow House of Books* on New Arbat, where I once tested my progress in learning Russian by poring over a bilingual copy of *Meet Elvis*. This consisted of a brief biography, accompanied on alternate pages by English and Russian versions of eighteen of the master's songs. As I compared the chorus of *Tutti Frutti* in both languages, I reflected with amusement on how my mother would take the fact that Communism's collapse had seen Burns evicted and replaced in the land of Pushkin and Tolstoy by the lyrics of rock and roll.

I never found a newly published copy of Burns in Moscow, but eventually came across an old Marshak edition downstairs in the second-hand section of the *House of Books* on Tverskai Street. In the basement they deal in coins and stamps, antique maps, engravings, and antiquarian books – many of them valuable artefacts from Tzarist times. My purchase however, a maroon 1960s volume bound in sturdy cardboard, cost only 300 roubles – and like the Elvis book had pages of original text set alongside Russian translations.

Devotees of Burns owe a huge debt to Marshak. After more than eighty years, his translations are still considered the best in Russian, and are unquestionably chiefly responsible for Burns' popularity in the Russian speaking world. Yet despite their classic status, it's doubtful how long they will continue supporting the poet's reputation. Artistically and politically, they are products of their time, reflecting Soviet ideology and preoccupations. Although

Marshak conveys in Russian the spirit and sentiments of Burns poetry, his versions are not close translations. A great deal is missing or distorted. Soviet patronage of Burns had as much to do with his standing as a socialist poet as with his aesthetic appeal, and Marshak's texts manipulate his art for political ends. Indeed, there's a clear socialist ring in his anniversary pastiche, when he contrasts Burns' posthumous honour with his lack of reward when living. The money, Marshak says, was found to raise statues after Burns died, but the poet saw *"ne'er a groat o' a' that gowd"* while he still alive.

(Burns' life, like his work, has long been conscripted by all manner of political ideologies. Marshak's sentiment though, echoes a memory from my own childhood, when on the drive back from a Sunday pilgrimage to Burns' birthplace in Alloway, my mother explained that the poet had died in poverty because "the man he worked for didn't pay him properly." I understood, even as an eight- or nine-year-old, that the poet was a victim of the capitalism regularly denounced in our house. Years later I discovered Burns was destitute on his deathbed not because of The System, but his own lack financial prudence. As an exciseman – a government employee – he had the income to live a comfortable bourgeois life. But the truth is not always revolutionary.)

Ironically, a key characteristic of Marshak's translations is that he removed Burns from his immediate social environment to deliver a "world poet" rather than a specifically Scottish one. There's no attempt to reproduce in Russian the dialect of the originals – which Marshak himself deployed so well in his birthday tribute. Similarly, geography becomes blurred. Events take place nowhere in particular, in some non-specific homeland, while mention of Scotland itself is absent. For the Soviets, Burns represented internationalism, and his patriotism is accordingly played down, while his love of liberty and equality are accentuated. When his poems feature people on the margins of society – beggars, robbers and the poor – they're idealized, but nowhere do we find allusions to the poet's aristocratic friends. God too is absent, together with the whole religious context of Burns' life. And in deference to Marxist prudishness, any sauciness in Burns' love poetry is diluted or eliminated altogether.

These are not just quibbles. His texts are often strikingly different in detail from the originals. Yet they're neither crude travesties nor wooden imitations. Native Russian speakers testify that he reads well. Marshak interprets Burns as much as translates him – but does so with artistry and sensitivity, producing genuine poetry. Fittingly, the Soviet state honoured Marshak with his own commemorative postage stamp in 1987, and I saw it on sale in a glass display case in the philately section of the same Tverskai Street bookshop in which I found my copy of Marshak's Burns.

One weekend, as I played the tourist and explored around New Arbat, I came across another Scottish literary connection. New Arbat is one of the busiest areas of central Moscow, and the street itself – a six lane highway running West from the Boulevard Ring at Nikitsky Boulevard to the Garden Ring at Novinsky Boulevard – one of the best-known. A row of Soviet tower blocks touched the skyline on both sides of the road, but at ground level very different scenes neatly exemplified conflicting characteristics of Russian life in the 21st century. The south side was a model of post-Soviet consumerism, a mix of fast-food outlets, tacky souvenir shops, and casinos reputedly run by the Georgian mafia. Foreign luxury cars were displayed on ramps out front, lures to tantalise the punters with the riches attainable at the tables. One casino incorporated a sports bar – Metallista – which showed English football and American baseball on satellite TV and was a popular expat hangout. In contrast, the opposite side of the street offered a more sedate, cultured Russia. Here was Europe's largest cinema, Moscow's largest bookshop, and rows of pavement stalls selling all kinds of second-hand books – from heavily illustrated art and history (elaborately protected in plastic covers) to cheap editions of Russian classics and out-of-print Soviet potboilers.

At the Nikitsky end of New Arbat a fork led off into Malaya Molchanovka, a quiet side-street where an attractive collection of "older" buildings – quaint 19th century stucco-faced townhouses – evoked an earlier Moscow, before the street morphed into a sequence of Soviet-era official buildings. In reality, the '19th century' houses were fakes, modern reconstructions which purists dismissed as the Disneyfication of Moscow – an unfair criticism I think, of a sympathetic and imaginative attempt at replacing some of the city's lost architectural heritage. However, beside the official blocks stood a genuine relic – a pink two-storey wooden house with a wall-plaque advising it was the Moscow home of one of the greats of Russian literature: Mikael Lermontov. Here Lermontov lived with his grandmother from 1829-32, while he studied at Moscow University and began to develop his literary career. Today it's a museum devoted to his memory, with displays of original furniture, manuscripts and memorabilia. I passed it often as I walked through the backstreets from my flat in Bolshai Bronnai to Arbat. But the first time I visited I was drawn not by its literary associations, but by the house itself – by its small size and wooden construction – as it stood in contrast to the heavy stone and concrete edifices that dominated the city centre. Two hundred years ago Moscow was predominantly a city of wooden structures like this, but most were destroyed by fire when Napoleon's army ransacked the city in 1812. The Lermontov house was built a few years later, a reminder of the old wooden Moscow, and its very presence today has the kind of momentarily cheering effect we experience when a horse and cart or a vintage car passes in the midst of modern traffic. Although Lermontov came from a noble family, and his grandmother was a wealthy landowner, it's no mansion, just a comfortable middle-class dwelling. Homely not grand.

In many of Moscow's museums, particularly the smaller, more intimate house museums, the attendants are elderly ladies. They guard their domains vigilantly, if with no great mobility. In bigger institutions like the *Museum of Contemporary History* on Tverskai Street they'll hover while you view the exhibits, then shuffle suspiciously behind as you move on – for fear you might touch something or breathe too heavily on a glass case. But in old houses like this, with their steps, stairs and narrow corridors, they often stick to one room – and a seat in a corner – and let visitors roam. Most are more than just guards – but well-educated enthusiasts, experts on the famous individuals whose homes they now watch over.

When I explored the Lermontov house for the first time a party of Russian school kids was being ushered around. Despite their teachers' efforts at enforcing a reverential silence, they capered beside display cases and ducked in and out of rooms. To avoid them I ignored the prescribed order for touring the rooms and wandered around randomly. Which meant I encountered the information cards provided for visitors out of sequence and context. These told in Russian and English Lermontov's story and linked it to exhibits in the house. As I knew little about him at the time, despite seeing copies of his works in the Russian Classics sections of every bookshop I entered, I had a sense of a learning opportunity lost. However, a curious attendant approached when she saw me peering at an English version of a card. My foreignness must have been obvious.

"You are English?"

"Yes – Well, Scottish actually."

"*Scottish*?"

To my surprise she rose from her chair and motioned me to follow her to the stairs. In a small study on the upper floor there was a glass case full of manuscripts and engravings.

"You can see," she said, and indicated a typed biographical note lying amongst the fading exhibits. The top half was in Russian and the bottom in English. It advised that Lermontov was fascinated by Scotland "*from where he believed his family originated.*"

"Mikhail Yuryevich also was Scottish," she said, referring to Lermontov by his Russian patronymic. This was an exaggeration, but as I'd later discover, there were good grounds for it.

When I left the house I walked through the small public garden opposite, where a bronze bust of the poet stood on a stone column, and down onto New Arbat Avenue, to search the bookshop for anything by Lermontov in an English translation. Here I came across an Everyman's Library edition of his single novel, *A Hero of Our Time* (1840).

As a poet, Lermontov is second only to Pushkin in the affections of his countrymen and the esteem of scholars. His legacy includes a body of lyrical, romantic verse that continues still to influence Russian writers. It was through *A Hero of Our Time* however, that I came to appreciate Lermontov's gifts. Unquestionably a fine novel by any standards, and for a 19th century work surprisingly fresh today. It depicts the travels in the Caucasus of Grigory Pechorin, a cynical, adventure-seeking Russian army officer whom Lermontov portrays – fashionably for the period – as a Byronic figure: bold, brooding, charismatic, amoral and reckless. *A Hero of Our Time* is credited with bringing psychological realism to the Russian novel for the first time – apparent in the complexity of Pechorin's character, and the turmoil and contradictions of his inner life. He's at the same time dashing, melancholic, fatalistic, and troubled with self-loathing. In a series of romantic intrigues, we see his relationships with women characterised by coldness and calculation, while in violent confrontations with local tribesmen he's fearless in the face of danger. The novel has a modern sensibility which resonates with readers familiar today with the concept of the anti-hero. Traditional heroes embody the higher values and morality of their societies, and project conventional virtues like goodness, honesty or kindness. But Pechorin plays by his own rules, foreshadowing the kind of nihilistic loners familiar in twentieth century literature.

In his *Author's Introduction* to the novel, Lermontov explicitly declared Pechorin was intended not only as a portrait of an individual, but of Russian society "built up of all our generation's vices in full bloom." Interestingly, when I lived in Moscow the runaway bestseller in the city's bookshops was contemporary novelist Sergei Minayev's *Dukh-less* (soulless): *The Story of an Artificial Person*, which Russian critics characterised as a modern take on Lermontov. Minayev's hero inhabits the post-Soviet consumerist world of Moscow's young elite – fast cars, flash clothes, nightclubs, drugs and beautiful women – but at heart embodies the same inner emptiness, dissatisfaction and detachment from society as Pechorin.

Aside from its exploration of personality, *A Hero of Our Time* is lauded for its lyrical descriptions of the rugged landscape of the Caucasus, and for the technical skill with which Lermontov handles its structure – with Pechorin's story told via multiple narratives, out of sequence, and in the voices of several narrators. My copy came with a scholarly introduction, and a chronological table that set Lermontov's career in a wider literary and historical context. A note on his birth in 1814 confirmed the Scottish connection – his father's alleged descent from a Scottish mercenary soldier and, still further back, from the medieval Scottish poet Thomas the Rhymer. But the Scottish reference was an aside, and for the Everyman editors unimportant. An interesting curiosity maybe, but incidental to Lermontov's literary achievements and his place in the Russian canon.

Yet, I was not content with this brief allusion and decided to investigate further. It turned out there's no definitive proof of his Scottish descent, although a host of circumstantial details point to a genuine connection. Lermontov himself clearly believed in his Scottish ancestry, making it explicit in a poem entitled *Yearning*, in which he imagines himself a bird of prey flying West to Scotland – to the fields of his forefathers, his 'native land' as he calls it. According to legend, his family descended from George Learmouth a 17th century Scot who was captured fighting for the Poles but changed sides and joined the Russian army, settled, married and Russified his surname. Scholars point to similarities between the Learmouth family crest of the time and the Lermontov crest which appeared a century later. Even more curious is the fact that in childhood, generations of Lermontovs learned snatches of Scottish songs and nursery rhymes which passed down orally within the family, although nobody had otherwise any knowledge of English.

In Russia today there's a Lermontov Society dedicated both to celebrating the poet's memory, and to exploring his links with Scotland. An article of faith is that the Learmouths and Lermontovs share a common ancestor, and the society organises regular gatherings of members of the 'extended family' from both countries.

I discovered the Lermontov family story was part of a wider pattern of historical connections between Scotland and Russia, with estimates that up to a quarter of a million Russians can trace their ancestry back to Scottish merchants, or soldiers who migrated to Russia in the 17th and 18th centuries. This led me to a wry reflection: how long before there's an attempt to enlist Lermontov or some of these other Russians as Scottish celebrities?

Over the past couple of decades, with the rise of political nationalism, ever grander claims have been made about Scottish literature. Like a flag and a football team, a must-have for an independent nation is a strong national literature with its own characteristics and traditions. It's a confirmation of identity. And there's a small, tempting step from the aspiration, to the convenient discovery that in fact such a literature already exists – it just hasn't yet been widely recognised. As a result, the Scottish literary landscape sees various efforts to assist the process of recognition – with the exhumation of forgotten works which on reevaluation turn out to be 'classics'. It's amusing to watch these attempts at bagging as many writers as possible, by including in the canon famous names with only tenuous links to Scotland. (In several literary histories, for example, Lord Byron becomes a Scottish Poet on the strength of his mother's roots.)

The answer to my question about how long it might take to enlist Lermontov, turned out to be only a few years. In the autumn of 2014, the bicentenary of his birth, and several years after I'd left Moscow, I saw a BBC news report about a bronze bust of Lermontov being erected in his memory in the village of Earlston in the Scottish Borders – which was once the home of his supposed ancestor Thomas the Rhymer. Underlining his Scottish roots, the anniversary was also marked with the creation of a new *Lermontov 200 tartan.* A claim to Lermontov as a trophy for Scottish culture had been staked!

An interesting footnote to the mystery of his ancestry was a project launched by an Oxford University genetics professor in the mid-2000s. He set out to investigate Lermontov's links with Scotland through DNA profiling, and appealed to Russians with the Lermontov surname, and Scots called Learmouth (and its variants Learmonth, Learmond and Learmont) to volunteer for genetic testing, in the hope of finding scientific proof of their common lineage. Unfortunately, the results were inconclusive, and failed to confirm a DNA link between the Russian Lermontovs and those Scottish Learmouths who took part in the project. But they did show that the Lermontov DNA shared a genotype very common in Scotland, indicating a strong probability of Scottish roots, if not proof of specific family links. This however has not discouraged the Lermontov Society, which remains hopeful of establishing a conclusive connection with the Scottish Learmouths. Society members argue that the number of Scots who supplied genetic samples was too small to provide the basis for a decisive study, and also point to factors in the history of the surname that complicate the picture: not all Learmouths descend from the same Scottish clan, some branches of the family have died out over the past couple of centuries and, more importantly, going as far back as the Middle Ages, many Scots with the Learmouth surname were never blood relatives of the family, but simply assumed the name when they settled on what had been Learmouth land.

23

In any society, the selection of official holidays is a political gesture that proclaims its self-image and core values. Contemporary Russia, stuck between two worlds and struggling for a post-Soviet identity, continues to tinker with the calendar inherited from the communists – to widespread confusion and controversy. Only two of the national public holidays which defined the Soviet year have survived on their traditional dates, or with their original meanings unchanged – Victory Day (May 9) and New Year's Day. The rest have had makeovers to align them with current Kremlin ideology. In addition, the host of lower-profile professional and commemorative days which proliferated in the USSR – days honouring specific groups of workers, or special events of lesser importance than those marked by public holidays – has undergone a similar modernisation. It's the public holidays which draw fire from disgruntled Russians, as I saw with Valeria's complaint about Christmas. But it was these other days, many of which I encountered as red footnotes in our company's pictorial wall-calendar, that seemed to me more curious and interesting. To a foreigner they offered a quirky dash of local colour, and at the same time demonstrated the essential continuity in mindset between Soviet political culture and its new Russian successor.

The contemporary list is a mixture of not-quite-dead-yet Soviet relics, and more recent inventions which self-consciously seek to connect with the spirit of the times. There's a series of Military

Glory Days that commemorate big anniversaries like the battles of Borodino (September 8), and Stalingrad (February 2), but also a plethora of obscure triumphs such as the Kulilovskaya Battle of 1380 (September 21), the 1790 Capture of the Izmail Fortress (December 24), two separate Victories Over Turkish Fleets: in 1812 (September 11) and 1853 (December 1) and so on…and on. What jars with Western sentiment is that these are not just anniversaries – but celebrations. Unashamed declarations of pride. They're not about remembrance – but about triumph. In the West the jingoistic tone is unfashionable today: glory is only for sportsmen – or the pages of boys' comics. It's just about permissible to fight in self-defence, or maybe even for freedom – but for glory? Russian society however hasn't yet undergone the same feminisation as post-war Europe and America, and its male dominated culture still holds martial values in high esteem.

Honour, victory, glory are serious anchors for a nation's holidays. However, many of the other commemorative days – the professional ones in particular – provide wry amusement for foreign observers. The full collection reads like a satire on officialdom – an odd blend of banality, petty bureaucracy, state pomposity and a febrile determination to keep up with the times. Citizens' hearts must surely stir with pride each September 24 when it's Systems Analyst Day. Or on the third Sunday of March – Sales Clerks, Housing & Community Services Specialists Day. Similarly, March 11 is the Day of Drugs Control Specialists, while June 5 is the Day of Ecologists and Environmentalists. For those who like their glory on the grand scale, December 17 is Intercontinental Ballistic Missile Forces Day. Every month has its roll call. In May for example, there are separate days for Librarians, Border Guards, Philologists, Chemists, Radio & Telecoms Workers, Lawyers and

Entrepreneurs. In July it's the turn of Traffic Policemen, Sea and River Fleet Workers, Metallurgists, Fishermen and Postal Service Workers. Nobody it seems is to be left out.

"Valeria," I once asked as an experiment, "do you know what day it is today?"

"Of course. It's Monday."

"Yes – but what other day? A special day?"

She gave me a puzzled look. "Special day? I don't think it's a special day."

"Yes it is! It's – the *Day of Radioactive, Chemical and Biological Defence Troops.* You didn't know that? Look -"

I pointed to the calendar, and she peered at the tiny legend printed beneath the date. Then blew a loud raspberry.

"Pfffttt…Nobody knows that! Except the soldiers maybe – if they get a holiday. Who else cares?"

"But look," I said, "here's more. Sunday's Rocket Forces and Artillery Day. And then next Tuesday – it's Tax Inspection Workers Day."

"You're laughing at us."

"No, no, I'm not. I'm just not used to the idea – of special days for all these workers. At home most holidays are religious – or they were originally."

"We also have religious ones now."

Which was true – and important. Since the end of the Soviet Union, a calendar of saints' days and feasts celebrated by the resurgent Orthodox Church has joined the template of state prescribed holidays

"Tell me about them," I said.

"I don't know much. There's Christmas of course. But the others…? Young people aren't so interested. When I was a child, every holiday was important. The newspapers and television told us their meaning, and the people they congratulated. Now it's different. The government creates new days but nobody's interested."

Valeria's recollection reached to the heart of Soviet ideology – the centrality of jobs to people's identities and their perceived value to society. Communism placed collective good above personal happiness, and a person's worth was as a unit of production. Occupational holidays, as public events, affirmed this ideology, eulogising work itself and commending specific occupations. By providing workers with time-off together as a group, they reinforced the supremacy of collective effort. The communal picnics and large-scale works outings once features of Russian life have now mostly vanished, but at an official level at least, and despite general apathy, the holidays themselves persist as institutions – with some gestures to modernity. Straining to celebrate every conceivable occupational group seemed ridiculous even in a Soviet context, but in the new cut-throat, capitalist Russia it's even stranger. Yet I was amused when living in Moscow to witness the continuation of the tradition – with the 2006 announcement that every October 31 would henceforth be the Day of Detention Centre & Prison Workers. (I never discovered who actually got the pat on the head. Current employees only? Or was there posthumous rehabilitation for retired KGB jailers, and guards from the Gulags?)

Less questionable are other professional days created since communism's collapse, such as Advertising Industry Workers Day (October 23), with which the Yeltsin government in 1994 acknowledged the new free market. Or Social Workers Day (June 8), established a few years later in a further pious sign of changing times. Aside from newly created holidays, many of the old Soviet ones had their names changed – for no obvious reason other than that the new ones sounded fancier. So, Cosmonauts' Day (April 12 – the anniversary of Gagarin's flight) became The Day of Space Travel Science, and Pushkin Day (June 6) recently became Russian Language Day.

Another communist holiday that was renamed was Soviet Army & Navy Day (originally Red Army Day), held on February 23. In the new order it became Defender of the Fatherland Day. This is one of Russia's high profile national holidays, and also popularly known as Men's Day (since most Russian males at some time in their lives do military service). Every year, like most of the rest of Moscow, our company's office closed in recognition, and on the day immediately before, held a ceremony in the office to mark the occasion. The company President and management team – myself included – would assemble mid-afternoon in the executive dining room, where the usual furniture had been removed to make space for a long table set with plates of finger-food and bottles of spirits. The format was the same every year. We'd pour a drink and stand together on one side of the table, waiting until the President signalled his bodyguard to open the room's double doors. Then a group of about twenty men would file in and line up facing us across the table.

"They're all veterans," Dmitri the interpreter whispered the first time I attended.

There was a stiff, uneasy air at the start, since many of those attending had no routine contact with senior management. But it was the one day in the year when a man's position in the hierarchy came second to his service record, and employees were invited for their military credentials rather than their current jobs. The room was therefore filled with retired career soldiers, rather than the legions who had suffered a couple of years' conscription.

"Maximov" Dmitri told me, glancing towards our Head of General Affairs (who managed the Visa, Travel and Transport Departments) "used to be a colonel. Gubarev and Filchenov were captains. And Sokolov was maybe a major – I'm not sure."

Sokolov was now Head of Facilities Management, and he spent his days supervising the office cleaners and odd-job men. All the old soldiers, as far as I knew, were in such support roles – not the key substantive posts which drove the company's business. And even here, although doubtless they performed well enough, most were not obvious candidates. But I understood performance wasn't the point. That they'd been hired not for their skills, but for their pasts – for their links with the military, and the web of connections they represented. (This was not about buying influence in the conventional sense – our veterans were not important enough to have that kind of access. Rather it was something subtler, less tangible, but in its way just as calculated – the company reaching out beyond the volatile world of business for allies, for anchors to something more solid and enduring in Russian society.)

In their civilian clothes, our soldiers were a motley collection. Undistinguished middle-aged men – with a few more elderly survivors (whose active service must have been well back in Soviet times). The fact they still worked, or needed to, meant they were either honest or unlucky. They must have retired on modest military pensions, without enriching themselves during their service years in the traditional spheres of military corruption – illegal arms sales, pilfered supplies, smuggling, or recruitment scams.

The event's dynamic intrigued me, for here were men of rank who had held serious posts in one of the world's top military machines. Now, in the second act of their lives, they deferred to a collection of accountants, lawyers and salesmen. But while the gathering was a serious affair, and proceeded with dignity, it was not unduly solemn. The President greeted them warmly, and indicating the table in front of us, invited them to fill their glasses. The wide variety of drinks available was itself a gesture of respect. Beyond the inevitable vodka were fancy whiskies and brandies, and an exotic array of coloured bottles that suggested a raid on an airport duty-free shop.

There followed a series of speeches and toasts. The President opened with a short address.

"He's thanking everybody for their service to the nation," Dmitri whispered. "And asking us to remember those who were lost. He also thanks our soldiers for their loyalty to the company."

Next came Mr. Kuznetsov, the most senior military figure present. Judging by his age he must have served at the height of the Cold War. When he began speaking the President, to underline his respect, made a point of placing his own glass on the table to listen.

"Kuznetsov was a full General," Dmitri told me.

The General's remarks were inclusive. He spoke about the brotherhood of men – and how each, whatever his job, served the nation in some way. There were a couple of affectionate jokes at the expense of those who had been in the navy rather than the army. And the General concluded with a toast to Russia. It was nicely done. Patriotic without being jingoistic. I was the only foreigner in the room, and my presence could have been awkward. But this was Russians at their best – hospitable, relaxed and courteous – and I was made to feel welcome. Even the General acknowledged me with a friendly nod and a handshake. Filchenov, who had served in military communications in the Yemen and spoke Arabic and English, sidled over and said: "Mr. Strachan, we're all on the same side now. We can celebrate peace together."

After a suitable interval the senior management diplomatically withdrew, leaving the old soldiers to drink their way through the bottles on the table. With something similar happening all over Moscow, it's unsurprising that Defender of the Fatherland Day has become a highpoint in the year for serious public drunkenness.

24

My all-time favourite Russian quotation comes from neither Tolstoy nor Pushkin, but an angry lady on an Aeroflot flight from Moscow to New York. Just before take-off one December day in 2008, the pilot appeared at the cockpit door, red-eyed, disheveled and walking unsteadily. Despite passenger alarm, airline officials insisted he was sober and fit to fly – until an outraged lady passenger loudly exclaimed: *"Everybody in Russia knows what a drunk looks like!"*

The episode was well publicised at the time. In his pre-flight announcement the captain slurred his way through a message in Russian, then followed up with an incoherent one in English. Drawing the obvious conclusion, passengers demanded a replacement crew – only to have their complaints brushed aside by cabin staff, who told them to either "stop making trouble" or get off. One passenger who called Aeroflot's head office by mobile phone was disdainfully told it was impossible for a pilot to be drunk. A group of Aeroflot officials then boarded the aircraft, hoping to quell the clamour, but things became even more farcical. A *Moscow Times* journalist who happened to be on board reported the following exchange:

"It's not such a big deal if the pilot's drunk," an official said. "Really all he has to do is press a button and the plane flies itself. The worst that could happen is he'll trip over something in the cockpit."

The captain himself chipped in with further reassurance. "I'll sit here quietly in a corner," he told the anxious passengers. "We have three more pilots. I won't even touch the controls – I promise."

Astoundingly, even this performance failed to move Aeroflot. It was only when a politically-connected TV celebrity in first-class called friends in high places, that Aeroflot backtracked and replaced the crew. Weeks later, striving to manage the PR damage, the airline made no attempt to deny the facts, but disputed the cause. The pilot it seems, had been ill not drunk.

The Russian skies are notoriously dangerous at the best of times. Crashes and near misses are common. Internal flights are still dominated by old Tupolevs, the workhorses of Soviet aviation, popularly derided as flying Lada. They were noisy and unreliable even in their heyday, but more than thirty years after production ceased in the 1980s, they are now often deathtraps, and there are regular reports of bits falling off in flight. Russian airlines are defensive about the condition of their planes and their lamentable safety records, and quick to blame pilot error when things go wrong – as if this provides any comfort. Indeed, it does the opposite, drawing attention to the extraordinary lack of professionalism of many Russian flight crews. The Aeroflot incident was no rarity. Even well-maintained Western-built planes are routinely crashed by Russian pilots – and the reason is usually alcohol. Time and again, accident investigations have exposed it as the prime factor in Russian air disasters. A few months before the Aeroflot incident, another plane went down in the Urals, killing 88 people. In remarkably similar circumstances, an uneasy passenger texted a friend in Britain just before take-off, saying the pilot sounded drunk during the pre-flight announcement. Black box recordings later revealed the cockpit crew squabbling as the plane plunged out of control, and an autopsy confirmed the presence of alcohol in the pilot's body.

The lady on the Aeroflot flight's comment about drunks resonates well beyond aviation and opens a window on a general truth about Russian society – alcohol is a huge problem. Of course, there's nothing surprising about this. The Russians, like the Scots, have always embraced strong drink as an essential element of their national culture. For centuries heavy drinking has been an accepted part of life at all levels of Russian society. Even the communist hierarchy dank copiously; Stalin and his closest henchmen would regularly collapse in drunken stupors, and Stalin's longest serving successor, Leonid Brezhnev, was virtually an alcoholic.

Despite their private behaviour however, the Soviet authorities periodically launched campaigns against drunkenness – although the degree of commitment varied with the leadership. The Brezhnev years (1964 -1982), were notably lax, leading commentators to call them the "era of the alcoholisation" of the Soviet population. Official figures for the period show an unprecedented rise in alcohol consumption, with the annual intake per head more than doubling, and over 40 million Soviet citizens – one in seven – officially classed as alcoholics. Brezhnev himself was lukewarm on state crackdowns, arguing that his countrymen couldn't function without their vodka.

In the 1980s Mikhail Gorbachov successfully cut problem drinking for a time, by increasing prices and restricting purchasing opportunities. But his measures were deeply unpopular, and ultimately just drove demand on to the black market. After the collapse of communism, the authorities again became concerned, as economic turmoil and social dislocation drove millions to seek consolation in the bottle. Even Kremlin opponents – who habitually took contrary positions on social policy matters – conceded drink was seriously undermining the development of a successful, modern society.

President Boris Yeltsin's own drink problems became emblematic of the period, and an incident at Shannon airport caused particular embarrassment, when he was reputedly too drunk to disembark a plane. The *Irish Times* the following day captured the mood of the Western press, in a cartoon that showed a vodka bottle toppling down the aircraft stairs, and an onlooker commenting *"at last a message from President Yeltsin."*

I saw daily reminders in Moscow of alcohol's hold on Russia. The kind of scenes apparent in most big cities: late night brawls, drunken rows in the streets, public bouts of vomiting. But the real story was in smaller, quieter details. Officially it was illegal to drink spirits in public – in streets, parks or on public transport – but beer, which was classed as foodstuff, was permitted. (On the metro both vodka and beer were banned.) The law however was widely ignored, and it was common at any time of day to see Muscovites standing at a tram stop, strolling along a street, or settled on a park bench with a bottle or a beer-can in hand. These were not the derelicts who haunt pedestrian underpasses or sleep in shop doorways, but respectable Russians, professional men in smart suits and fashionably dressed women, for whom drinking while commuting, shopping, or in the course of business was normal behaviour. They generally caused no trouble, but summer or winter could be spotted enjoying alcohol for breakfast or unwinding with an open can on the evening walk home.

They were the respectable tip of a huge iceberg, a symptom of deeper alcohol problems in Russian society. At work, I regularly witnessed drinking that carried echoes of Scotland a generation ago

– but would not be tolerated in today's more austere business environment. For too many of my Russian colleagues, incapacitating hangovers destroyed their mornings, and boozy lunchtimes wiped out any possibility of productivity in the afternoons. Absenteeism was rife – particularly early each month, when employees still had money left for drink. As HR Manager, I routinely reviewed attendance statistics, and shocked by the numbers, reacted at first with textbook fussiness.

"Can't we do something?" I asked Grishin.

"What should we do?"

"Anything – fire the worst offenders. Arrange an absence management program – that kind of thing."

I had in mind the kind of attendance initiatives used in Western public organisations where it's difficult to sack people.

Grishin shrugged – too polite to comment. But the look on his face said I was hopelessly naive.

"There must be something," I said.

"Yes – we can fire them. But then we'll have no workers. New hires won't help – they'll be the same. This is Russia. Every company's the same."

I discovered he was correct. Russian industry was plagued by chronic, drink-related absenteeism, which through necessity all employers tolerated. A well-documented cycle of fluctuating productivity, linked to salary-payment dates. Huge numbers of feckless workers regularly disappeared for part of every month, returning just in time to qualify for the next pay cheque. Manual and lower-level clerical employees were the worst culprits. Senior professionals drank just as much, but were less prone to absenteeism, and at least turned up to work – to linger in dazed, unproductive hibernation.

I changed tack with Grishin. "OK then, what about Marina Bolotova?"

Grishin raised an eyebrow and nodded, recognising where I was going.

"And the others like her," I said. "Shouldn't they get help?"

"With Bolotova nothing will work."

Bolotova was Head of Marketing and the most senior woman in the company. Short, dumpy, and aged somewhere between forty and sixty, she dressed expensively, but her defining feature was a permanently red face which heavy make-up failed to camouflage after 9.30 in the morning. An alcoholic's complexion of blotches and broken veins, whose colour heightened in the course of the day. Her notoriety however rested on her erratic behaviour. She was known for drunken, late-night phone-calls to subordinates, berating them in a slurred voice for some failing or other. Occasionally victims would hear her husband in the background, gently coaxing her to hang-up, or to hand him the receiver. He was not always successful, and a fierce row would be heard, which inevitably featured in the following morning's office gossip.

I was present only once when Bolotova disgraced herself at work. At a boardroom lunch in honour of some visitors she dozed off and slumped forward, her face landing in the soup in front of her. It might have been comical in a sitcom, but in real life was sad and embarrassing.

Moscow has twelve drunk tanks, where those passing out in the streets are taken to sober up. They are never short of customers, and on any evening legions of unsteady figures can be seen tottering around in public places. On the metro, I learned by experience to be wary of seats miraculously available in crowded carriages. Too often a dash to the space revealed it wasn't luck that reserved it, but a pool of vomit other passengers had already spotted. Similarly, a clean empty seat might reveal its mystery a few minutes after you sat down – when a fishy smell wafted from the gentleman dozing next to you, and dribbles of piss collected around his shoes.

But it wasn't public drunkenness that was Russia's main problem with alcohol. Bar and club culture were the preserve of the young and the relatively affluent. The bedrock of its alcohol crisis were the old-fashioned adult drunks who did their drinking hidden away – at home, in their workplaces, or in unlicensed drinking dens. And despite the growing popularity of beer, especially amongst the young, their drink of preference remained vodka. Large scale beer consumption in Russia is a recent phenomenon. Soviet brewing had a poor reputation, but the industry was transformed by the expansion into the country of Western companies such as Carlsberg and Scottish & Newcastle, whose beers are marketed under suitably Russian brand names. With government encouragement, beer was heavily promoted as a safer alternative to vodka.

During my first two summers in Moscow, beer tents offered refreshments in several spots around the city centre, including Pushkin Square and Tverskoi Boulevard. The beer was on draft, served in plastic glasses for safety, and temporary *al fresco* tables and chairs ensured a pleasantly relaxed atmosphere. They were well-organised ventures, and problems were rare. In my third summer, however, the tents failed to reappear. Why, I asked Valeria – what happened?

"Officially it's to stop people drinking alcohol. But everybody knows the real reason. The vodka companies are losing business because people prefer beer. So they complained."

In Russia's ruthless and paranoid business world this was plausible – official interference marshalled to do-down competitors. But on this occasion Valeria's cynicism was misplaced. The disappearance of the beer tents was part of wider reforms that included new regulations on alcohol labelling, and the production and supply of spirits. These changes proved a fiasco. Instead of tightening control, a bungled implementation resulted in all kinds of alcohol disappearing completely from shops for weeks. The sudden unavailability was a minor inconvenience for many, but for Russia's serious drinkers a calamity that sparked a flight to dangerous alternatives – such as disinfectant, cologne and industrial alcohol. The law of unintended consequences also meant that to the dismay of Moscow's women, the city's shops ran out of hair spray, deodorant, cheap perfume and other alcohol-based cosmetics, as desperate drinkers stocked-up on substitutes. Official hikes in the price of legal spirits compounded the problem, putting them beyond the means of drinkers at the bottom of Russian society. The retail price of half a litre of vodka rose from 65 to 95 roubles, while the same volume of industrial alcohol cost only 25 roubles. Pharmacies saw a spike in demand for another perennial favourite: *Tincture of Hawthorn.* This cost 15 roubles for 100 ml, less volume than the smallest bottle of vodka – but cheaper per unit of alcohol as the hawthorn is 90% alcohol while the vodka is only 40%. Even further down the price scale were positively lethal concoctions, featuring anti-freeze and cleaning fluids.

In the years since I left Moscow, the picture has allegedly changed. The World Health Organisation in 2019 reported a 43% reduction in Russian alcohol consumption since the beginning of the century, and health improvements that see a remarkable rise in male life expectancy – from the 57 years of the Yeltsin era, to 68 years currently. Supporters of Vladimir Putin cite the President's sporting profile as key in promoting a healthy lifestyle. Others point to new controls on alcohol sales that echo Gorbachov's Late-Soviet initiatives, including restrictions on advertising, pricing and availability. These include a ban on shops and supermarkets selling drink after 11pm, and a clampdown on bootleg booze, which is often the most poisonous and destructive.

***

Russia's alcohol problems illuminate a paradox at the nation's heart. A country full of feckless wasters and drunks, is also home to a disproportionate number of world-class creative artists, who realise their genius through intense effort and personal discipline. Between the two extremes are the many in the middle, who drink intemperately, but through luck and guile nevertheless stay afloat. One of these featured in a little cameo of Moscow life I experienced personally. I was watching television one evening when I heard a loud crack – like a single gunshot. A mafia hit on the staircase? A few minutes later water began seeping under the living-room door, and I dashed to the kitchen to investigate. The gunshot had been a weld bursting on the connector from the cold-water pipe to the dishwasher. Unable to turn off the supply, and with a serious flood on my hands, I called my landlord who dispatched a plumber. About twenty minutes later, a van pulled into the yard behind the building, and I watched from the window as a man clumsily hauled out a toolbox and stumbled unsteadily towards the entrance. When I opened the door, it was obvious the plumber was blind drunk. Yet he managed to quickly locate the cold-water valve behind the bath and stop the flow. Then he stood back and took stock,

248

fumbling in his jacket pocket for cigarettes. His hands shook and he struggled to open the packet, but finally pushed a cigarette between his lips. His degree of intoxication became clear however when he tried to light up, waving the lighter dangerously, unable to focus enough to align the flame and the cigarette. With a flash of good sense, he suddenly gave up, and handed me the lighter, and I completed the task without burning his face or setting his hair alight. When he'd finished smoking, an even scarier pantomime ensued. Muttering incoherently in Russian, he disappeared downstairs to the van and returned lugging a gas canister and a welding torch. It's unwise to be conventionally fussy about health and safety in Russia, but a drunk wielding a gas torch indoors posed a dilemma. Should I intervene? Or retreat from a possible explosion behind a sofa? In the end I played safe, and nervously helped light the torch, holding it steady while the plumber somehow mended the weld and reconnected the dishwasher. Job done, he had another cigarette – for which we followed the same process as the first time. I helped him carry his kit to the van, gratified that he seemed to sober-up momentarily when we hit the cool air in the yard. But it was an illusion, his hands shook on the steering wheel, and the gears crunched alarmingly as he drove out onto the city streets.

***

Russia's difficult relationship with drink is apparent in the succession of anti-alcohol posters the state issued over the years. These have a long history. The first were published soon after the revolution, and new versions continued to appear until the collapse of the USSR. Original Soviet propaganda posters of all kinds are collectors' items today, with rare copies in good condition commanding high prices in dealers' salesrooms. They're sought-after as relics of social history, and for their clever artwork and decorative appeal. Fortunately, reproductions of popular examples are widely available at reasonable prices.

My favourite is a cartoonish illustration from 1959. Drawn with great bravado, it depicts a drunk who has passed out at the dinner table. His head rests on a plate (shades of Bolotova), while the remains of his meal – including a half-eaten fish – lies staining the tablecloth. Tellingly, there's an empty bottle at his side. His face has the stock characteristics of a drunken slob – red nose, podgy jowls, heavy eyes. The drunk's swinish quality is no accident, for the top third of the poster features a contrasting scene: two fresh-looking pigs standing in a green field, peeping down at the dinner table carnage below. A legend in Cyrillic speaks for them: *And They call us Pigs.*

A second poster that caught my attention was very different. Serious in tone and humourless, but a fascinating historical curiosity which unintentionally evoked something darker of Soviet society – signalling distress, control, censure and menace. In the forefront a man buries his face in his hands. Behind him, in the distance, he's shown again, this time at the site of an overturned barrel and a damaged sapling. A stern figure in some kind of military tunic confronts him, and the legend explains: *He destroyed a tree while drunk and is now ashamed.* It's a warning about drinking – but in the hint of official retribution carries an unmistakably sinister dimension. In its somber tone it's more representative of the genre overall than the one with the pigs.

As anti-alcohol posters evolved over the 20th century, their design mirrored developments in the wider art world. Published collections record styles ranging from *avant garde* modernist, to pictorial realism and stylised caricature. The message itself though, and the props underscoring it, remain remarkably constant over the years. A parade of degrading situations: neglected children, reproachful wives, the unpleasant consequences (often medical) of drinking. Slogans such as *Drunkenness is wasteful! or Remove drunks from the workplace!* are typical. It's the same finger-wagging sanctimony typical of Victorian temperance movements in the West. Drink is dangerous. Nothing to laugh about. Drunkards come to a bad end.

With the USSR now history, Soviet posters have become retro-chic – fashionable pieces of home decor. Idealised portraits of Soviet heroes, or slogans which mocked Russia's citizenry for most of the 20th century, now hang on living-room walls. Yet I suspect their true appeal is limited. Foreigners and affluent young Russians may find them ironic and amusing, while ageing, die-hard communists still revere their Lenins and Stalins. But how comfortable are ordinary Russians with old-fashioned reminders of a difficult past? At the same time, the posters repay study as pieces of cultural, political and art history. Personally, I absorbed a deeper sense of Soviet society from the era's posters than the written word – a testament to the skill and intelligence of Soviet propagandists. Temperance posters also help humanize their world. Soviet PR generally was about myths and upbeat messages: socialism was thriving; the masses were happy and prosperous; their leaders strong and benevolent. Images of barrel-chested workers or industrial achievements spoke to an idea of continuing progress. But drunkenness is negative. It involves guilt and shame and requires a different mood, and anyone viewing the Soviet period through its posters will find the acknowledgement of frailty a breath of fresh air. In the end, although the propaganda machine was successful in moulding public attitudes across many areas of life, as all the statistics show, it failed dismally to make any enduring impact on alcohol abuse. A portent maybe for today's seeming improvements?

25

One miserable January morning, wet sleet stinging my face, I trudged determinedly down Tverskai Street in the direction of the Kremlin. It was a day for remaining indoors – bleak, shivery, and heavily overcast – but as there were few people around it was ideal for my purpose. I was on my way to Lenin's mausoleum in Red Square, nudged into action by a conversation I'd had with Valeria.

"If you want to see Lenin," she'd said, "go soon. There may be no more chances. The government's proposing to bury him. It was on television yesterday."

"Is it just talk again – or serious this time?"

"Who knows? But there's a risk."

I'd heard speculation of the kind before. Indeed, since the fall of communism politicians and Orthodox clergymen have regularly called for the body to be removed for burial and the mausoleum closed.

"Is it really worth a visit?" I asked. "Have you been inside?"

"At school the teachers brought us to Moscow for a special visit. Celebrating our history but -" Valeria hesitated. "It's not so interesting – just like a yellow doll."

Nevertheless, I was determined go, if only to tick a tourist box. I was well into my second year in the city but had yet to enter this iconic landmark and see Lenin's mummified corpse. One of the world's great tourist attractions, the mausoleum, like Big Ben and the Eiffel Tower, is familiar from television to millions who will never visit in person. Soviet-era news footage from Moscow regularly included shots of the Politburo on its roof balcony, inspecting some military parade, and Western Kremlinologists famously calculated the political fortunes of individuals according to their proximity to the leader.

"What's your opinion?" I asked Valeria. "Should he be buried?"

"Of course! I'm not religious but it's – like a circus. Russia's a modern country and this shames us."

Public debate on the issue peaked during the Yeltsin years but has never gone away. It's not only right-wing figures and Orthodox churchmen who support a burial, but a majority of the general population, particularly the young. The stumbling block is the communists, who threaten mass civil disobedience if the body is moved. Lenin's own wish was to be buried in St Petersburg beside his mother. But Stalin ignored this, along with the wishes of Lenin's widow, and had him embalmed and displayed in the Red Square tomb, deliberately manufacturing a quasi-religious relic for worship by the communist faithful.

Over the decades millions of Soviet citizens filed past the body, including school children like Valeria on officially organised pilgrimages. The symbolism of the mausoleum's physical location, at the very heart of the Soviet Union, together with the sanctity of its occupant, ensured that this – the only building ever erected on Red Square by the communists – became the most important site in Moscow. A shrine. The significance of politburo members standing on top of the founding father of the Soviet state was a powerful declaration of legitimacy. Vladimir Putin, while reportedly personally in favour of a burial, has acted cautiously and postponed plans indefinitely. "Many people" he said, "connect their lives with the name of Lenin.... burying Lenin would mean...that they had lived in vain."

My failure to visit until now was down to the queues. The mausoleum's normally open to visitors five mornings a week, from 10am till 1pm, when the immediate Red Square area gets barriered off and the police control access. Entry is free, but bags and cameras are forbidden, and visitors must line up for a security search at a gate beside the Kremlin wall. Typically, the queues are long and slow moving, a mixture of foreign tourists and Russian out-of-towners visiting their nation's capital. I'd always baulked at waiting in line, telling myself there'd surely be a better opportunity another day. I'd also resisted the alternative – handing $20 to a tour guide to be escorted directly to the front. (Maybe I should just have queued and accepted it as a personal taste of Soviet life.)

On this morning, as I'd hoped, there were only a handful of visitors at the security gate, and the queue which usually spills well back into Manage Square was absent. I could have gone straight to the mausoleum but decided first on a little detour. In fine weather Manege Square bustles with shoppers from the underground fashion mall, courting couples (who rendezvous around the statue of Marshall Zhukov) and hucksters of all kinds. Today, however, the souvenir venders and street photographers were absent, along with the inevitable herds of tourists. The only evidence of normal activity was a huddle of figures sheltering at the brick archway at the Historical Museum, which separates the Manege area from Red Square. Even at a distance, and despite their heavy winter overcoats, I recognised them as a group of historical lookalikes – professional impersonators of characters from Russia's past. They were a favourite Moscow sight, and I went towards them, intent on looking at a live Lenin before visiting the dead one.

The offer of these lookalikes was simple: if you wanted a souvenir photograph and were averse to sharing it with a monkey wearing human clothes, or a hooded bird of prey, you could, for the rouble equivalent of a few dollars, pose instead with Lenin, Stalin, or Tzar Nicholas II. It was a competitive trade, and in summer I counted as many as four rival Lenins vying for attention, along with a couple each of Stalins and Tzars. The best of these living waxworks combined a natural physical similarity to the originals, with painstaking attention to details of dress and appearance – mimicking the public images familiar from photographs, and decades of propaganda posters. Every Lenin had a peaked workman's cap, a red ribbon in the lapel of his dark suit, and a trimmed goatee beard. The Stalins were short, like the real man, and depicted the elderly WWII dictator in his general's uniform – khaki tunic with red trim, gold epaulets embossed with stars like those on the Kremlin towers, rows of medals on their chests. They sported heavy grey moustaches, and had authentically sallow complexions. One even had pock marks which uncannily resembled those disfiguring the real Stalin's face. Were these, I wondered, a remarkable natural coincidence – or self-inflicted attempts at verisimilitude?

Fittingly, Nicholas II (in both his incarnations) was the most elaborately dressed – in expensive, tailored costumes of Ruritanian excess which would done credit to a film or theatrical performance. One Tzar wore a splendid, heavily-decorated white ceremonial uniform; the other, a marginally more military version in khaki. And both featured sleek, black riding boots that exemplified vanity and arrogance. Yet it was not their sartorial extravagance which best evoked the last Tzar, but the remarkable likeness in their faces – the perfection of their Romanov beards and whiskers, as famously echoed in photographs of Nicholas and his British royal cousins.

Less impressive I think, was the man who did Karl Marx – all wild white hair and unkempt beard. In a different context he'd have been indistinguishable from any number of scruffy old men walking Moscow's streets. He just about got away with it there, since the company of the other impersonators signaled he was a historical figure, and a huge granite bust of Marx nearby reminded tourists who he was supposed to be. My favourite turn, however, for his sheer opportunism, his cheapskate, creative effrontery, was a brown-suited man who played Mikael Gorbachov. His get-up was rudimentary: Gorbachov's distinctive birthmark inked on his bald head with a purple felt-tipped pen.

When the lookalikes were out in force, people-watchers lingering in the square were rewarded with quirky, sometimes surreal, cameos that offered a variety of counter-historical photo-ops. Nicholas II chatting amiably with Lenin, or sharing a cigarette with Stalin. Lenin playing with a photographer's monkey, or lounging with a pigeon on his shoulder. A Tzar enjoying a can of Coke, while beside him Stalin munched a burger from the McDonalds above the fashion mall. What wasn't seen, however, was such good fellowship manifested between direct competitors. I never spotted two Stalins together, nor two Tzars. And on days when all the Lenins were working, they carefully took up pitches far enough apart to avoid stealing each other's thunder.

I once read a *Moscow Times* profile of Anatoly Koklenkov, a Lenin impersonator who claimed to be the first, as well as the most authentic, lookalike. Koklenkov hailed originally from Uzbekistan and began impersonating Lenin as a hobby after a friend in Tashkent commented on his remarkable resemblance. In 1990 he sent a photograph of himself to a Moscow competition for impersonators and was invited to appear at a performance in the theatre of the Rossiya Hotel. There his earning potential became apparent, when people continually approached during rehearsals and offered money to pose with him in photographs. A few years later, during the turmoil that accompanied the collapse of the Soviet Union, he left Tashkent permanently for Moscow, determined to capitalize on his appearance. By the time of the newspaper story – 2007 – his career as a lookalike had brought him financial security, and he confessed to earning on good days upwards of 5000 roubles from posing with tourists. Not a fortune by Western standards, but a decent enough sum in post-Soviet Russia.

In his newspaper interview, Koklenkov admitted to frequent quarrels with rival Lenins, and of competition for customers which at times bordered on violence. Yet he also spoke of his friendship with one of the Tzar impersonators, and of how he helped him attract customers by permitting him to stand beside him. It seemed that when the Tzar waited alone, few tourists would approach, but when he allied himself with Lenin, he prospered.

Disappointingly, what's potentially most interesting about Koklenkov is entirely absent from the interview – his thoughts on Lenin. There's nothing about his views on Lenin's politics, life or legacy. Celebrity impersonators in the West, especially those styling themselves as tribute acts, not only mimic appearance, but typically pay homage to their heroes – and seek to capture something of their spirit and values. Many identify and empathise with them, adopting mannerisms, speech patterns, and attitudes. But what of those haunting central Moscow's tourist spots? Elvis impersonators commonly idolise Elvis – but Stalin impersonators? There's surely a fascinating book to be written about the world of Russia's historical lookalikes. About how they see the characters they mimic, and what it says about contemporary attitudes to the country's past. Is it possible to masquerade as a famous figure for any length of time, without developing sympathy for the original? Do they judge their crimes – or simply dress up and play pantomime villains? Is it even valid to use interchangeably, as I have done, the terms lookalike and impersonator? Is there a distinction between those who offer portraits of individuals – performances even – and mere moving statues?

Some of these questions were again in my mind as I crossed Manège Square. The full complement of lookalikes is a summer phenomenon, and in today's sleet only a hard-core trio was present: a single Lenin, Stalin and Tzar. Koklenkov might have been the Lenin – I neither knew nor cared. But I did want a closer glimpse, a reminder of Lenin's appearance before I saw the real thing, so I deliberately cut a path past the little group. A bulky overcoat covered Lenin's trademark dark suit, his face was blotchy red in the cold, and his beard and famous cap were flecked with melting snow flakes. But I was satisfied.

After passing through the security gate, the entrance to Lenin's tomb is approached via a path that runs alongside the Kremlin wall, flanked by memorials to the other Soviet potentates whose graves lie here. Some are buried in the earth at the foot of the wall, while the ashes of others lie in urns interred in the wall itself. The honour of a Red Square resting place was given to many of the great names of the communist era – Felix Dzerzhinsky, Maxim Gorky, Leonid Brezhnev and Yuri Gagarin lie here. Stalin is now buried close to the mausoleum that for a few years he shared with Lenin, in a plot marked with a grey granite bust.

For all the mythology and fuss surrounding Lenin's corpse, the reality was something of an anti-climax. He lies on his back under glass, fully clothed, arms by his sides, his right hand clenched, the other at ease. His eyes are closed and a spotlight casts white light on his face, deliberately invoking an air of saintly dignity. When my mother visited Moscow in the 1970s, she came back gratified to have connected with her hero. "He looked just like he was sleeping," she said. "As if he's still alive." She had found what she wanted. Maybe it's a question of belief, but I did not find him especially lifelike. He was fuller in the face than in most photographs, his skin smoother, and I fancied I detected hints of plaster or plastic. Indeed, a yellow doll. But my assessment was hasty, as there was no time for detailed study as I filed silently past. The guards were vigilant and ensured visitors kept moving. I was in and out in less than five minutes.

It hadn't always been like that. The mausoleum underwent something of a revival when Putin became president, after standards slipped during the Yeltsin era. The marble fabric became shabby with neglect, and official indifference extended to the behaviour of the guards, who at times conducted themselves in a manner that would have seen their Soviet predecessors shot or dispatched to the Gulag: scruffy uniforms, slouching on duty, slackness that permitted visitors to talk, sip soft drinks, and linger beside the body. However, Putin's push to foster national pride with a revival of Soviet symbols, ensured the premises were smartened up and discipline restored.

A couple of weeks after my visit, the police, on the anniversary of Lenin's death, closed off Red Square, and arrested twenty-five Russian Monarchists attempting to hold a banned demonstration. The Communist Party was scheduled to lay flowers at the mausoleum that day, and the Monarchists had planned to dress as mummies and parade a cardboard coffin, in protest at the continuing failure to give Lenin a normal burial.

Ever since 1924, when he was first embalmed, the condition of Lenin's body has fascinated observers. He was pickled with glycerol and potassium acetate, a treatment that's refreshed annually, and the scientists responsible for his upkeep claim he can last like this for another hundred years. Understandably there's speculation about just how much of the original Lenin remains, given the acknowledged priority of Russian scientists to maintain the size and outward appearance of the body rather than preserving biological tissue. With his internal organs removed early in the preservation process, his brain taken for dissection by the *Moscow Brain Institute* in order to study the characteristics of genius, and a catalogue of further body parts replaced as they decayed over the years, skeptics argue that there's now little more on display in Red Square than a wax-work replica – an idealized recreation of Lenin rather than the real man. They say he looks better dead than he did when alive. Photographs of Lenin in later life appear to validate this. One in particular, taken by his sister six months before his death, shows a wreck of man – thin, wild eyed, obviously very ill and possibly deranged – strikingly different from the serene figure in the mausoleum.

A few months after my visit, I came across a second-hand copy of a book published in the 1990s, when debate in Yeltsin's government about burying Lenin was at its height. Entitled *Lenin's Embalmers*, it was written by Russian biochemist Ilya Zbrasky (assisted by American journalist Samuel Hutchinson), and it tells the story of the Zbrasky family's involvement over a thirty-year period with the mausoleum's laboratory and its efforts to preserve

Lenin's body. It's a curious little book – part social history, part autobiography, part treatise on the science of embalming. Ilya's father, Boris Zbrasky, was one of two key figures who during the 1920s developed the embalming process used on Lenin. He became a senior figure in the preservation team and was joined in the laboratory a decade later by his son Ilya. Both Zbraskys worked there until they were caught up in one of Stalin's purges in the early 1950s, when the father was arrested and jailed, and the son dismissed from his post. Prior to this calamity, however, such was the importance to the state of their work on Lenin's corpse, that throughout their long years of employment, they enjoyed the privileged lifestyle of the Soviet elite.

During World War II, with the German army threatening Moscow's Western outskirts, Lenin's body was evacuated for safe keeping to the city of Tiumen 2500 kilometers to the east. Here the Zbraskys set up a makeshift laboratory on the first floor of a decrepit building in the local agricultural institute. The body itself was installed in a 'funeral chamber' converted from an adjoining room, in which the windows were bricked up to keep out sunlight. Chemicals and equipment were shipped in from Moscow, but the working conditions were difficult, and the scientists found it challenging to maintain standards. Paradoxically, however, as there were no regular public displays of the body, more time was available to carry out repairs, and at the end of the war Lenin returned to Moscow in noticeably better condition than when he left. Ilya Zbrasky proudly informs us that in recognition of their wartime service his father was awarded the Order of Lenin, while Ilya himself received the Order of the Red Flag of Labour.

Zbrasky's book is a fascinating insider's portrait of life in the USSR's upper echelons during Stalin's reign. A life that mixed luxury, opportunity, intrigue, and paranoia – with the ever-present threat of denunciation. Against all the evidence, including the experiences of acquaintances in their social and professional circles (which included secret policemen, academics, writers, senior politicians and high-ranking officials), the Zbraskys believed their connection with Lenin and the mausoleum would protect them from the kind of arbitrary, state-directed persecution that destroyed the lives of millions of their fellow citizens. In the end it didn't. And as Ilya recounts, although they kept their lives, they lost their careers and livelihoods. The older Zbrasky's health was irretrievably damaged by prison, while the son struggled with poverty for years. It was an archetypal 20th century Russian fall from grace.

In the latter sections of *Lenin's Embalmers* Zbrasky describes the laboratory's activities in the period after his own involvement ended, when its scientists took on the mantle of international consultants in the field of embalming dead communist leaders. They were responsible for preserving the bodies, amongst others, of Vietnam's Ho Chi Min, North Korea's Kim Il Sung, Bulgarian Communist Party leader Georgi Dimitrov, and Czech Communist Party leader Klement Gottwald. The laboratory came close to cornering the global market; only the Chinese declined their services and chose to mummify Mao Tse Tung themselves. Some preservation projects were trickier than others. In 1979 for example, there were unforeseen problems when attempting to preserve Angola's President Neto. It was their first experience with black skin, and it took three months of experiments with different chemicals before they got the colour right. This job had a final twist when the time came to dress Neto. In life he'd worn spectacles, and Angolan officials insisted that authenticity required a pair on his corpse. But the embalmers worried that light refracted through the glass would fade his carefully tinted skin. A compromise was agreed: Neto kept his spectacles – with the lenses removed.

The collapse of the USSR ushered in a new era for the mausoleum's scientific staff. Faced with cuts in state funding for their work, they were allowed to freelance, and a venture named *Ritual Service* was set up to sell embalming services to private clients. Russia's nouveau riche, together with families and associates of murdered gangsters, provided most of their business. The changed nature of demand meant a different focus for the embalmers. In the old days, when they treated dead tyrants, the priority was to ensure the long-term preservation of a body. They were manufacturing relics intended to underline a regime's legitimacy for decades to come. But the modern requirement was for a more cosmetic approach. Lengthy survival was rarely a concern. Looking good for a funeral or a wake became the priority, and the expertise of the biochemist was secondary to the beautician's skill in covering up bullet holes and stab wounds. Nevertheless, the effectiveness of the chemical processes developed for Lenin meant that decay was dramatically arrested in bodies treated by the laboratory, and many remained well-preserved in their coffins for months, even years, after burial – whether the clients wished it or not.

Ilya Zbrasky was in his mid-80s when he published *Lenin's Embalmers* in 1997. Looking back on his career he gave a final verdict on the practice of embalming. Despite the scientific achievements it represented, and the personal prosperity it brought for a time, he concluded it's barbaric, anachronistic and alien to Western culture. As a Russian citizen, he believed Lenin's body should now be buried.

26

When my daughter left home for university, my wife joined me in Moscow. Her arrival changed how I used my free time. There was less random exploring, more shopping and more socialising with other expats. She joined the *British Women's Association* and became part of a circle of English-speaking wives who had their own sightseeing routines.

"Do you know the *Natasha Gallery*?" she asked me one day.

"No. Where is it?"

"Patriashy Prudy. Karen says it's really interesting. It's an art gallery and they're doing her portrait."

I tried to recall a gallery in the streets around the pond but failed.

"She found it by accident," my wife continued, "Henry's a bit arty apparently, and they were out walking one night when he said *let's look in here*. He's a designer or something – so he's interested in that kind of thing. Anyway, they went in to some exhibition, and the woman running it asked if they wanted to be in a competition – and get their portraits painted for free."

"What's the catch?"

"There's none. If they don't like them, they don't have to buy them. They're under no obligation."

"Yeh, sure."

"No, really. Karen says there's been no pressure. It's a competition's called *Mysterious Stranger*. They just have to pay for framing – so they can be exhibited."

The deal was that a group of artists would paint portraits of complete strangers. They'd know nothing about the sitters and interpret only what they saw. Then there would be an exhibition, with everyone who visited the gallery voting for the best painting.

"The prize for the winner's a holiday in Egypt. Karen's hoping she'll win."

"What do they mean by *winner*? The artist or the person being painted?"

"The person being painted."

"That's ridiculous. It's a painting contest – not a beauty contest. Surely an artist should win?"

"It's to encourage people to sit for them. They're hoping to exhibit about sixty paintings. It takes hours to sit. Karen's already been twice – and has to go once more. I know it's a marketing ploy, not a real competition. Getting people to have portraits done in the hope they'll buy them. For the artists the prize is selling their paintings. Anyway, I think it's a good idea!"

My wife was curious to see her friend's portrait, which was already on a gallery wall awaiting finishing touches. Karen apparently was pleased with the result, but Henry had not liked his own, and confided he'd never buy it whatever the price.

"Does that mean it's a bad likeness?" I said. "Or too good a likeness?"

"If you're so interested let's go and have a look."

Although I'd been to Patriashy Prudy dozens of times I'd never noticed the gallery. It was on the ground floor of a block overlooking the pond, but the floor-level was several feet above the street, meaning the windows were above head-height, and it was easy to walk past without seeing what was there. As there was no entrance from the street itself, access was via an archway in a lane

266

at the side. We rang a bell for admittance and waited until the door was unlocked.

"Can we see the exhibition?" I asked.

"Ah – English! Give me four hundred roubles."

The speaker was a bohemian looking lady of uncertain age, who glanced at my wife and added: "And four hundred for your woman."

She thrust a catalogue at me. *Imperial Hunt* it said in both English and Russian, and featured reproductions of hunting scenes.

"This is the exhibition?"

"Very beautiful Russian art!"

"We thought it was portraits," my wife said. "My friend's having one done."

"Ah, our competition. Who is your friend?"

"Her name's Karen."

"Karen? Yes, yes. Here – come look!"

Forgetting the eight hundred roubles, she led us up a short flight of stairs into the gallery itself. Most of the walls were taken up with old pictures in heavy frames, but in one corner a young girl posed in an armchair while a painter sketched. On the wall behind her was a group of what were obviously works in progress – unframed portraits in various stages of completion.

My wife pointed at one. "That's Karen. It looks really like her. But -"

"But what?"

"Well, it's very realistic. The painter's caught her likeness. But I'm not sure I'd want it. Look at her clothes."

The picture showed a middle-aged lady in a heavy knitted jumper.

"Are you a painter yourself?" I asked Natasha.

"I am actress," she said, and added grandly: "And I have my gallery."

Then turning to my wife she asked: "Do you want plastic surgery?"

"What?"

"Some treatment? I know very good doctor."

Natasha, it seemed, was also a tout for a private clinic. A useful connection, I guessed, in theatrical circles. She went on to explain how difficult it was for Moscow girls to get a man. Too many provincial beauties it seemed, flocked to the city seeking their fortunes, and to compete local women sought surgical improvements.

"I already have a man," my wife said. "So thank you, but no."

"OK – You want be in our competition?"

We agreed to return the next evening, when there would be artists available to paint us. Each of our sittings would last about an hour and a half, and Natasha promised repeats later in the week. I was assigned to a youngish man who worked in quick bursts – of about fifteen minutes at a time. He then stood me down for a similar period, while he tinkered with his efforts. He worked without sketches or outlines, glancing from me to his easel, and applying colour directly to the canvas. He made no objection when I sidled up behind him to check progress. During our short breaks I also wandered around the gallery, watching the other painters working on their competition pieces. There were three or four present each evening we attended. Most were young, probably recently out of art school, and almost all favoured a traditional portrait style which never strayed too far from photographic realism. I saw only one impressionistic example – painted by a woman for whom the sitter was clearly not a mysterious stranger, but a blood relative. A sister maybe – their faces were too similar for coincidence.

I also took the opportunity to browse the stock of pictures Natasha had for sale. She offered a mix of 19th century and modern works which, like the competition pieces, were largely traditional in style. Landscapes, portraits of children and animals, street-scenes. I saw nothing abstract. Her hunting exhibition was displayed separately in a small alcove and featured thirty or so mid-late 19th century compositions, that presented a picturesque version of Russian rural life. The kind of images that look good on expensive lacquered boxes. Cossacks on horseback pursuing a stag – with dogs at heel. A horse-sledge in a snow-covered forest, hauling the carcass of a newly shot bear. A fashionable hunting-party enjoying a summer picnic: military officers, horses and hounds, ladies in period dress. Yet for all their nostalgia and romanticism, none were merely formulaic, decorative pieces – but art of genuine quality, realised with a high degree of technical competence. It's easy to decry the limitations of the gallery's range, and its crowd-pleasing, conservative aesthetic. But it was a business. Natasha knew what sold and tailored her offer accordingly, leaving anything challenging or groundbreaking to the big public galleries and the specialist avant garde dealers.

Moscow has a thriving art scene, and wealthy New Russians spend freely on paintings and sculpture. The Natasha Gallery sat somewhere in the middle market, a serious player, well above the street venders of the Arbat who target tourists and weekend shoppers – but not in the same league as the major dealers. At the higher end of the trade the last two decades have seen such an appetite for 19th century Russian masters, that there is now a problem with fakes. A common scam is for dealers to buy works by minor 19th century Western painters, change a few details to 'Russify' them, and pass them on as paintings by Russians of the same era. Landscapes, usually by Danish, Dutch or other northern European artists, are a favourite as they are easily doctored. A few brushstrokes and a Western building can look Russian, and a figure in Western dress becomes a Russian peasant. Fraudsters avoid detection because canvases and most of the paint are correct for the period, and because it's credible in Russia, with its history of upheavals and looting, for quantities of previously unknown works to suddenly appear on the market.

One evening, as I circled Natasha's exhibition of hunting paintings, I spotted a middle-aged army officer in full uniform. He sat stiffly in a leather chair, while an artist hovered only a few inches away, carefully scrutinising his medals and military decorations. Absolute precision here was clearly essential. I glanced at the easel as I passed, and the officer caught my eye and said something in Russian. Fearing he thought me rude, I responded with a shy wave and a "*Good Evening.*"

"Ah, you're English," he said. "Come and look. How do you like my picture?"

He rose from his chair smiling and gestured towards the easel. The portrait was almost complete, awaiting only the addition of his military honours. It was an excellent physical likeness, yet revealed a subtly different character from the affable man beside me. He had been given an imperious air – a touch of haughty, martial dignity.

"It's very good," I said. "You look great."

"Yes, I like it. But my friend here" he said, indicating the painter, "makes me look like Napoleon. I think I'll buy it."

My wife and I were also pleased with our portraits, and a month or so later we returned to the gallery to see them in Natasha's

Mysterious Stranger exhibition. Each visitor was given a coloured sticker on entry, to fix to the frame of their candidate for best picture. There were no stickers on mine, my wife's, Karen's nor Henry's. But the army officer had collected a respectable tally and looked a contender for Natasha's prize.

"What's the price of a picture?" I asked Natasha.

"You want the Generali?"

"No – I want my own of course."

"I like the General's better," my wife said.

"Anyone can look good in uniform," I said. "You should judge the quality of the painting. Not the sitter's clothes."

"Mmmm."

"After show I will ask artist the price." Natasha said. "Maybe get you good deal. Price for the Generali painting will be high – but not for you. The Generali is very handsome man."

***

Over coffee in my office Morrison entertained us one morning with an item from that day's local newspaper. "Listen to this," he said. "It's from a lady called Tatyana Andreyeva who says Russia's famed for the beauty of its women. Apparently it's the only country in the world where female beauty's in the blood. According to Tatyana – and I quote – "it's a natural resource." She's the director of some pageant called '*Beauty of Russia*' which celebrates it. Not a bad way of looking at things – *natural resources*. What makes country rich? Oil? Minerals? Agriculture? No – it's the fanny count."

Norman spluttered with laughter in spite of himself. He was not given to crudity, and often found Morrison's comments tasteless.

"Beauty contests are still big here," Morrison went on. "Back home they're pretty much killed off."

"True," Norman said. "Every county fair used to have one – but now…"

"It's refreshing to hear Tatyana. She can publicise her contest without getting attacked."

"Is she correct?" I asked. "What do you guys think?"

As they both had Russian wives, I expected agreement with Tatyana.

"She *is* on to something," Morrison said. "Just look around in the street. Did you ever see so many gorgeous women?"

I did not deny it. "Around here certainly. But -"

"Everywhere!" Morrison was emphatic. "All over the country!"

There were certainly a disproportionate number of young, expensively dressed women in central Moscow. But I doubted the same was true of less fashionable areas.

"It could be a trick of the mind," I said. "Of perception. Only noticing the attractive ones – editing out the rest."

"That happens everywhere," Morrison said. "It's life – and doesn't explain Moscow's body count."

"There's truth in what John says," Norman observed. "But the beauty in the blood theory's a bit much. The fact is – women here *make an effort*. Always try to look good. It's to do with the end of communism. Access to clothes and cosmetics their mothers couldn't dream of. It's no big deal for Westerners – but think how amazing it must seem here. Transformative."

"And the Sushi bars?" Morrison chipped in. "They're a sure sign."

"*What?*" Norman and I asked, almost in unison.

"I'm serious! Haven't you noticed how many? More even than Tokyo it seems."

There was indeed a huge craze for Sushi in Moscow at the time, and specialist restaurants proliferated in the city centre. Their significance however escaped Norman and me.

"So? – What's your point?"

"They're part of the same pattern – all about beauty," Morrison said. "Don't look at me as if I'm crazy – think about it. What's the key thing about Sushi?"

"The taste of fish?"

"No – *you don't get fat eating it!* That's why it's so popular. Russian women watching their figures. Am I right? OK, so their mothers didn't have fancy cosmetics – but they did have dumplings and sausage. But now...Anyway, you get the point."

We did.

"I never thought of that," Norman admitted. Then echoed Natasha. "But I guess the big city factor's more important. Moscow's a magnet for small-town beauties from all over Russia. They come looking for a job and a man. Seems like there's a never-ending supply."

"Exactly!" Morrison said. "Look at Chugunov for example. It's the reason he gets away with it. Purely because there's so many to choose from. Beauty's cheap here."

Mr. Chugunov was a minor legend within the company. A focus of amusement and admiration to macho males – but annoyance and frustration to HR. He was notorious for affairs with his secretaries, and for changing them regularly. Our Recruitment Group had recently worked on his latest replacement and offered fourteen candidates for interview. Not one passed muster – despite each meeting his essential specification: blonde and under thirty. I was astounded by his brazenness. In other environments managers might communicate a preference with a quiet nod and a wink. But Chugunov was open and forceful, and made a fuss if 'unsuitable' candidates slipped through the net. Yet even more surprising was the general absence of outrage amongst female staff. Our company was no back-street sweat-shop, but a respectable, modern, international business, and Chugunov's antics were the stuff of old-fashioned TV sitcoms and comedy films – a *Carry On Recruiting* scenario. In an equivalent Western organisation, they would spark a lawsuit or a scandal – but my Russian colleagues thought them normal, even acceptable. At times like this I felt the true culture shock of Moscow. The big, obvious differences quickly fade into everyday reality, but a myriad of small things – prejudices, attitudes and habits – lie hidden, unseen but ready to suddenly surface and remind us we're in a very different world.

A common sight in the bars and restaurants of central Moscow is expatriate men with much younger Russian women. One evening in the *Hard Rock Cafe* my wife indicated a couple at a table opposite – a man of fifty something and a girl in her twenties. They sat largely in silence – constrained likely by mutually inadequate language skills – but every few minutes the man would put down his drink and stroke his companion's chin.

"Disgusting," my wife said. "*How old is she*? Talk about an ill-matched couple."

I nodded wisely in agreement and said nothing.

The episode reminded me however of Norman and Morrison. Were our two *Hard Rock* diners any less suited than my colleagues and their partners? More than once I pondered the chances of their marriages lasting. I'd never met Morrison's wife, but I guessed at an even bigger age difference than between Norman and Ina. The occasional throwaway comment hinted she wasn't his first – or even his second – but simply his current wife. I never asked about his personal life, but once, when we heard one of our Russian colleagues was marrying a Syrian, he spoke about foreign wives in general. His perspective was typically forthright and unembarrassed.

"It's a complicated subject," he said. "With different schools of thought. People can get sniffy. Everything hinges on the wife's nationality. An Englishman with a French or Spanish wife's a bohemian character – to be envied. But an Asian wife's different – there's always a stigma. A suspicion of mail order – even when there's cast-iron romantic provenance. Is it a passport job or just economic convenience? An older Western man with a younger Asian wife? Definitely mail order. A young Western guy with a young Asian wife? Possibly mail order – but equally it might be the geek effect."

"Geek effect?"

"You know the type. Guys too nerdy or weird to get a woman back home. But a Western credit works wonders in Hanoi or Jakarta. To be fair, it's sometimes not the whole story. Language and cultural differences cut both ways. They make genuine romance – a meeting of minds – difficult; but they also camouflage problems. It's harder for women to detect bores and creeps when they can't understand what they say. A nerd's nerdiness gets smoothed out. Their very foreignness seems romantic. Look how women go weak at the knees when some non-descript TV celebrity speaks English in a French accent. Foreign's sexy.

"Just after the Soviet collapse, Russian brides were in the mail order category. Thousands of beautiful women desperate for a ticket out. Not now. The economy's improved. Life's better and most women want a Russian guy – preferably with loads of money. A lot of foreign men who married Russians in the early days regretted it. They were hypnotised by their glossy appearance. Gorgeous looking women who seemed as Western as them. But it was usually a mirage. Culturally they came from a different planet – and most hadn't even the language skills of a Filipino bar girl. Things have settled down now and everybody's more selective. Men and women alike. But it's still possible for us older guys to hook up with younger local women."

27

It was Valeria who alerted me to the ceremony.

"If you want to see some history, go to Red Square tomorrow morning," she said. "There's a communist march."

"A march? – Why?"

"To celebrate Stalin – it's here in the newspaper."

The story reminded readers that the following day – March 5 – was the anniversary of Stalin's death, and the communists were meeting in remembrance.

"Is it a public holiday?"

"Of course not! Nobody cares except the communists."

The next morning though, I slipped out of the office to walk the ten minutes to the square. "If anyone looks for me, say I've gone to the bank."

It was cold, but Red Square was clear of snow. I took up a position in front of the GUM shopping arcade, from where I could easily watch the cordoned-off area to the right of Lenin's mausoleum, which seemed the focus of attention. As the participants assembled it struck me that nothing denoted more clearly communism's decline in Russia than the appearance of its adherents. Most were elderly and shabbily dressed – ancient heavy coats, woollen hats, and a fair ration of walking sticks. No more than a hundred or so took part, and they looked lost in the wide spaces of the Square. It was less a crowd than a straggling, shuffling band, which evoked a Saga Tour more than a revolutionary movement. The handful of police in attendance were unnecessary. But of course, I reflected, it was a weekday, and maybe the more youthful followers were at work.

A few of the communists held flowers, while others clutched red flags or placards displaying portraits of Stalin. Occasionally, a marcher waved one aloft, but for a few moments only, as if the effort was too much for weary arms. The placards in particular underlined the tired, almost forlorn air of the proceedings; some were home-made, crudely fashioned with sellotape and pictures torn from magazines; others were battered, dog-eared relics that told of being exhumed for the occasion from dusty cupboards, or under the beds of believers. A far cry from the huge official portraits visible in archive films of Red Square gatherings in the past.

When Stalin died in 1953 his body was embalmed and placed alongside Lenin's in the Red Square mausoleum. Eight years later however, in the wake of Khrushchev's de-Stalinisation campaign, it was quietly removed and buried nearby, in front of the Kremlin wall. It was to this grave that these Soviet pilgrims now headed, and I moved closer for a better view, leaving my spot at GUM and crossing the square, to join the onlookers collected at the edge of the barrier.

There's a stone bust of Stalin on a pedestal behind his grave, and on either side that day stood a military figure, providing a guard of honour. Their dated uniforms, and white hair visible beneath their military caps, indicated however that these were not serving officers, but veterans dressed for the occasion, in the attire of their earlier lives. I watched them stiffen to attention when a middle-aged man in a civilian coat approached with a wreath. He was balding, and despite the cold, bare-headed – a sign of respect? Presumably a senior communist. Unlike most of his companions, he was still young enough to be genuinely politically active. When the wreath was laid, he took up a megaphone and began a short but energetic oration. At first, I listened intently, trying to understand, but between the crackle of his device and my shaky Russian I caught little. I soon abandoned the attempt and allowed my gaze to drift. As I scanned the square, I was struck by the indifference of most of those present. The speaker had the attention of his followers, but few others.

The police were clearly bored; shoppers entering and leaving GUM cast passing glances, but few slowed or altered their paths to watch. With the exception of a handful of curious individuals beside me at the cordon, not even the tourists were interested. They clustered as usual to photograph St. Basil's and the Kremlin but ignored the ceremony as if it were a dull piece of street theatre.

When the formalities were over and the participants gradually dispersed, I reflected on Valeria's remark about witnessing something from history. But what had I seen – a historical curiosity? The last sputtering remnants of a lost cause? Here, on its most sacred ground, communism, one of the key forces of the twentieth century, embodied only irrelevance.

Was I dismissing it too easily? Maybe this spectacle misrepresented the reality of communist support? Besides, had the marchers been honouring Stalin himself – or the whole Soviet system? Back in the office I sought some insights.

"Valeria" I asked, "Who are the communists? What's their background?"

"They're a mixture. Many are old – and believe what they've always believed. Some are angry or jealous. It's complicated."

She was disdainful. But as I'd later discover, her assessment is shared by many Russians, who see the communists as simply losers. In the sense of having lost both the ideological and political struggle – and the personal battle of life. Modern Russia's failures. People incapable of thriving in a market economy, who therefore reject the whole notion of such freedom. It's the harsh verdict of opponents, but in essence also of mainstream economists and political commentators, who note that support for the Communist Party of the Russian Federation (CPRF) – the successor to the of Communist Party of the Soviet Union – comes predominately from the lower reaches of Russian society: unskilled workers, pensioners, former state employees (often mourning lost prestige, or even lost jobs) and the generally disappointed and disgruntled. And despite the feeble turn out in Red Square that morning – there are millions of them.

While the Kremlin now embraces market capitalism, significant numbers of Russians are unshaken believers in the principles of the revolution and the vanished Soviet state. The communists may have lost power, but they continue as a presence on the political scene – and as the main opposition to Vladimir Putin's ruling United Russia party. For many of the poorest Russians it's about material concerns – resentment at the loss of state benefits that in theory still exist (such as universal medical care, or pensions that people can actually live on), but which in reality disappeared with the Soviet Union. Yet there's more to the communists' survival than economics or ideology. Looking to the future with optimism, Valeria had a young person's outlook and dismissed them as an irrelevance from yesteryear. Yet her Russian roots meant she also recognised the deeper emotional influences at play, even if she shied from unpicking them – the cocktail of nostalgia, denial, ignorance and pride which sustains many older communists.

There's an obvious paradox in the fact that the Red Square marchers were predominantly Stalin-era survivors – the generation which suffered most under totalitarianism. On one level their constancy defies logic, but on another testifies to the potency of nostalgia, and the universal human capacity for self-delusion. To repudiate Stalin and communism would have been to repudiate their own pasts, and to diminish the significance of their lives. Throughout years of struggle and hardship they were relentlessly told – and to varying degrees believed – that they were building something worthwhile, something special. When a changing world exposed the madness, incompetence, viciousness and lies behind the Soviet dream, many simply refused to listen and kept their beliefs intact. I saw the same protective psychology closer to home, in my mother's continued attachment to all things socialist – in the face of reason and worldwide evidence of its failure.

Yet a sentimental attachment to an ideology is one thing, worshiping Stalin, the man, is another.

"What about Stalin?" I asked Valeria. "What's your opinion?"

A reproachful look said I'd asked a stupid question: "Really – you don't know?"

"I can guess. But I'm interested in your thoughts."

"He was very cruel of course. Many Russians hate him. He killed so many people and made life terrible. But…" She paused.

But…The but is crucial to understanding Stalin's reputation in Russia today. In the West, beyond the ranks of left-wing intellectuals like H G Wells, Bernard Shaw, and their modern-day counterparts, he's long been simply a monster. There are few buts. In Russia however, a surprising number of those who condemn his tyranny also praise his wartime leadership, and his role in the defeat of Nazi Germany. This was Valeria's view.

"He saved us," she said. "And gave us a great victory."

"What about your family Valeria? You father? Your grandfather? What do they think?"

"They don't like Stalin – and don't speak about him. But I'm sure they think the same."

It was ironic that Valeria should have directed me to Red Square that morning, since I was often struck by her ignorance of Russia's recent past. She was educated and intelligent and had a shrewd grasp of the realities of contemporary life, but was hazy about the history of the Late-Soviet world – the world of her childhood – and the preceding Cold War decades. Day-to-day life she could describe with clarity and insight, but the wider canvas seemed blank. I found it curious that as a foreigner I'd heard of people and events of which she seemed wholly ignorant. In retrospect I recognise my expectations were unfair and unrealistic. She was my secretary – not a historian or political activist. Present-day life was her interest. (Would a British secretary have been any different?) Nevertheless, I was disappointed, imagining that because Russian history had been so momentous, she might be more aware. Crucially, I also failed to grasp the extent to which Soviet-era propaganda and disinformation still colour ordinary Russians' knowledge of their country. It's not that official concealment continues to bury the past, but that Soviet orthodoxies and taboos linger on in the popular psyche, in the absence of any general resolve to correct them. Apart from genuine state secrets, information on most aspects of Russia's 20th century history is readily accessible to those willing to look. Most ordinary Russians however have little interest in doing so.

Stalin's public reputation at home received a mortal blow in February 1956 – three years after his death – when his successor, Nikita Khrushchev, delivered to the 20th Congress of the Communist Party his famous, so called "secret speech", denouncing Stalin's crimes and his cult of personality. Living in Moscow in 2006 I devoured the press comment generated by the speech's fiftieth anniversary. The English Language *Moscow Times* ran a series of articles and debated its long-term significance. But when I mentioned Khrushchev to Valeria, she was vague. She'd heard his name and confessed to seeing a story in a newspaper – but paid little attention. She knew nothing about his speech. Stalin was lodged in her consciousness as a historical figure, Khrushchev simply did not feature.

This was a generational issue. Those who lived through the fifties and early sixties, Khrushchev's years in power, recognised his place in modern history. But to younger Russians he was a non-person. When Leonid Brezhnev and his henchmen deposed him in October 1964, he was quickly airbrushed from the picture. And even today, continuing Kremlin unease with his speech means he's largely ignored by the official media, and his public reputation in Russia is uncertain. I had the advantage of Valeria here, for he featured alongside Stalin in the textbooks used in Scottish schools during my teenage years, to teach European history. What now interested me most was how the *Speech of the Century*, as an article in the *Moscow Times* labelled it, still sharply divides Russians. That it's one of the 20th century's seminal events is rarely disputed. But there's fierce debate about Khrushchev's motives in delivering it, and on its continuing reverberations in Russia. To the communist faithful, it was a massive betrayal that ultimately led to the Soviet Union's implosion. On its 50th anniversary, Gennady Zyuganov, the CPRF leader, denounced it for dividing society by airing in public the Party's dirty secrets. He did not deny Stalin's crimes, but argued exposure went against the greater good. Stalin had legitimised communism domestically and internationally, and challenging him was a challenge to communism itself. By damaging its prestige at home and abroad, Khrushchev had cracked its armour, paving the way for Mikael Gorbachev, perestroika, and the calamity of the USSR's collapse. In this analysis, Zyuganov is remarkably close to many Russian liberals, who see the same cause and effect. Three decades after Khrushchev, Gorbachev himself acknowledged his own reforms would not have been possible without the example of the speech.

Beyond general agreement on the speech's importance, in the myriad of articles I read around the anniversary, there was no consensus on how to judge Khrushchev. Zyuganov believed his motivation was personal spite against his old boss – not idealistic attachment to the truth. Yet for others Khrushchev performed a courageous act. In openly confronting the horrors of the Stalin era, he allowed a measure of recovery and healing in Russian society. The "Khrushchev thaw" which followed saw thousands of political prisoners released from the gulags, and the Kremlin allow some social liberalization, confirming to many commentators that his motivation was essentially altruistic. Khrushchev, they argued, was the only close colleague of Stalin to retain any genuine humanity – and could now act on it. His speech was an act of repentance – amends for wrongs he'd been forced to commit under Stalin.

Amongst the most interesting anniversary pieces were contributions from Khrushchev's daughter and great granddaughter, both of whom, naturally, espoused positive interpretations. In a newspaper interview illustrated with a photograph of the old lady seated in her Moscow apartment, a portrait of her father on the wall behind her, Khrushchev's daughter Rada looked back fifty years to when she first heard about her father's speech – fully two weeks after its delivery at the Congress. In line with the process for dissemination decreed by the Kremlin, a Party official arrived and read it aloud to her university class. No questions were taken, no comments permitted. Like so many in the Soviet Union at the time, she was stunned by its content. Her father, true to the habits of secrecy prevailing in Stalin's court, had never said a word about it at home.

In contrast, the piece by Nina Khrushcheva, his great-granddaughter, is more analytical and more curious – a mix of family history and professional commentary. Her memories are of a later era, two decades on from her grandmother's. Now a New York academic, she recalls being at school in Moscow with the children of Party VIPs during the Brezhnev years. While classmates boasted about their parents' important jobs, she would remain silent, unable to mention her own illustrious great-grandfather. He was now a non-person, written out of the official records. At home she learned about his speech and of how, for a time at least, the state relaxed its inflexible grip on every aspect of life. Nina's article moves from personal recollection into a critique of contemporary Russian politics and accuses today's Kremlin of continuing to trash Khrushchev's reputation to shore up public support for Vladimir Putin's autocracy. Central to this, she argues, is the myth of strong leadership focused on a rehabilitation of Stalin. The man who denounced his bloody reign is therefore traduced, and at the same time cast as a scapegoat for all the ills that befell post-Soviet Russia. So, Khrushchev, along with Gorbachev, is blamed for Yeltsin era chaos, for corruption, insecurity, economic dislocation, and the loss of national pride that followed communism's collapse.

In this context a strong leader prepared to impose order is attractive, but Nina sees more at play than just temporary political expediency. Russian history and psychology, she believes, make her countrymen infinitely more comfortable with tyranny than freedom. It's a characteristic deeply rooted in the national psyche. Russians may fear dictators, but ultimately find them less threatening than the existential challenges posed by democracy, personal responsibility and individual choice. After all, if you're responsible for your own actions, who do you blame when things go wrong? This is not an original observation; many commentators have said something similar, and it's not at odds with Putin's own concept of what's required to effectively rule Russia. Curiously though, there's also no shortage of Russians who think Putin fatally weak, who shudder at the memory of the 1990s and yearn for a leader like Stalin to run things properly.

Nina's thoughts on Khrushchev's image today cast poignant light on her family history. No longer, she tells us, is his speech generally considered in Russia a brave step in confronting Stalinism – but more commonly dismissed as a shabby exercise in revenge by a man with a grudge. Old rumours about Khrushchev's eldest son Leonid – Nina's grandfather – circulate again, blackening both their names. Nina's sketchy with the details, but I was intrigued enough to investigate further, and found various independent accounts that flesh out the story. Officially Leonid Khrushchev died a hero in 1943, when the fighter plane he piloted was downed by German fire. Sometime during the Brezhnev era however, stories began to surface, allegedly fed by the KGB, that Leonid had not died in battle but was executed by Stalin for treason. It was said he'd bailed out and deserted, or surviving a crash, was captured by the Nazis and changed sides. A different version had him flying direct to a Nazi airfield to defect.

It's impossible to uncover the truth of any of this. No body was ever found, and short of a secret file emerging from official archives, it's unlikely the mystery of his death will ever be explained. However, as Nina sees it, the allegations are still being used to discredit Khrushchev – with the claim his speech was revenge for the execution of his son. It's a good story, chiming with popular notions of Kremlin treachery and intrigue. But is Nina correct about her great-grandfather's reputation in modern Russia? My own impression is that she exaggerates. That the press is generally more balanced than she admits. Many anniversary articles certainly damned Khrushchev – but were only part of the picture. Others took a more nuanced approach, including several that argued what seems to me the most plausible explanation of Khrushchev's motives – that he was driven by neither revenge nor altruism, but a pragmatic determination to save communism by reforming it. According to this theory, criticism of Stalin was a tactical ploy. Blaming Stalin for everything, absolved the rest of the Soviet leadership and the system itself. That it stirred currents that ultimately wrecked the Soviet Union was an unintended consequence. Western leftists have long used Stalin in a similar manner, arguing in the face of history that there's nothing inherently oppressive, totalitarian or unworkable about communism. It just got a bad name because of Stalin. He's a useful sin-eater – a decoy without which more evasion, wriggling and explaining would be necessary.

An interesting footnote to Khrushchev's speech is what its aftermath shows about the malleability of Soviet public opinion.

Every account speaks of widespread shock and surprise at the revelations. But then what? Historians taking the long view see the eventual destabilisation of communism. But what of the months and years following the Party Congress? Stalin loyalists retreated into denial – but the overwhelming public response was simply acceptance. The Russian people accepted what they were told and got on with life – in the same way they had for decades accepted without question Stalin's lies. The party had spoken and they believed what it said – just as they believed scares about traitors, spies and saboteurs used to justify Stalin's purges. Stalin had gone from God to disgrace quickly, but without, it seems, provoking undue intellectual turmoil. Most of the public absorbed the disclosure of his crimes as just another fact of life.

The truth about Soviet public opinion is a tricky subject, and yet to be fully examined in histories of the era. What people truly thought and believed is notoriously opaque. A Soviet-era joke gives one perspective on how average citizens regarded the dictator: *One evening Stalin's wandering the streets of Moscow in disguise, observing first-hand how ordinary Russians live. He goes into a cinema and takes a seat near the back. At the end of the film the screen is filled by a huge picture of Stalin, and the whole audience stands up and begins singing the national anthem. Delighted by this show of loyalty, Stalin nods his head contentedly and relaxes back in his seat, when he feels a tap on his shoulder. "Comrade," a voice whispers urgently. "We all feel exactly the same as you. But it's much safer to just stand up."*

***

Conforming in public was rational – pretence the price of survival. Yet what is truly astonishing is the fact that for millions of Russians, no such dissembling was required – because Stalin ruled not only through fear but also through love. It's easy to dismiss as propaganda the gushing praise, the adulation and the tributes that surrounded him during his years in power. All the sycophantic slogans, the poems in his honour, the adoration of schoolchildren. Russians of all kinds played the game to save their lives. But there were huge numbers who *volunteered* these sentiments. Who *meant* them. Who loved Stalin and felt real gratitude for what they believed he'd done for them. Remarkably, this was true even of his victims. Relatives of those executed or imprisoned, as well as inhabitants of the gulags, often believed that somehow their misfortune was all a mistake. That Stalin had no knowledge of what was really going on.

This is juicy territory for psychologists. Recent access to Stalin's archives showed that claims of his ignorance of the evils perpetrated by his regime are nonsense. Document after document demonstrates not only the extent of his knowledge, but his personal responsibility in ordering, directing and approving many of the worst crimes. Yet millions of believers still refuse to acknowledge his guilt, more comfortable persisting with a delusion than admitting a whole belief-system is trash.

One evening, stuck in traffic on the hill leading into Trubnaya Square on the way home from work, Nikolai gestured out of the side window, and making conversation told me something of the street's past. The gist of his remarks – he spoke in Russian – was that it was an important place in Russian history. His father, he said, remembered when more than a hundred people were killed there when Stalin died. Later I checked the facts. On the first day of mourning, as thousands of grieving citizens made their way to the House of Unions where Stalin's body lay in state, sections of the crowd were crushed to death in the confusion in the streets. From the perspective of the early 21st century, such a public display of grief recalls the mass hysteria in Britain at the time of Princess Diana's death. Historic Russian newsreels of crowds weeping in the Moscow streets are a reminder that, however incomprehensible, sorrow at the death of a stranger is not a new phenomenon. Crucially though, millions of ordinary Russians did not regard Stalin as a stranger – but as a father figure, a protector and a benefactor. The Stalin myth may have been a triumph of propaganda, but the sense of loss his death engendered was no lie. The grief was genuinely felt.

In Russia, Stalin's death has the same kind of clock-stopping significance as Kennedy's assassination in the West. Elderly Russians invariably remember where they were when they heard the news. Published reminiscences of 70 and 80 year-olds – who were school children and college students at the time – recall emotional scenes: whole classes in tears, their teachers in shock, funeral music playing in school rooms. At home, parents numb or weeping. A constant refrain was the widespread feeling of helplessness – of how could life possibly go on? Occasionally, however, witnesses report more complex, more human responses – the relatives of gulag prisoners for example, masking with fake tears carefully suppressed glee. But these were unusual – for most of the public the sorrow was real.

Ordinary Russians' love for Stalin is marvellously depicted in *The Inner Circle* (1991) a little-known Hollywood movie by expatriate Russian director Andrei Konchalovsky. In the final days of the Soviet Union Konchalovsky was granted permission to film in the Kremlin, and using both Western and Russian actors, made a picture based on the true story of Ivan Sanshin, Stalin's personal projectionist from 1939 until the dictator's death in 1953. Konchalovsky captures the madness, fear and paranoia of the era, setting Sanshin's personal life against a background of national events and domestic Kremlin intrigue. We get glimpses at close quarters of Stalin, his household, and his immediate political circle. Tom Hulce plays Sanshin as a gullible peasant, foolish and conceited but essentially good-hearted. Bob Hoskins is thuggish and sinister as spy chief Laverenty Beria, the Russian actor Alexandre Zbruyev impersonates Stalin, and Lolita Davidovitch is Sanshin's wife Anastasia.

When the film opens, Sanshin, a projectionist in Moscow's KGB club, is about to get married, and the plot hinges on events triggered on the evening of his wedding. After celebrating with other occupants of their communal apartment, Sanshin and his new wife are disturbed by the arrival of a KGB detail which has come to arrest their Jewish neighbours. When that couple are bundled away, their four-year-old daughter is left behind in the apartment, and Anastasia, hoping to save her from an orphanage for children of "Enemies of The People", makes an impromptu but futile attempt to adopt her. Although the child is removed to an institution, Anastasia maintains contact, and her growing love for the girl, and guilt at abandoning her to the authorities, will become one of the film's key story lines.

Later the same evening the KGB visit the apartment again, this time seeking Sanshin, who understandably thinks he too is being arrested. But it turns out that he's needed in the Kremlin, where Stalin is scheduled to watch a film. The usual projectionist has dropped dead and Sanshin is to be a last-minute replacement. From then on, he becomes part of the dictator's "inner circle", a witness to daily life in the Kremlin and an unquestioning devotee of Stalin.

291

This devotion is at the centre of the film – what it's about: the love, loyalty, adulation which ordinary people – in their ignorance and stupidity – willingly gave the tyrant. Konchalovsky shows that despite a pervasive undercurrent of terror, love and devotion were as important as fear in sustaining the dictatorship. A decade and a half after the events Konchalovsky depicts, Stalin's death underlined how millions of Russians could love – or think they loved – a stranger who was a prime cause of their country's misery. In the film, as personified in Sanshin, this devotion is shown as absurd. As he parrots official scare stories about foreign spies and saboteurs, or drools over a bust or portrait of Stalin – whom he refers to as The Master – Sanshin takes on a quality that comes close to idiocy. In one scene his wife asks him who he loves most – herself or Stalin. Without hesitation Sanshin answers: "Comrade Stalin of course." And we know he's speaking the truth.

Konchalovsky's verdict on the Stalin years is delivered by one of Sanshin's neighbours, an old professor, who observes that Satan sits in the Kremlin and has hypnotized Russia. Damningly, he points out, that this is only possible because of the existence of good but naive characters like Ivan.

For all its serious message, *The Inner Circle* is gloriously entertaining, and at times hugely comic. The comedy though is more than light relief; we see that farce and absurdity are as much inherent characteristics of the regime as brutality and megalomania. During the arrest of Sanshin's neighbours, KBG officers search their room for incriminating material, and seize personal photographs, letters, and books in foreign languages. A senior officer picks up a child's doll, and in a serious official voice adds it to the inventory: "A toy of foreign make – depicting a woman – with a red nose – make a note of it!"

The film works through a series of contrasts and parallels. The luxury we see in the Kremlin interiors, plush reds and golds, contrasts with the shoddy lives of the inhabitants of Sanshin's communal department. The projectionist's delight in his career and proximity to Stalin, is set against his wife's growing despair and eventual decline. Allegorical parallels which sound clumsy and obvious in print, have a different effect on screen – where lighting, colour and movement make them less crudely explicit. (Sanshin's apartment for example is in Slaughterhouse Street, and jostling herds of cows regularly pass his bedroom window on their way to execution – obviously the Russian people during the Great Terror. At the end of the film the fate of the animals is echoed in the scenes of a stampeding crowd at Stalin's funeral, showing mourners crushed to death.)

Konchalovsky got the idea for *The Inner Circle* when he met the real-life Sanshin in the Moscow film world many years after Stalin's death. He was struck by his unfaltering devotion to The Master's memory. When the film appeared, the old projectionist was still alive, and even then remained as constant as ever in his devotion to his old boss.

***

The communists I watched marching in Red Square on that anniversary of Stalin's death were Sanshin's people. Unreconstructed Stalin loyalists. Survivors from an earlier era. It's claimed their influence is waning, that the Communist Party is modernisng under a new generation, in keeping with its role today as the chief opposition to Putin's United Russia. That it's moving with the times, leaving behind its troubled past, forging a new identity for the 21st century. But it's a claim that neither sat well with leader Gennady Zyuganov's old-fashioned rhetoric, nor the Party's reluctance to distance itself from Stalin. Observors argue that contemporary Russian politics are blighted by the country's failure to openly come to terms with its past. That despite piecemeal acknowledgement of horrors and injustices, there has been no full accounting. Russia has never embarked on the kind of "truth and reconciliation" processes other nations emerging from tyranny have used to exorcise their ghosts and heal their societies. Alexander Zakatov, a Russian Monarchist and spokesman for the heirs of the executed Imperial Family, publically complained that "if in Germany people went on the streets with portraits of Hitler they would be punished, but in our country, it happens at every step." On the 90th anniversary of the death of the Tzar and his family, Zakatov, and his fellow Monarchists unsuccessfully lobbied the Moscow authorities to change the name of the Voikovskaya metro station on the green line. When it was built in 1964 the station was named after Pyotor Voikov, the man who arranged for the Tzar's murder, to stop his rescue by advancing White Russian troops. To the disgust – but not the surprise – of the Monarchists, the authorities refused, citing not ideology, but the cost and complexity of a name change. This despite the fact many Moscow Metro stations have changed names over the years, according to fashion or the political mood of the day.

The hesitancy about the past does not mean ordinary Russians are uninterested in their history – just that there's reluctance at official levels to confront it. In the *Dom Knigi* across the street from Moscow's City Hall, I glimpsed intense curiosity about one aspect of the past. On the bookshop's table of 'recent publications', the most-thumbed item was an album of monochrome photographs from the Stalin era. Despite its heavy polythene cover, the display copy was stained and disintegrating from constant inspection, and I witnessed huddles of Russians in animated discussion as they studied the pages. The book used photographs newly acquired from Soviet archives, to illustrate how state censors rewrote the past – by removing from the record individuals who fell from favour. Although common knowledge in the West for decades, after the USSR's collapse this came as a revelation to many Russians. The book's concept was simple – the juxtaposition of doctored official photographs against the original versions. Most were similar in format – Stalin at some event, flanked by senior associates. In the original everyone present is clearly visible; in the revisions, certain individuals, often old Bolsheviks, have disappeared. Replaced by sky or a hazy background. Removed from sight and thus from history.

That nothing much really changed with the Russian Communist Party was brought home to me by a weird episode in June 2007, when the Party posted an internet statement publicly denouncing a Trotskyist saboteur, Anatoly Baranov, the editor of the Party's own website, in language that carried more than a whiff of old-style Stalinism. In echoes of Stalin's 1930s show trials, they accused him of plotting to further Western interests by spreading views online that were contrary to official Party policy. The Party's Central Audit Committee declared that Baranov headed a group which demonstrated "clear signs of Trotskyism as defined by J.V. Stalin in his article *Trotskyism and Leninism*." These traitors, the Committee explained, were pushing the Party away from Leninism onto the "false Trotskyist path of a rapid revolution." This was being done in the interests of the bourgeois West rather than

Russia, and would lead to the country's complete occupation by NATO forces.

Delicious stuff. Paranoia, conspiracy, treachery, old fashioned Marxist rhetoric flourishing in the 21st century. Living history indeed. As evocative of the Soviet past as a stay in the Rossiya Hotel.

28

A wealthy Russian and his wife are eating Sunday Brunch in a hotel restaurant, when a beautiful blonde girl approaches, kisses the man and saunters off.

"Who was that woman?" his shocked wife asks.

"That's my mistress," the man says.

"Mistress? You have a mistress? I'm leaving!"

"Well, before you do anything drastic" he says, "just think about what you're giving up. The new dacha. The skiing in Courchevel. The shopping in London. Our apartment in Nice."

Before he can say any more, his wife's attention's distracted when the husband of one of her friends walks past, accompanied by a young lady.

"Who's that woman with Vladimir?" the wife asks.

"That's his mistress."

The wife's silent for a moment then says: "Well our mistress is better than theirs!"

It took three tellings before my own wife got the point of the joke – the materialism and one-upmanship endemic in modern Russia. With citizens free for the first time in a century to be uninhibited consumers, extravagant spending and showing off are widespread. There's no old money in Russia – and little of the restraint and good taste that sometimes accompanies it in the West. New Russians are brazenly materialistic, and acutely status-conscious. The very rich spend lavishly, and not always with discrimination. And the simply wealthy copy as far as they can. The Soviet world of course had its own version – apparent in the flourishing black markets, and legendary appetite for Western consumer goods. But the fall of communism saw the foundations of status and prestige shift. Traditional sources, like service to the state, or artistic, sporting or military accomplishments, remained valid, but were dramatically overshadowed by the power of money. As wealth trickled down to an expanding middle class, competitive spending – spending for show – became ubiquitous. Unlike the USA, however, where financial success is often equated with moral worth, in Russia the rich are envied, but rarely liked or respected.

In the midst of Russia's new materialism, some old obsessions live on. When I spotted a new face at work I stumbled on an interesting phenomenon.

"Who's that guy?" I asked Grishin.

"Mr. Gavrilov" he said, and lowered his voice to a whisper. "He's the President's helper."

"Helper?"

"Like a Research Assistant. He's an economist."

"They're working on some deal?"

Grishin gave a knowing laugh: "No. He's helping Mr. Ivanov with his Ph.D."

The helping was loaded with irony.

It seemed that our President was due to deliver a thesis and collect a postgraduate degree from Moscow State University.

"What's the topic?"

Grishin shrugged: "I don't know exactly. Some business thing – maybe about this business."

"But why?"

I was genuinely puzzled. Why bother? He was head of a major company – with an oligarch's lifestyle. What did he want with some dreary academic credentials?

"In Russia, these things are important," Grishin said. "Many powerful men want higher degrees."

His voice dropped again and he became confidential: "Of course he won't write it himself. That's Gavrilov's job. But he'll contribute some ideas. I think it's OK. It's still the President's project. He'll decide what's written. And he must defend it personally in front of the Academic Board. Gavrilov will coach him for that."

At the time, I was unaware of how common this was in Russia – successful businessmen, government officials, and others in public life burnishing their images with higher academic qualifications. But alerted by this conversation, I later noted a series of academic scandals, where the press had fun at the expense of prominent figures accused of plagiarism, or of employing ghost-writers to complete academic assignments. Fingers were even pointed at senior figures in the Kremlin.

Such is the appetite for postgraduate degrees that a lucrative industry of 'educational consultancies' has grown up to serve aspiring graduates who have no intention of doing any work themselves. Reputedly, the first time many candidates read their 'own' dissertations is when they mug-up on the contents to prepare for its defence before an academic board. The majority of those produced by consultancies are in economics, education and law – rather than technical or scientific disciplines, where hard data and genuine research is more important than recycling material already published.

The pursuit of unmerited scholarly awards is the stuff of comedy. Pride and self-importance eternal targets for jokes. Yet there's something very human about it. In Britain the same impulse – the desire to be taken seriously, respected for more than just money – once saw wealthy arrivistes acquire coats-of-arms proclaiming them gentlemen. Today, businessmen and public figures, from entrepreneurs to TV game-show hosts and celebrity hairdressers, scheme for decorations and titles. A high-profile charitable donation is no less a purchase than a Russian research assistant's fee, and it's tempting to scorn them all equally. Yet I had a niggling respect for the Russians. There's something admirable in the fashion for academic recognition. Rich men who claim degrees they don't deserve at least aspire to something worth having. Awards of substance – which are not simply *bestowed* but, in theory anyway, *earned* through scholarship. It's a cultural marker, a demonstration of a continuing regard for learning in Russian society, that goes hand in hand with a genuine interest in the arts and high culture amongst ordinary Russians that is rare in the West. Englishmen want knighthoods, Russians doctorates.

In parallel, Russia of course operates a national system of official honours, designed to bolster allegiance to the state. There's a hierarchy of fancy titles of the kind presidents and royalty universally confer on worthy citizens. At the top of the tree today is the *Hero of the Russian Federation* the successor to the old *Hero of the Soviet Union.*

When I witnessed a protest in Tverskai Street by some of the latter, it made me reflect on the inherent transience and absurdity of such honours. A band of demonstrators, medals prominently on display, shouted slogans and waved placards at bemused, though largely respectful, shoppers. The following day's newspapers told their story in detail. They came from all sectors of Russian society – and included Olympic athletes, retired scientists and technocrats, military veterans and representatives of the old Soviet arts world. Their complaints centred on the loss of benefits and privileges once guaranteed by their status. Beyond resentment at falling pensions and poor medical care however, they also felt a deep sadness at the disintegration of their world. Many were clearly bereft, their sense of self undermined by the demise of the institution from which their prestige derived. In the new order their Soviet titles had no more value than Confederate banknotes, or share certificates in failed companies, raising existential questions about the nature and permanence of honour and recognition. The line that separated respect from indifference – or even derision – was shown to be perilously faint.

When my interest in Soviet Moscow drew me to the biographies of the old Bolsheviks, I reflected again on the issue of titles. In their turbulent life stories, I was struck by their preoccupation with self-adopted names and titles. *Lenin, Stalin, Trotsky, Molotov* – all these familiar names were aliases. Amongst the senior figures who vied for power during and after the revolution their use was common. Lenin (real name Vladimir Ilyich Ulyanov) reputedly used over 160 pseudonyms in the course of his career as a political journalist and activist, before settling on the one the world recognises today. Socialist historians explain it as a security measure – necessary to avoid detection by the Tzar's secret police. And there's undoubtedly truth in this. But for some Bolsheviks an alias was also useful camouflage – obscuring their origins and protecting their credibility. Lenin, vocal champion of the workers, was himself no proletarian, but came from a family of minor nobility. Trotsky (Lev Bronstein), Zinoviev (real name Hirsch Apfelbaum) and Kamenev (Lev Borisovich Berkovich) were all Jews operating in a society scarred by anti-Semitism – not least amongst the class whose interests they loudly claimed to promote.

The choice of revolutionary pseudonyms raises interesting psychological issues. For some, the alias was simply a disguise with no underlying meaning, but for others, a deliberate statement. Trotsky reputedly copied his from a jailer who had guarded him in Odessa, while the name Lenin derived from the Lena River in Siberia, where the revolutionary was once exiled. (A facetious reference, or some kind of political allusion? – evoking perhaps the power of flowing water, forces of nature, etc.?) With other Bolsheviks, however, the self-dramatization is clear. Joseph Vissarionovich Dzhugashvili became Stalin (*Man of Steel*). His henchman Molotov (*The Hammer*) was originally Vyacheslav Mikhailovich Skryabin, and writer Alexei Maximovich Peshkov took the name Gorky (*Bitter*). There's something more than faintly ridiculous about these grandiose *nomes de guerre*. They smack of the playground, of comic book superheroes and schoolboy pranks. Their very childishness nudges us deep into the territory of the psychologists. Are they a clue to character, hinting at a lack of mature humanity? Do they function as spiritual cloaks, empowering their owners to act like conscienceless schoolboys? Does a persona – playing a part – release the actor from moral constraints? Half-convince him that *it's only a game after all*......? Did an alias make Molotov capable of atrocities from which plain Mr. Skryabin would have recoiled?

29

Ivan Turgenev succinctly evokes the arrival of spring in Russia when he writes of the "steam and glitter of an April thaw." At last there's warmth in the sun, the ground softens, and dirty white gives way to green. At the same time, the card-racks in the bookshops undergo a sudden seasonal change, and for a few weeks the usual rows of birthday and anniversary greetings are eclipsed by a new collection of *Victory Day* cards. These go on sale in the run up to the most important public holiday in the Russian calendar – the commemoration on 9 May of the Soviet Union's World War II victory over Nazi Germany. The cards come in many styles, from the schmaltzy (lots of gold and red) to the dignified and nostalgic. Some are documentary in style – reproducing old wartime snaps of military parades, or scenes of Red Army soldiers mingling with civilians in the streets. Others are still-lifes – arrangements of flowers, medals and ribbons. One of the most popular I spotted was an artist's sketch of a fresh-faced boy in uniform, being hugged by a woman in a shawl. Others were emblazoned with the simple legends: *1941-45* or *9 May* (the date of the German surrender).

It wasn't until I lived in Moscow, and repeatedly encountered such reminders, that I appreciated just how important the Great Patriotic War, as the Soviets styled it, continues to be in the Russian psyche. For Russians of all ages – not just the veterans who took part – it has a significance and contemporary relevance now absent in the West. In Britain, annual remembrance ceremonies are conscientiously held, but the tone has become elegiac, and the public mood, in truth, largely indifferent. Memories are fading; the world has moved on and genuine remembrance is evolving into detached ceremonial. In Russia, however, the war has not yet slipped into history. It still speaks directly and powerfully to the country's citizens – about pride and sacrifice, and above all about being Russian.

Foreign visitors can find this unsettling. The dominant sentiment is distinctly triumphalist. May 9 is not just about marking the end of hostilities, or even paying respect to the dead, but about actively celebrating victory. It's a public display of pride in a defining event in Russia's history – the crushing of Germany. And victory is glorified with a jingoism no longer fashionable in much of the rest of Europe. For Moscow's foreign residents, the continuing immediacy of the war in Russian life surprises, and at the same time forces a re-examination of our own assumptions about 20th century history. Like most of Britain's baby-boomer generation, I grew up convinced that Britain had won the war – with some belated assistance from the Americans. It was the orthodoxy of popular culture, and the largely unchallenged narrative of those who lived through it – the parents and grandparents of my contemporaries, whose reminiscences shaped our world view. It provided the context for the heroics depicted in war films of the 50s and 60s, constantly repeated on TV, and for schoolboy comics of the time like Victor and Commando, full of stories of military derring-do. Unsurprisingly, most of the country still believes it today. Curiously, even my own family, despite our left-wing allegiance, largely subscribed to this consensus. Albeit with reservations. That Britain had won the war was an unchallenged fact – but my parents contemplated that victory with grudging silence. At a time when the rest of the country still felt the kind of pride Russians feel today, they were ambivalent, and largely ignored the war. It was a tricky subject for Scottish socialists. On the one hand ideological pacifism decreed all wars – even just wars – were wrong, and this was my parents' lifelong creed. Occasionally it produced cranky displays of principle, like refusing to buy remembrance poppies, which allegedly condoned fighting, or scorning the Boy Scout and Girl Guide movements as irredeemably militaristic. On the other hand, fascism was also undeniably wrong. But what to do beyond hang-wringing? It was a dilemma they never resolved.

There was also a huge element of political embarrassment, which I now recognise they never quite overcame. When war broke out in 1939 it was opposed by significant numbers on the British left, largely because of the lead given by Stalin when he signed a Non-Aggression Pact with Hitler in August of that year. It committed both sides to avoiding military action against each other for the next 10 years, leaving Germany free to act aggressively elsewhere in Europe, without fear for its eastern borders. In British radical circles the Pact caused consternation. Their champion, the standard bearer of socialism, was now in bed with the fascist enemy. Soviet cheerleaders of all hues, from the Communist Party of Great Britain and assorted fellow travellers, to sections of the Labour Party, were unprepared for the thunderbolt. Badly shaken, and with their certainties overturned, socialists squirmed and performed moral contortions, abandoning principles to rationalise support for Moscow and oppose war with Germany. It wasn't only hardline Marxists who quickly got in step with Uncle Joe, but wider swathes of the left. Less than two years later however, when Germany invaded Russia, most did an immediate about-turn and got behind the war effort as promptly as they'd previously opposed it. For most it came as a relief – they were back on the side of the angels. But the smell of hypocrisy, betrayal and shame never quite cleared, and influenced the Left's attitude to the war for decades. What in retrospect I find very strange is that my parents, despite their obsession with Russia and its achievements, never once mentioned its wartime role. Surely Russian heroics should have exorcised any queasiness about the war itself? I can only think that like most of their countrymen, they simply knew very little about the USSR's involvement. While professional historians have long acknowledged Russia's crucial role in Hitler's defeat, more general awareness never permeated the popular consciousness. More than two decades after the war ended, a rare cultural reference for my generation was a running joke in *Hogan's Heroes*, a TV comedy series set in a German P.O.W camp, where wily American prisoners battled wits with their captors. In every episode a gluttonous and incompetent guard named Sergeant Schultz was threatened by the Kommandant with a transfer to the Russian Front – where crucially there was a shortage of salami. Hardly incisive historical analysis. But typical of the sketchy, unreal comprehension of Russia's wartime presence that was common at the time.

The end of the Cold War saw a wider understanding in the West of Russia's WWII role. Greater access to Soviet archives helped, but more importantly shifting propaganda demands reduced the need to take partisan positions, encouraging historians on both sides to write more objectively. This resulted in a flow of notable Western histories documenting the scale of the debt owed to the Soviet Union for Germany's defeat. A little reading about Russia's war goes a long way to explaining its continuing hold on its citizens. Quite simply the trauma was so great that the nation has yet to get over it. The conflict was too costly, and too painful – and eventual success such a relief – for it to be digested and forgotten in a couple of generations. To those of us previously exposed to an exclusively Western slant on history, there's much to ponder. Even a perfunctory exploration of Russia's wartime experience is enough to induce a major revision. I now recognise that instead of believing Britain won the war, we should recognise Britain was on the winning side. We may have stood alone in 1939 and forced Hitler to pause, but the heavy lifting for victory was done by the Soviet Union.

The casualty statistics alone are staggering. Somewhere between 25 million and 40 million Soviet citizens died as a direct result of the war. There is no consensus on the figures. Although estimates at the top end, promoted by some revisionist historians, are generally considered too high, different methods of calculation, and difficulties in verification, mean no definitive number is possible. The present balance of opinion settles on losses of around 27 million, of which just under 9 million were military casualties, and the rest civilians. Comparison with US and British statistics puts the Soviet losses in perspective. Total American deaths were around 420,000; British deaths, nearly 450,000. The scale of the Soviet tragedy is underlined when losses are expressed as percentages of each nation's wartime population: US – 0.3%; UK – 1%; Soviet Union – 14%. Mind-numbing as they are, figures alone only hint at the full horror of the Soviet wartime experience. They do not include the additional millions who survived, but were maimed for life. Nor do they reflect the long-lasting emotional dislocation inflicted by the invading armies' destruction and atrocities. The Nazis considered Slavs an inferior race and treated Russians with particular savagery. When Western politicians today condemn

Russian territorial aggressiveness and military adventurism, they ignore the war's continuing grip on the Kremlin. In light of its wartime experiences, Russia's paranoia and ruthless drive for self-protection is understandable.

Counting wartime losses is one thing, explaining victory another. In general, Western historians approach this with greater objectivity than their Russian counterparts. For decades, the Soviet position was that victory was due to the Red Army's valour, the Soviet people's steadfastness, and the military genius of Stalin. Although more a slogan than an explanation, this is still close to the current official Kremlin line. And it's only partly myth – for vast numbers of both military and civilians indeed fought bravely and ferociously in defence of their homeland. Often missing from the storyline however are the dark realities of the Soviet war. There's an anti-heroic underbelly in any conflict – cowardice, treachery and incompetence are universal – but what sets the Soviet war effort apart is the leadership's murderous brutality towards its own side. Russians fought to save Russia, but they also fought from fear of what the men in the Kremlin and the military command posts would do if they faltered. Coercion was as important as patritotism. Those who retreated, surrendered or simply showed insufficient appetite for sacrificing themselves as cannon fodder, were summarily executed. Marshall Zhukov wanted to go even further, and advocated shooting not just recalcitrant soldiers, but also their families. It's estimated that over 200,000 Red Army soldiers were shot by their own side as a deterrent against surrender. The early battle scenes in *Enemy at The Gates*, the 2001 film starring Jude Law as a Russian sniper during the battle of Stalingrad, capture some of this ruthless savagery. Red Army political officers with megaphones drive their troops forward, threatening execution for those who hesitate. When boats carrying soldiers across the Volga are attacked by German aircraft, we see officers shoot their own men in the back when they take refuge in the water. The highest profile illustration of the Soviet determination to deter capitulation, was the fact that when his own son was captured, Stalin refused to negotiate his release. The resolve against surrender continued even after the war was over, and many thousands of returning Russian POWs were executed or sent to labour camps.

Soviet-era historians argued that victory showed their system's flexibility, its capacity to mobilise personnel, and to direct industrial resources to military production when required. This was partly true, but it also ran counter to the official myth of a peaceful Russia caught off guard in June 1941 by the treachery of the Nazi invasion. In reality, Soviet industry had been on a war footing from the early 1930s, and by its outbreak Stalin had five times as many tanks as the Germans, and four times the number of aircraft. The problem for the Soviets was a shortage of trained personnel able to use them. This lack of preparedness early in the war, was evidence of the failure rather than triumph of Soviet organisation. By autumn 1941 nearly four million Soviet troops had been killed or captured, and 80% of their tanks and aircraft destroyed. Most damning was the fact that two-thirds of these tanks were not battlefield losses, but vehicles abandoned or destroyed by their own crews because of mechanical problems they couldn't fix. Responsibility for these debacles sat with Stalin himself. His purges in the 1930s had stripped the military of experienced senior officers, leaving it unable to effectively counter an attack. Equally disastrous was his refusal prior to the invasion, to heed intelligence pointing to German intentions, and his unwillingness to prepare a defence.

Some Western historians claim that Hitler's eventual defeat was simply a numbers game. What really mattered were not the actions of US and British forces, but Soviet willingness to accept staggeringly huge losses. (Stalin himself believed Western powers failed to provide full support to the Soviet war effort, in a deliberate strategy to weaken the Soviet Union.) There's a credible argument that democracy could not have stopped the Nazis, that only another dictatorship, with no respect for human rights, or qualms about sacrificing millions of lives, could have prevailed.

Of course, none of this sits well with Russia's official glorification of the war effort. Academic and popular histories, published memoirs, and a host of TV documentaries have ensured that facts impossible to air during the Soviet era are now widely known in Russia. But they disappear in the fuss and pride surrounding Victory Day, in favour of military heroics and battles won. In recent years the popularity in the West of *Enemy at The Gates*, and Anthony Beevor's multiple-prizewinning *Stalingrad* (1998), have cemented in our popular imagination the idea that Stalingrad saw the bloodiest fighting of the war. This is wrong. For all its savagery and suffering, Stalingrad came nowhere near the Battle of Moscow for the scale of destruction and loss of life. The German attack on the capital is often called the Forgotten War. A prolonged and complicated series of assaults, which took place over a wide area, during many months, and involved several fronts, attacks, and counter-attacks. Defying easy focus or explanation, it failed to capture the imagination of historians on all sides. Yet it was the biggest battle in human history. Lasting from September 1941 until April 1942, at some stages it involved over 7 million men – double the number who fought at Stalingrad. Likewise, losses were twice those of Stalingrad: 2.5 million killed, missing, taken prisoner or severely wounded. Of these losses, 1.9 million were on the Soviet side.

***

When the Germans invaded the Soviet Union in June 1941 they anticipated an easy victory, and at first this seemed inevitable. By October Hitler's troops had advanced to within 130 kilometres of Moscow, and the city looked about to fall. Panicked citizens fled, law and order collapsed, and looting was rife; the NKVD burned their files and the government initiated plans to evacuate beyond the Urals. Stalin himself was on the brink of leaving, and witnesses reported him pacing indecisively up and down a railway-station platform, while a train waited ready to take him east. In the end he decided to stay and fight.

During November 1941 an event of great symbolic significance took place in Moscow, when Soviet strategists decided to deploy 100,000 reinforcements to the battle. To boost military and civilian morale, Stalin ordered that these troops take part in a military parade already scheduled to celebrate Revolution Day (November 7th), and famously had them march from Red Square straight to the front. As propaganda it was a spectacular success, demonstrating Soviet resolve and calming the nerves of civilians spooked by the panic of early October. The parade has become part of Russian folklore and ensures that 7 November now ranks just behind Victory Day as the second most important date in the Russian calendar. On the parade's 65th anniversary in 2006, the Kremlin staged a reenactment, and I watched the troops in WWII uniforms marching through the Square as if going off to war.

Back in 1941 however, Stalin's reinforcements were not enough to halt the German advance. By early December the Wehrmacht had reached Moscow's western outskirts, within sight of the centre less than 15 miles away. But this was as far as they would get. The spot where they finally halted is today just within the city limits, close to the turn-off for Sheremeteva Airport on the St Petersburg highway. It's overlooked by a shopping mall dominated by a giant IKEA superstore, but at the roadside the momentous events of 1941 are marked with a memorial fashioned from huge iron anti-tank crosses, reminding travellers how near the Germans came. Many times, as I passed en route to the airport, I fleetingly studied the crosses. But after reading evocative accounts of the Siege of Moscow I asked Nikolai to drive me out one Saturday morning for a better look. On the spot, I pictured in my imagination the German commanders studying the city through binoculars, close enough to pick out the towers and domes of the Kremlin. But as I stood beside the memorial and looked east towards Moscow, my own view that morning was obscured by heavy Autumn mist. I could have returned on a clear day or lingered until the sun burned through. But it suddenly seemed more fitting to settle for the spectral scene confronting me. A panorama of indistinct shapes behind the veil of mist. The varying shades of darkness more evocative of the past than any clear view of the modern city.

***

Victory Day is public property, a focus for official patriotism and rejoicing. But for millions of ordinary Russians, it also continues to inspire intense personal emotions. The state organises the big displays – the military parades, the wreath laying, the speechifying and TV coverage. But it's private citizens who buy and exchange Victory Day cards, in individual acts of remembrance. The war touched every Russian family, and each has losses to remember and mourn. The sanctity of the day is undiminished in the post-Soviet world, because the authorities deliberately harness the wartime experience as a unifying motif for modern Russia. It's a rallying point, the one episode in the nation's twentieth century history around which all sections of Russian society can still unite. For much of the population the Revolution was a tragedy; others lament the fall of communism and the passing of Soviet power. The new Russia of oligarchs and free markets inspires widespread ambivalence and cynicism. But the story of victory in the Great Patriotic War remains untarnished, capable of uniting Russians of all ideologies and backgrounds in shared respect and pride. The massive $220m the authorities spent on celebrating the day's 60th anniversary in 2005 testified to its importance.

It has become the custom to annually mark May 9 with a military parade, and Red Square hosts a familiar march-past of troops, tanks, and missiles. But the day is also about nostalgia. A time for older Russians to remember their younger selves, and for history to come to life. Modern soldiers are joined by young servicemen wearing WWII uniforms, and carrying historic weaponry, while civilians in the watching crowds dress in clothes of the time. Military music and popular wartime songs are broadcast over loudspeakers, and buildings close to the celebrations are decorated with wartime signs and patriotic posters. I missed the 2005 jamboree, but the following year witnessed a less lavish but still impressively evocative display.

***

313

There are permanent memorials to the Great Patriotic War all over Moscow, but the grandest and most dramatic is at Park Pobedy (Victory Park) in the city's southwestern suburbs. Standing on Poklonnaya Hill, it's accessible from the Park Pobedy Metro station on the dark blue line, or by the road which runs alongside – Kutuzovskiy Prospect. Covering a large area of mainly green space, it's a public park and a tranquil recreational area for Muscovites, but also one of Moscow's premier landmarks, a must-see destination which needs several visits to do it justice. I was a frequent visitor, though attracted less by the trees, fountains and gardens than its war museum and extravagant sculptures. The site was earmarked for a memorial in the 1960s and was gradually developed during the following Soviet decades. Significantly however, its major expansion, and the installation of many of its key features took place after the fall of communism – a further reminder of the importance of the war in the creation of a national myth for contemporary Russia. Today, the park is dominated by a 142-metre-high obelisk which stands just outside the Great Patriotic War museum. At the obelisk's base there's a statue by sculptor Zurab Tsereteli, of Moscow's patron saint – St. George – slaying a dragon embossed with Nazi symbols. Tsereteli also sculpted the park's holocaust monument, entitled *Peoples Tragedy*, which depicts a vanishing queue of forlorn, naked, figures. Elsewhere in the grounds are several memorial religious buildings – an Orthodox church, a Catholic Church, a synagogue, a mosque and a chapel that commemorates Spanish volunteers who died fighting the Nazis. And with the park still evolving, a planned Buddhist temple will be added shortly.

To my mind, however, the War Museum is the park's most interesting venue. Just behind there's an outdoor exhibition of military hardware – tanks, armoured vehicles, artillery and such like – while inside the building itself are displays typical of many museums of this kind: battle relics, historical documents, flags, photographs, and items of military history – together with memorials to the fallen. It's the six stunning dioramas situated on the museum's ground floor however that bring history to life. These depict key battles of WWII – including the Battle of Stalingrad, Siege of Leningrad, and Defence of Moscow. Each takes the form of a huge painting mounted on a semi-circular wall, fronted by naturalistic models, and strewn with rubble and battlefield debris to give a 3D effect.

Although Park Pobedy's focus is primarily Russia's wartime experience, it's not an entirely jingoistic venture. There's generous acknowledgment of the international contribution to the defeat of Hitler, with several statues celebrating anti-Nazi coalition soldiers. Across Kutuzovskiy Prospect, however, there's another, smaller, museum that's more purely a Russian affair – the Borodino Battle Panorama Museum. This is a little gem, more modest in scale than the one to the Great Patriotic War, but also more compelling. It's a memorial to the 1812 encounter 70 miles west of Moscow, between the Russian Imperial Army commanded by General Mikhail Kutuzov, and Napoleon's invading troops. The battle itself was a confusing, inconclusive affair, which has for two centuries been the subject of debate and myth-making. Notionally, the Russians intended it as a defence of Moscow – a set-piece action to stop the French in their tracks. Afterwards both sides claimed victory – although by conventional measures the French won, inflicting significantly greater casualties on the larger Russian force.

Nor did the battle prevent Napoleon's advance on the city – his army entered Moscow a week later. Yet in the wider picture Borodino was a crucial turning point for the Russian war effort. By confronting the French directly, proclaiming victory while at the same time managing an orderly withdrawal that left the Russian army, although badly mauled, sufficiently intact to fight again, Kutuzov delivered a vital boost to Russian morale, and gained a pause in hostilities in which to rebuild his forces.

The museum's site on Poklonnaya Hill is especially symbolic, for before he entered Moscow it was here that Napoleon waited for the Russians to present him with the keys to the city. They never did, and their act of patriotic defiance inspired the Soviet decision to locate their Victory complex on the hill. The Borodino Museum delivers one of the best visitor experiences in Moscow, in a building specially designed to house its key offering – a cyclorama that places visitors in the very heart of the battle. From an observation platform in the centre of a purpose-built theatre, they can view a huge 360-degree panoramic portrait of the battle. It was painted in 1912 by artist Franz Roubaud, to mark the battle's centenary, and is 15 metres high and nearly 115 in length. The canvas is displayed around the theatre's circular wall, and like the dioramas in the Great Patriotic War museum, a 3D effect is achieved with scenes in the foreground populated with props and models illustrating in creative detail the carnage of the battle. The visual experience is reinforced by accompanying sound effects.

I preferred the Borodino museum to the WWII one. It's not only more colourful – in all senses – but eschews the understandable solemnity of the other. Dealing with events beyond living memory, it is more historical epic than hallowed memorial.

Visitors arriving via the Park Pobedy Metro station are reminded by painted panels that decorate the station's walls, that the Russian heroes who fought at Borodino were the forerunners of those who defeated the Nazis. Tsereteli is again the artist, and along with his portrait of Russians cheering victory in 1945, there's a tableau of Napoleonic-era generals in the uniforms of the time.

***

For all the pride and patriotism, there are now symptoms of a diminishing reverence for the past that would have been unthinkable during Soviet times. Characteristically, in today's Russia, there is often a commercial dimension. The activities of the *diggers* for example, are widely castigated for bad taste and disrespect for the fallen. A mix of hobbyists and professional scavengers, the *diggers* use metal detectors, and picks and shovels, to trawl battlefields that are also mass graves, in search of both Nazi and Soviet wartime artefacts. Although technically illegal, and denounced by the church as sacrilegious, little is done to stop them, and their booty is offered to collectors on internet sites and in the shops of specialist dealers. Almost certainly they are the source of much of the military memorabilia on sale at Ismailova market. Even more repellent than this shabby trade, however, is a growing fascination in Russian society with Nazi symbols and ideology. Ironically, in the nation that did most to defeat the Nazis, this often goes beyond a purely historical interest, and becomes a glorification of Nazi values and beliefs. Nor is it simply an underground phenomenon, confined to the fascist fringes of Russian nationalist groups. Human rights campaigners complain about the availability of fascist propaganda in mainstream outlets. Alongside serious studies of the war, respectable bookshops carry eulogistic histories of the Third Reich, profiles of Nazi leaders, and a range of holocaust-denial literature. (Jewish organizations claim Russia is becoming a world centre for holocaust denial.) A cursory examination of book jackets and advertising blurbs in Moscow's bookshops, shows a popular market for lavishly illustrated histories of the SS, and sensational accounts of Nazi crimes. DVD copies of wartime German newsreels, and movies that include explicit Nazi propaganda, are widely available from up-market full-price video shops, as well as pirate vendors in metro underpasses and street markets.

Who in 1941 would have thought that Moscow in the 21st century would be home to increasing numbers of Russian extremists, who would openly mark the birthday of Adolf Hitler each April, and celebrate with hate crimes against ethnic minorities? I saw a stark illustration during my years in the city, when it was reported in the press that for their own protection, Moscow's Sechenov Medical Academy was confining all its foreign students (around 500 of them), to their dorms for three days, in the run up to the anniversary on April 20th. It was a precautionary measure. For several years, Hitler's birthday had seen the Academy attacked by skinheads shouting fascist slogans, giving Nazi salutes, and hurling firebombs at the building.

30

I was woken by sunlight creeping between the bedroom curtains, and as my eyes adjusted, I sensed something amiss – it was snowing. My brain struggled momentarily with the puzzle. Winter surely was behind us, but the air outside was white. When I moved closer to the glass, however, it was clear these weren't snowflakes drifting in front of me, but *puch* – a sure sign that summer was here. *Puch*, as the Russians call it, is the fuzzy white pollen that the city's poplar trees produce for a few weeks every year, when spring turns into summer. It gets everywhere. Dusts the pavements, invades buildings through air-vents and rickety window-frames, causes sneezing, and torments those with allergies. Overnight, it seemed to have exploded and now oppressively filled the air. Its presence was a result of Moscow's rebuilding efforts after WWII, when to compensate for the ravages the Battle of Moscow inflicted on the countryside around the city, a massive tree-planting programme was launched. Poplars were favoured as they grow quickly, but at the time no thought was given to selecting between male or female trees. Most of those planted were female, and these produce the *puch* that now heralds the arrival of Moscow's summer.

A few mornings after the puch appeared, I had another intimation of the arrival of summer. Turning on the shower, I was hit by an unexpected blast of cold water. I grabbed the shower head to divert the spray, and frantically turned the hot tap. But nothing changed, and I understood that summer was officially here. There would be no more centrally supplied warm water for months. I called my landlord, who said: "I will bring boiler tonight!"

For the next four months, a temporary water-heater hung from a hook in the corner of the bathroom, its outlet connected to the plumbing for the shower. The city's Water Department had pasted a notice at the entrance to our communal stairs, advising when the supply would stop, but thinking it an advertising leaflet I ignored it. A final introduction to summer in Moscow came a few days later, when Valeria entered my office followed by a sheepish-looking Nikolai. She was clearly present to translate.

"Nikolai's asking permission to leave the office tomorrow," she said. "Maybe for most of the day. He'll return by the evening and take you home. Is it possible?"

"That's ok. There's nowhere we need to go tomorrow. Is there a problem?"

"Not a problem. Nikolai has some business. He's buying a small house in the country and must take documents to an official office – far away."

"A *dacha*?" I said.

Both their faces lit up at my comprehension.

"Yes, a dacha!"

When he'd gone I asked Valeria about Nikolai's property. How could a driver afford a dacha?

She laughed. "It's not so unusual. It's not a house like you imagine – maybe more like a wooden shed. And far from Moscow – too far I think – more than one hundred and fifty kilometres. It'll be very cheap to buy."

"What about you – have you got a dacha?"

"No, and I don't want one! I came to Moscow for city life. I enjoy weekends here. I don't want to go to a cold shed with no toilet or electricity. I'm not crazy."

Valeria affected a shiver, but her tone softened and she added: "Anyway, I'm too young. First, I need to buy an apartment in Moscow. Then later maybe…"

Dacha life it seemed, might be less undesirable than first indicated.

Of course, the idea of a cottage in the country, an escape from traffic noise and summer heat, is attractive to city dwellers everywhere. What's unique about Moscow is that it has been achievable, in one form or another, for people of all classes. The city noticeably empties on summer weekends, as thousands of Muscovites head to their rural retreats, confirmation of just how deeply the dream has embedded itself in the Russian consciousness. The tradition of the dacha began in the eighteenth century, when the Tzars granted the privilege of a place in the country as a reward for loyal service. The word *dacha* itself derives from *dat*, the Russian verb to *give*. The tradition of a gift, of a reward, continued in Soviet times, when dachas were allotted not only to senior state officials, but used to encourage loyalty and support more generally across Russian society. Critically it was a privilege that could both be given and taken away – its removal a quick, sharp indication of disfavour. Many victims of Stalin's purges had their first intimation of impending doom when they discovered their dacha had been assigned to someone else.

The size and quality of Soviet dachas varied enormously, just as they do today. The elite had spacious villas of timber and glass in peaceful locations not far from Moscow. Internally, the furnishings could be luxurious, but externally the decoration often incorporated elements of traditional Russian rustic design, that not only linked the dacha aesthetically to its setting, but deliberately harked back to a rural past. Possession of a dacha today continues to evoke in Russians deep feelings at a psychological – perhaps even mystical – level. For a dacha is not simply a rural retreat, but a means for owners to connect with the soil, and through it their roots. With old Russia, and their Russian souls.

Soviet era dachas were regularly provided to employees by factories or other state organisations, resulting in the spread of occupation-specific 'colonies' – compounds of dachas – where workers from a single industry, or similar jobs collected together for weekends and vacations. There were colonies for a plethora of groups – artists, writers, military officers, musicians, railway workers, etc. – with various levels of facilities depending on prestige and luck. For Russians lacking this kind of official sponsorship, the privilege of a dacha might simply mean access to a patch of land, on which to build with their own hands some kind of rough and ready shack, from whatever materials they could scavenge. Eventually the state settled on a standard size of land grant for ordinary Russians – 0.06 hectares – which was big enough not only for a dwelling, but also a decent-sized vegetable patch. During the Soviet years the produce grown at Muscovites' dachas were an important element in the economy. And in the difficult early Yeltsin era, the dacha's harvest was the saviour of many a family.

Over time dachas passed down through families, and a large number of today's owners inherited their forebears' Soviet-era properties. Nikolai's new dacha had originally been the property of a provincial self-builder, who decades earlier erected it on a plot allocated by local communist officials. It was tumbledown and neglected and of no interest to the long-dead owner's surviving family, who eagerly sold it off at the first opportunity. Fortunately for Nikolai the distance from Moscow meant there was no competition, and he acquired it at a low price. His dilemma on purchase was whether to knock it down and construct a new building from scratch, or to renovate the hovel already there. He decided on renovation, and for as long as I knew him he spent every vacation and every summer weekend on the site, working at his improvements.

After dropping me home on a Friday evening, he'd swap the company Mercedes for his own battered Lada and drive north-east out of the city for three and a half hours. More often than not he'd arrive at his destination after dark. On Sunday evenings he'd make the opposite journey, joining the inevitable traffic jams that formed in the approaches to Moscow, as all the returning *dacherie* converged on the city at the same time. The best part of eight hours driving every weekend – to spend a day and a half in hard manual labour? Madness, I thought. But of course, that is to seriously underestimate the power for Russians of the rural myth, the pull of the soil. I got into a habit of asking on Monday mornings about his renovations, and he'd show me with satisfaction the calluses and cuts on his hands, as if these in themselves were evidence of progress. On one special Monday he arrived very weary but jubilant. Over the weekend he had achieved an important goal – he'd finished digging a well. It had yielded clear, fresh water, and his next step would be to lay some pipes and pump it into his house.

The criteria for dacha ownership today, whatever the size, location or level of luxury, is simple – ability to pay. For Moscow's wealthy it's both a status symbol and a local alternative to foreign vacations. There's a thriving market in the construction of new luxury dachas, in countryside easily accessible from Moscow. Some are on developments or compounds that echo the old Soviet colonies, with the more luxurious examples offering facilities similar to up-market country clubs. Many dachas are for hire by the season, and wealthy Muscovites who want variety take different rentals every year.

Berkovich told me of his experience with a rented dacha when he was with a previous employer. "Their remuneration package was better than here," he said. "As well as a Moscow apartment they gave me a dacha to use in July and August. Rented of course. There was a swimming pool in the compound, and a restaurant. Very nice – classy. But my wife nearly ruined it with her big mouth."

"What did she do?"

"Interfered. All the other dachas were taken by rich people – businessmen and oligarchs. Maybe a few gangsters. And every Sunday evening the restaurant put on a fashion show. They *called* it a fashion show. The models were all teenagers – officially showing clothes – but everybody knew they were prostitutes. My wife wasn't happy, so I suggested we just avoid the restaurant. But she said *we have to eat!* So, we went most weeks, and she got to know the girls. She'd talk with them when they weren't working. Give them advice. And started saying things like – *why do you want to do this? A girl like you could have a better life*. I told her to take care. *You'll get me killed*, I said. *These are dangerous people*. But she just kept on nagging the girls. Nothing did happen – but it always worried me. It was a relief when we gave up that dacha at the end of the season."

"You were still alive," I said.

"Exactly."

31

I rarely saw Valeria angry, but at the height of the Grigori Grabovoi affair she showed her outrage. With the story dominating the news, I asked her opinion and her face darkened. "He's a devil," she spat. "A very evil man."

Grabovoi's photograph stared out from that day's newspaper, and she struck it with the back of her hand, muttering more condemnations in Russian.

"Anyway," I said, "he's locked up in Lefortovo now." (Moscow's notorious prison.)

"He deserves it – he should suffer."

Grabovoi's story was peculiarly Russian. His notoriety stemmed from the 2004 attack on a school in Beslen, in Russia's North Ossetia region, where terrorists demanding the withdrawal of Russian troops from Chechnya took over one thousand people, mostly children, hostage.

After a three-day siege they began executing adult hostages, and Russian commandos stormed the building. All but one of the terrorists were killed, but over 300 hostages, including 186 children, also died. Eyewitnesses claimed the Russian assault was chaotic – the carnage exacerbated by disproportionate force, the use of heavy weapons and high explosives, and it quickly became a PR disaster for the Kremlin. Survivors and relatives of those who died blamed not only the soldiers involved, but President Putin himself for mishandling the situation. The tragedy became one of modern

Russia's most sensitive political contoversies – a high-profile state failure that sparked public condemnation.

Along with the officials, journalists, and security experts that flocked to Beslan in the aftermath, was a motley collection of spiritual groups seeking to minister to the traumatised and bereaved. These included a cult with several hundred followers, led by Grigori Grabovoi. Grabovoi was a modern version of an age-old Russian phenomenon: a spiritual leader with self-proclaimed supernatural powers. As a mystic, miracle worker, clairvoyant and healer, he claimed the ability not only to cure cancer and AIDS, but to harness mind-over-matter to deliver unbelievable results. In this he differed little from a host of similar figures haunting the margins of contemporary Russian life. Belief in the supernatural, and a willingness to engage with paranormal practitioners, have long been features not only of peasant tradition, but of wider Russian society. When religion was banned under the Soviets the occult flourished under the surface, and immediately after the collapse of communism enjoyed a boom in the anything-goes environment of the Yeltsin era, when psychics were even permitted on TV – to perform magic on a nationwide audience.

What set Grabovoi apart from competitors in Beslan, and ultimately brought official retribution, was his most outrageous proposal – he would, for a fee, raise from the dead the children killed in the siege. It was this that so shocked Valeria. Most Beslan parents reacted with revulsion and denounced him as a charlatan, but others yielded to his offer, and began gathering together the 40,000 roubles each he charged for a personal interview. Grabovoi never revealed details of his resurrection process, but he offered to teach parents how to do it themselves. He told one mother it would be easy to bring back her daughter, because the girl's twin-sister was still alive. At the same time, he made it clear he would accept no blame for any failures. The dead, he argued, are sometimes unwilling to be brought back to life. Or they might reappear in other people's bodies, or return elsewhere in the world.

Observers reported that in Beslan's febrile atmosphere, stories circulated that indeed a way of moving between the worlds of the living and the dead had been discovered – but the government was keeping it secret. Beyond Beslan Grabovoi was widely condemned as a monster and a fraud, a heartless crook preying on the grief of stricken parents. Russian press coverage was vitriolic, but Grabovoi claimed the attacks were politically motivated. That media hostility, and an official prosecution for fraud, were engineered by the Kremlin to stop him running for President of Russia in the 2008 election.

Bizarrely though, Beslan was not his first encounter with the authorities. In the mid-1990s the government had actually hired him as a consultant, seeking his paranormal expertise for a project hoping to harness supernatural powers to control public order. His mistake at Beslan was straying into national politics, dabbling in matters that embarrassed the Kremlin, and supplying the Beslan story with oxygen. Curiously though, there was also an opposing conspiracy theory – which held that Grabovoi's antics were deliberately orchestrated by the Kremlin, to discredit by association Beslan parents who criticised the military operation, and continued to press for the truth of what happened.

When the government filed fraud charges and consigned Grabovoi to Lefortovo, everybody knew a guilty verdict was certain. Criminal cases that get to court in Russia rarely result in acquittals. Civil rights activists claim the nation's 99% conviction rate makes a mockery of justice. But it has remained steady over the years and reflects an enduring Soviet attitude to delinquency – the presumption that an accusation is in itself evidence of guilt. It also demonstrates a lack of independence in the courts. Apologists for the legal system repeat the old chestnut about excellent detective work, and thorough pre-trial preparation, ensuring only rock-solid cases get to court. But independent experts acknowledge the reality of political interference. Paradoxically, one of the strongest pressures on prosecutors and judges to deliver convictions is the fear of seeming corrupt. A criminal court with too many acquittals would inevitably arouse suspicion that defendants were bribing their way out of trouble.

After his arrest Grabovoi turned his attention to the policemen guarding him, and offered to use his magical powers to get one promoted to the rank of General, and another to Minister of Defence. He also confided that if he chose to release himself from custody, nothing could stop him, as he possessed powers of teleportation that could spirit him away at will. There's no record of any of these miracles materialising.

"Can he get off?" I asked Valeria. "Buy his freedom?"

"Never! It's impossible."

She was right of course. The statistical odds were certainly against him, but Grabovoi's case was also special. It was public hostility that made it inconceivable he'd be free any time soon.

***

There's something in the Russian psyche that draws them to marginal, quasi-religious movements and eccentric cults. For centuries the country has been home to a proliferation of sects, holy men, miracle workers, psychics, prophets and charlatans. They have flourished within the mainstream Orthodox Church, and outside. Grabovoi was simply the most outrageous contemporary example. Cults are usually about money and power, and a few years before Grabovoi came on the scene, another mystic who briefly hit the headlines achieved both. Sergei Tropp, a former traffic warden from Siberia, became a spiritual superstar when he renamed himself Vissarion and announced he was a Messiah – even convincing his followers he was Jesus Christ returned. His message of salvation through austerity was nothing new, but it caught the imagination of idealists disillusioned with the materialism of Boris Yeltin's Russia. Disciples had to hand over all their wealth and submit without question to the demands of Vissarion's leadership. Thousands did – and retreated with him to a life of simplicity and contemplation in the Siberian wilderness. Unlike Grabovoi, however, Vissarion avoided antagonising the authorities and was left undisturbed. Some commentators argued that the Vissarian phenomenon was driven by nostalgia for the old Soviet world. That for those unable to cope with the new Russia, his appeal was less about religion than a return to communism. His community provided the essentials of life, but also an environment in which adherants had no need to think for themselves.

The most famous of countless predecessors of Grabovoi and Vissarion were Leo Tolstoy and Grigori Rasputin. It feels almost sacrilegious to mention the idealistic Tolstoy alongside a scoundrel like Grabovoi, but if nothing else they shared similar messianic tendencies. When Tolstoy in later life gave up writing fiction, he devoted himself to religion and morality, developing a philosophy of asceticism, pacifism and opposition to private property, which sought spirituality via the inner man rather than organised religion. Many contemporaries regarded him a living saint, and like

Grabovoi he inspired a devoted band of acolytes who cherished his teachings. Independent holy men have often had difficult relationships with the Russian authorities, and Tolstoy's dismissal of the Orthodox Church, and criticism of state authoritarianism, provoked official hostility that to this day has never fully disappeared. The Church excommunicated him – an act it has never rescinded – and as a result his reputation burns less brightly in his homeland than the rest of the world. The 2009 film about his final days, *The Last Station*, with Christopher Plummer as Tolstoy and Helen Mirren as his wife Sophia, depicts the tensions in his household as his followers scheme to build a religious community based on Tolstoian philosophy, while his wife struggles to retain the copyright of his works, and resulting income, for the benefit of his family. The film's most interesting feature is its portrayal of cult life: a mix of genuine spirituality, contrariness, mercenary intrigue and sheer crankiness.

Tolstoy never claimed for himself any of the special powers attributed to other religious leaders. There was no healing or prophesy. His contribution was as a thinker and spiritual teacher. By the time of his death in 1910, another figure closer to the Grabovoi mould was establishing a career as a religious mystic – Grigori Rasputin. Rasputin is of course one of the great pantomime villains of Russian history: the 'mad monk', notorious for his influence over the royal family, his spectacularly debauched lifestyle, and alleged possession of magical powers which made him nearly impossible to kill. Through his mesmeric personality, and a healing ability that seemed to control Crown Prince Alexei's hemophilia, he developed a hold over Tzarina Alexandria which allowed him to interfere in national politics. Yet comparing him with Grabovoi doesn't do Rasputin justice. The former was simply a greedy showman, charlatan and fraud. Rasputin despite his evil reputation and personal flaws, had genuine religious convictions, and a real concern for Russia's well-being. The latter caused him to warn the Tzar against taking the nation into the First World War. Photographs of the two men show very different characters. Rasputin, with his penetrating eyes and wild hair, projects a personality we might just believe possesses mysterious powers. Grabovoi on the other hand, in a jacket and tie, looks like an accountant. Clean-cut, respectable and nondescript. There's nothing in his face that hints at charisma, or ironically, explains how he managed to influence those who followed him.

As a tease I said to Valeria: "I guess Grabovoi's the new Rasputin – have you heard of Rasputin?"

She looked at me with scorn. "Of course. I'm Russian."

"Are the stories true?"

"Probably. But who knows. I've also heard the song."

Would she now share an authentic piece of Russian folklore?

"Song?" I said.

"Yes, do you want to hear? Ra…" And she rolled off a verse from the 1970s pop hit *Rasputin*.

"But that's just Boney M!"

She looked at me: "Who?"

"Never mind."

Although curious about Valeria's religious beliefs, I had never questioned her. Once she had told me personal matters were more important than politics. But her list of competing interests made no mention of religion. I never saw her with a rosary or heard her express pious sentiments. Religion is a difficult subject to broach directly. Too personal and sensitive for work colleagues. Especially in a foreign language. Yet I was curious. Several years of living in

Moscow had given me little insight into Russians' spiritual or religious lives, and I wondered if something of Valeria's beliefs – and by extension those of other ordinary Russians – might emerge from the Grabovoi controversy.

I took my chance when a newspaper reported some new allegations about Grabovoi's promises to a Beslan family.

"Look at this, Valeria," I said. "It's getting worse."

She read the story with grim concentration, then said: "He should burn in hell."

"Do you believe in hell?"

She looked at me with surprise. "It's an expression," she said. "Just an expression."

And the subject went no further. So much for my subtle interrogation. Valeria's spiritual side remained mysterious and enigmatic – like Russia itself.

There's been a lot of talk of a religious revival in Russia since the collapse of communism, and public displays of religious allegiance are common in Moscow. But it's unclear how many adherents are new believers, or just the faithful emerging from the shadows after decades of suppression. Religion was not completely absent from communist Russia. Although repressed and discouraged, the state for practical reasons tolerated a small group of approved clergy, who were expected to control the attitudes and behaviour of their followers. At the same time, although all kinds of religious cults were officially banned, many continued to flourish underground, reservoirs of long-standing belief which surfaced when the times allowed.

It suits the Kremlin today to talk-up the revival, particularly the role of the Orthodox Church, whose conservative social philosophy and traditional values are politically useful. Its ideals of national pride and respect for authority are a foil to Western notions of free speech, government accountability and democratic reform. Cynics doubt the extent of true religious conviction in modern Russia, arguing that professions of faith have become lifestyle statements – as much about fashion as belief.

Russian liberals also express alarm at the growing political influence of Orthodoxy in a supposedly secular society. They cite in particular a landmark trial of the organisers of a Moscow art exhibition entiled *Beware Religion*, who were prosecuted for blasphemy. The Church, offended by a collection of avant-garde artworks with a religious theme – an image of Jesus in a Coca-Cola advert, a church made from vodka bottles (seen as a sly comment on the tax exemptions on alcohol sales the church used to enjoy) – pushed for convictions. The court's guilty verdicts aside, that the case was brought at all was a key concern for secularists. Soviet censorship of artistic expression, it seemed, had been replaced by state suppression of anything challenging Orthodox religion. A sign of the Church assuming the kind of role in Russian society the Communist Party once occupied. The Church's hostility to competition from rival religions exacerbated concern. Clerical antipathy towards most cults, also extends to other mainstream faiths. The Russian state itself officially recognises the rights of Jews and Muslims, and tolerates the presence of various Western churches – Roman Catholics, Jehovah's Witnesses and some protestant denominations – but the Orthodox establishment is deeply antagonistic.

On Sundays the Orthodox faithful are on display on Moscow's streets, making their way to church. And on any day of the week, pious Muscovites mingle with tourists in the city's cathedrals and monasteries, lighting candles and praying. Vladimir Putin himself is a declared Christian, and famously attends services in the FSB's own chapel; photographs of him alongside Orthodox priests appear frequently in the press. Putin not only puts his personal commitment on public show, but openly acknowledges the political dimension of his religious allegiance. The Kremlin sees the Orthodox Church as a force for national unity, filling the ideological vacuum that followed the collapse of communism. Recent official statistics put the number of Russians who consider themselves Orthodox believers at 50% of the population – compared with around 16% in the dying years of the Soviet Union. But the same source offers other more telling figures: regular attendance at communion or confession is 1.5% -2% of the population, no higher than in Soviet times.

During my years in the city, I passed almost every day an Orthodox priest who made himself a fixture outside the *Tiffany* jewelry shop on the corner of Tverskai Street and Pushkin Square. I'd watch him with curiosity as I waited for the crossing lights to change. He was a conspicuous figure in black vestments, with a white wooden collecting-box that hung at chest height around his neck. A tall well-built man in his early thirties, he sported the heavy, untrimmed beard customary for Orthodox clergy. He never preached, nor begged directly, but just stood waiting for donations. He seemed open and friendly – I often saw him chat affably with passersbys – but I found him in a way more troubling than the religious old women who make themselves deliberately pathetic and beg theatrically on the city's streets. (Beggars are a fact of life in Moscow and come in various guises: amputee ex-servicemen, derelict alcoholics; piteous old women. Amongst the latter, is a sub-category who cloak their entreaties in religious fervor. They kneel in underpasses and at the entrances of metro stations, ostentatiously clutching rosaries and tattered bibles, muttering biblical phrases, keening melodramatically and touching their foreheads to the ground. In rain or snow, instead of retreating to sheltered corners, they make a point of positioning themselves in puddles or patches of ice, where their wretchedness is accentuated. Good business or spiritual significance? Self-abasement as an act of piety? It was never clear if the theatrics were actually beneficial. My Western sensibility reacted with impatience, and I suspect the charitable impulses of most Muscovites were similarly dampened. But one surprising truth I noticed time and again, was that by far the greatest generosity to street beggars came from young women – often fashionably dressed young women.)

Although the priest at *Tiffany* kept his dignity, standing passively at his pitch, never giving the collecting box even an occasional rattle, a tiny, sceptical, sanctimonious voice in my head made me regard him with disapproval. Some vestige of Scottish Calvinism no doubt. He was a big man in his prime, and I could imagine my mother saying something like: "*What a shame! A strapping lad like that should be doing something useful. Some real work that benefits people. Not that! He wouldn't have got away with it in Soviet times.*"

The real story of religion in Russia today is not Orthodoxy, but the growth of Islam. For Russians this is a sensitive and highly political issue. The state officially recognizes four religions: Orthodox Christianity, Buddhism, Islam and Judaism. However, to the alarm of the Orthodox Church and Russian nationalists, Islam is flourishing while the numbers professing Orthodoxy are static or falling. The Church itself claims to have around 80 million adherents, but in reality, it has probably half of that. Like the Russian population in general, their numbers are in decline, and according to statisticians if the pattern continues, within a couple of generations Russia will become a majority Muslim society. The official estimate today is that 10% – 15% of the population is Muslim, but the true figure is commonly agreed to be higher, possibly approaching 20%.

Muslim clerics point out, provocatively as far as nationalists are concerned, that unlike Muslim populations in Western Europe, which are the product of immigration, the majority of Russian Muslims are indigenous, having coexisted with Orthodox Christians for centuries – and in some parts of the country were there even before the Christians arrived. In Moscow itself there are an estimated two million Muslims today, more than in any other European city. A mixture of Russian citizens from Russian republics like Tatarstan and Chechnya, and immigrants from former Soviet republics – in particular Azerbaijan, Uzbekistan and Kazakhstan. Many are illegal, and work in casual jobs where no papers are required, providing essential labour for Moscow's construction boom, and manning the city's food and fruit and vegetable markets. Their presence is evident in the numbers of dark-skinned, non-Slav faces in the streets, and the proliferation of halal butchers and ethnic shops. The Moscow authorities have licensed four mosques in the city, but it's no secret many others operate unofficially.

It's not only extreme nationalists who fear the growth in Muslim numbers. Many European Russians worry about social stability, and Islam's impact on Russian culture. But the trend is as much about the population crisis affecting European Russia as Muslim demographics. The high death rate and falling birth rate in European parts of the country contrasts with Muslim areas, where due to less alcoholism and drug abuse, the death rate is lower and large families are more common. The average male life expectancy in some Muslim republics is ten years higher than in European Russia.

The state's relationship with Islam is complicated by the experience of terrorism. With radicalised Chechen Muslims continuing to commit atrocities in pursuit of an independent Caliphate in the Caucasus, the central authorities in Moscow, together with much of the population, view their Muslim fellow-countrymen with fear and distrust. Paradoxically, Muslims in Russia now have more freedom than at any time in their history. They were persecuted under successive Tzars, and by Stalin, who heightened their oppression to the extent that anyone found with a religious text in its original Arabic might be sent to the Gulag. Today, Kremlin unease harks back to Soviet-type controls, with the establishment of a Muslim Spiritual Department that vets and appoints Islamic leaders and monitors mosques. Muslim organizations operating without official endorsement can suffer discrimination and police harassment.

32

"Have you seen this movie?"

I handed Valeria a copy of David Cronenberg's *Eastern Promises* (2007) which I'd picked up at Ismailova. The film was in English, but the packaging a Cyrillic version for the local market.

She read the blurb and shook her head. "I don't know it."

"Take it and watch it – then tell me what you think. It's very exciting. It's set in London, but really it's about the Russian mafia."

"Gangsters?"

"Yes gangsters – but a lot more than that. I won't spoil the story. But after you've seen it, I'll ask your opinion."

When she returned the DVD a couple of days later, she was enthusiastic. "You were right," she said. "It is very exciting. And for me very interesting – to see London."

"What about the criminals – are they realistic?"

"Maybe Nikolai's more beautiful – handsome – than a real gangster. But in general, it's realistic."

Nikolai, the film's hero, was played by Viggo Mortensen.

"Have you ever known a real gangster?"

"Of course." She hesitated. "But not as a friend. They were in Kirov. They're in every city. Everybody knew who they were. But it wasn't my business."

"And the tattoos?"

"That's true."

It was the tattoos which fascinated me. Cronenberg's film depicted a criminal sub-culture that intrigues both cultural historians and ordinary Russians: the world of the Vory, the brotherhood of criminals whose members use an elaborate iconography of tattoos to denote rank, and to record their personal histories.

The Vory: *vor v zakonye* (literally thieves-in-law, or thieves who operate by a code) – had their roots in the labor camps of the Stalin era, where they developed as organized gangs controlling the Gulag underworld. Unlike the political prisoners alongside them, the Vory were hardened criminals proud of being outside normal society. Joining them today still requires strict obedience to a code which emphasises their separateness. Vory cannot marry, must support themselves through criminal activity, and never take legitimate jobs. They may not cooperate with police or prison authorities and must avoid politics or contact with the government. Joining the Vory requires demonstrating courage, intelligence and leadership – but also a criminal record that includes at least three prison terms. Punishment for Vory who break their own laws can be severe – including death.

The Vory's heyday came after the collapse of the Soviet Union, when the economic and political chaos allowed them to expand their crime networks, and infiltrate politics and business. Observers argue that since the 1990s their influence has waned, as more sophisticated players, with the education and skills necessary in a complex capitalist economy, gradually supplanted them. Nevertheless, their myth remains powerful, and they are a potent presence in popular culture. Even Valeria had an ambivalent attitude, as I saw when I continued with my questions.

"Have you ever seen Vory tattoos in real life?" I asked.

She thought before she answered, then gave a measured response.

"It's not difficult to see tattoos. On the metro. In markets. You'll see them. And some may be on criminals. But who knows if they're Vory? Vory are famous in Russia – like a legend. Everybody knows about the marks on their bodies."

Beyond scriptwriters of crime thrillers like *Eastern Promises*, Vory tattoos have lately become a fashionable subject for serious academic study. Although the first learned article about them appeared, remarkably, as early as the 1930s, interest has intensified during the last fifteen years – and a stream of papers in academic journals, as well as several books, have been published on the phenomenon. The most comprehensive is Danzig Baldaev's three volume *Russian Criminal Tattoo Encyclopedia*, the first part of which appeared in 2005. Baldaev was a former prison guard who spent thirty years copying, cataloging and researching the meaning of prison tattoos, and his Encyclopedia reproduces over 3000 examples. His illustrations are mainly drawings, but a number of documentary films have also appeared recently which show the artwork on display on the bodies of real prisoners. The best is Alix Lambert's *The Mark of Cain*, which went inside Russian prisons to film interviews with prisoners, and secured extended shots of convicts stripped to the waist, their torsos covered in tatoos.

To the uninitiated, a striking characteristic of the art on display is the lack of colour. In ordinary life tattooists use coloured inks generously, to create what can be subtle and intricate patterns. But prisoner tattoos use only black ink. Although officially forbidden, most are applied in the prisons themselves – by other prisoners using homemade tools. Their quality varies from very crude to genuinely artistic. In *The Mark of Cain*, a prison artist demonstrates his improvised tattooing equipment, made from a mechanical shaver, a ball pen, and a piece of sharpened guitar string.

A Vory's tattoos are more than just decoration. They tell the story of his life, and each one has a meaning often intelligible only to other afficionados. Common designs include an eight-pointed star and a spider. A star's meaning changes depending on its location on the body; on the knee it says that the wearer will not kneel before the authorities; on the shoulder it declares the individual is a thief. If the spider faces upwards, it means he's still active; but downwards indicates he has left his life of crime. Another favourite design is a church, with a familiar onion-shaped Russian dome. These may look like religious symbols, but in reality, they are a summary of a Vory's criminal career – the number of domes indicating the number of times he has been imprisoned.

In Russia, popular attitudes to the Vory are ambivalent. As a foreigner, I thought them violent hoodlums, little different from the Italian Mafia. But with tattoos that made them more sleazily exotic. For Valeria and other law-abiding Russians, the Vory were all of this. They were feared and despised as a criminal conspiracy that had taken over much of the country. Yet at the same time, many honest citizens granted them a lingering respect – as symbols of resistance, of opposition to a tyrannical state. Their origins in the camps and their lack of cooperation with the communist authorities gave them prestige. They were a rare fragment of Russian life that had not collaborated with the system during Soviet times. From the earliest days of the Gulag, political prisoners regarded them with curiosity, and respected their refusal to work. More recently, despite their involvement in crime and corruption at senior levels of the state bureaucracy, they have acquired in some quarters new esteem, as symbols of opposition to the authoritarianism of the Putin regime.

Akin to this glamorization of the Vory is a peculiarly Russian passion for prison songs – *chansons* as they are popularly known. Russian chanson is an officially discouraged, but wildly popular musical genre (doubtless official disapproval is part of its appeal) that developed in prisons and labour camps during both the Tzarist and Stalinist periods. In the later Soviet era it blossomed out, to capture a wider audience in the underground music scene of the time. It continues to evolve today, and contemporary forms are a mix of musical influences – from traditional folk-style ballads to pop. Highbrow critics scorn chanson as redneck music, pointing to similarities with American country music. With its gritty commentaries on crime, and protests about injustice, it also has echoes of gangsta rap. Above all, chansons are emotional. They can be mournful or hopeful, upbeat or sad, as they recite their perennial subject matter: prison life, punishment, redemption, lost freedom and lost love. Russian politicians officially denounce them as criminal propaganda or indecent trash, and the main radio and TV stations ban them. Yet there's a flourishing chanson recording industry, as well as a live music scene. Several small independent radio stations specialize in the genre and thrive despite the hostility of the authorities. Although you won't hear chanson acts on state TV, the music is everywhere else. It's impossible to avoid in Moscow. Background (and sometimes foreground) in bars and restaurants; it drifts over markets and lingers around street kiosks; taxi drivers serve it to their passengers, and it seems to flow from the open windows of every truck driver's cab. A St. Petersburg DJ once described its popularity as follows: "Russian chanson is like a pornographic magazine. Everyone reads it, everyone listens to it, but they're afraid to admit it." His comment highlights the strange schizophrenia surrounding the music. It's scorned by the authorities, but at the same time tolerated. Official hostility coexists with widespread public affection. Nothing illustrates this paradox more than the figure of Alexander Rozenbaum. Rozenbaum is one of the genre's biggest stars, a performer who fills large-capacity venues on a regular basis. Yet, incredibly, he also has a second life – as a member of the Russian parliament and supporter of Vladimir Putin. The most famous of all exponents of Russian chanson was actor and singer Vladimir Vysotsky who died in 1980, but he remains an enduring influence in Russian culture. There's a statue of him standing Christ like, arms outstretched with a guitar slung at his back, at the bottom of Strasnoy Boulevard – the very image of a minstrel and romantic rebel.

"What about chansons?" I asked Valeria.

She laughed. "Yes, I like them. They're very sad but – romantic."

"Are they fashionable – with young people?"

"Maybe not so much now. Some people laugh and say they're old fashioned. But I like them. My father listened to them, so they're familiar. When I was a student, we sang them at parties. They're good songs for drinking."

To cultural historians chansons are more than just honky-tonk anthems. Like the glamorization of the Vory they offer an insight into the national psyche. In the West respectable citizens may occasionally flirt with prison sub-culture as a vicarious walk on the wild side – criminality as cool. But in Russia the relationship is deeper and more complex. It's a communion with the past, and with history's continuing scars. Prison there has a different meaning. During the 20th century the lives of few Russian families, irrespective of any guilt or innocence, were not in some way touched by prison, or the fear of prison. Serving time therefore does not carry the same stigma as in the West. Rather than a source of shame, it can represent a triumph of the individual over the system.

The worlds of the Vory and the chansons are simultaneously sordid and romantic. Yet whatever the Vory's popular appeal, they are dangerous and unsavoury, and like Valeria, few ordinary Russians wish to encounter them in real life. Viggo Mortensen has spoken of how he once unwittingly sparked fear in a London restaurant, when playing the gangster Nikolai Luzhin in *Eastern Promises*. He had arrived direct from the film set, without first removing the tattoos he sported for the role. These were reproductions of authentic *Vory* designs, and when some Russian diners caught sight of them a visible chill settled on the group. Thereafter he conscientiously removed all make-up at the end of each day's filming.

For a few weeks after watching *Eastern Promises* I looked around purposefully in Moscow's streets, hoping to spot prison tattoos. It would have been hopeless in winter, when there's little bare flesh on display. But in early summer I felt confident of seeing some criminal artwork. But I cannot claim success. The sheer proliferation of tattoos surprised me, but anything with a genuine Vory look eluded me. It's possible that in my ignorance I just failed to recognize them, but the vast majority of what I saw were unmistakably commercial creations. Shrek, Homer Simpson, any number of intricately-coloured bouquets of flowers – all from a catalogue in a city tattoo parlour and not a prison cell. In the Arbat's pedestrianised area alone, several parlours touted for custom with advertising boards strategically positioned to attract strollers.

Occasionally, my attention was caught by the dark smudges on the arms of drunks out cold on benches in Tverskoi Boulevard – Vory art? I thought not. Would authentic gangsters sleep it off in a public park? I also peered at passengers alighting from flash cars outside expensive restaurants, surreptitiously scanning their hands and wrists as they guided their female companions inside. But again, without success.

***

Most foreigners in Moscow never knowingly come in contact with the Russian mafia. But Norman was a rare exception and told me of an encounter he'd had in the late 1990s. At the time he was doing the accounts for a Moscow company that imported clothing, then distributed it to the provinces. The economic depression had hit business, cash-flow was a problem, and the company struggled to pay its bills. One day, as he waited on a metro platform, Norman was approached by a swarthy stranger.

"American – pay your company's debts!" the man said and stared into his face before walking away.

Norman was taken aback but dismissed the incident. A few days later however, the same man confronted him again, this time outside his office.

"Last warning American. There will be no more."

Shaken, and now grasping the seriousness of the situation, Norman told Vladimir, his Russian boss.

"*He threatened you twice?* Here and at the Metro?" his boss said. "You should have told me earlier. What did he look like?"

Norman described the man's Southern – or Eastern – appearance.

"Ah!" his boss said. "Now it's clear who we're dealing with. Don't worry. He won't trouble you again after today."

And he didn't.

"It crossed my mind," Norman told me, "that Vladimir might be planning a hit. But the truth's less dramatic."

The bad guy, it turned out, was from the Chechen mafia. Vladimir's business had some kind of facilitation deal to send goods to Chechnya but had missed a couple of payments.

"Not deliberately," Norman said. "A cash-flow issue. We just had no money. I wasn't paid myself for months. So, Vladimir spoke to the Russian mafia, and they spoke to the Chechen mafia, and it was sorted out. That's how it works."

Norman's boss had been paying-off the Russian mafia – standard practice for companies at that time. The arrangement bought protection. But the Chechens had ignored underworld protocol, and instead of going through the Russians controlling the local turf, had approached the defaulters direct.

"It shouldn't have happened," Norman said. "But Chechens are real bad news. Undisciplined. You never know where you stand with them. They shouldn't have bothered me at all. I was only the accountant – an employee. It wasn't my company. Assholes! The Russian mafia were reasonable. They knew times were bad and were patient. They understood Vladimir couldn't pay money he didn't have, and they were prepared to wait – not kill the golden goose. But the Chechens... Do you know what Stalin did to the Chechens?"

"What?"

"Deported them from Chechnya to Siberia and Central Asia. Millions of them – whole families. During the war – as a punishment for fighting with the Nazis. I guess Old Joe got some things right. Anyway, in our case the Chechen mafia apologised to the Russian mafia – but nobody ever apologised to me."

33

The longer I lived in Moscow the more the city grew on me. I was never one of those expats who fixate on the calendar, marking off the days until the end of their contracts. Yet life was not uniformly agreeable, and although I had no wish to leave, I became increasingly frustrated and disillusioned at work. Viewed objectively there was more to be positive about than otherwise. The salary was good, the tax-rate low, and my workload light, if erratic. Yet somewhere in the middle of my fourth year, my mindset changed and my mood darkened. The resilience which previously left me untroubled by the annoyances of office life, gradually started to wither. There was no single breaking point, just an increasing weariness with the never-ending cycle of misunderstandings, obfuscations, arbitrary changes of plan, office sneaks, and bureaucratic shenanigans. These of course are present in workplaces worldwide, but they seemed to me to flourish in Russia to an extraordinary degree. Incidents that would have once seemed comical local colour, became serious exasperations. Morrison sensed something of my malaise, and surprisingly tried to restore my equilibrium with some wise words.

"You're looking at things all wrong," he counselled. "Like we're in a normal business. Just accept that the usual expectations don't apply – and recalibrate. Remember," he added, repeating a mantra he'd voiced before, "we're not paid for what we do – but what we have to put up with."

"Easier said than done. Habits of a lifetime."

"Think how Soviet dissidents used to act. They conformed in public – but escaped mentally into a kind of internal exile. Do the same. Pretend like you care – but don't take work too seriously."

Good advice. But I had not yet acquired Morrison's levels of stoicism or cynicism. One event around that time particularly depressed me. The annual Staff Assessment cycle was nearing completion, and dissatisfied individuals had the right to appeal against their performance ratings. Most did not bother, recognising that complaints rarely did any good. Nevertheless, there were always a handful of appeals, which were handled with a maximum of bureaucratic fuss. I had once recommended simplifying the process, saving time and energy by steering staff to their direct supervisors for an informal chat in the first instance, and escalating matters only if this failed to produce a resolution. The President however had vetoed any change, insisting – as Dmitri translated it – that international standards required robust and detailed processes.

Appeals were therefore heard in a formal setting, by a panel of senior managers in a room arranged as if for a US Senate hearing – or a show-trial. The panel sat behind a long table, and the complainant addressed them from a chair a few metres away. Representatives of HR, together with any staff acting as witnesses or providing information, sat at the back wall. Ivanov, the President, never attended, but delegated the Chairman's role to Mr. Pryadkin. The first time I took part my heart sank at Pryadkin's long-winded introduction, which demonstrated he meant to make a meal of the event. His Soviet soul relished lengthy meetings, and he gladly presided over sessions that could run for days. They were characterised by the same mind-numbing focus on trivia he brought to our Weekly Management Meetings. It was exhausting, messy, at times embarrassing, and above all extremely boring. A dismal catalogue of claims, counter-claims, denials, grumbles and recrimination. Russian business life at its worst. Dmitri sat beside me and whispered a running translation of the proceedings, but often I paid little attention, and struggled to keep awake. The staying-power of my Russian colleagues amazed me; they seemed unfazed by such life-sapping events. More than once I wondered if appeals were deliberately made as unpleasant as possible – as a deterrent. Ninety-five percent failed anyway, and the few staff who managed to get their performance scores increased rarely derived any benefit.

My last appeals session followed the same pattern I'd witnessed previously, and by mid-morning my attention was wandering. I reconciled myself to a long, tedious day, then an unexpected element of drama enlivened the proceedings.

"Who's next?" Pryadkin asked. "Zernov? – Tell him to come in."

Zernov was ushered into the room, installed in the hot seat, and instructed to summarise his complaint. It was unfair, he argued, to be marked down for failing to meet his renewals target.

"Do you deny you failed?" Pryadkin said.

"No, I don't deny it."

"Then why are you here?"

"Because it wasn't a valid target."

Pryadkin frowned, but I noted a matching hint of defiance in Zernov's face.

Looking at him sternly Pryadkin said: "Mr. Radayev set your target?"

"Yes."

"And Mr. Radayev's your supervisor?"

"Yes."

"Do you think you know better than your supervisor?"

"No – but...In this case I believe the target was unrealistic. Impossible to achieve."

Pryadkin turned to Radayev, who was sitting with us at the back wall. "What do you say Radayev? Zernov says his target was unachievable."

A clearly uncomfortable Radayev got to his feet and muttered his disagreement. Zernov's target was perfectly achievable. It was, he said, just a matter of commitment.

"*Commitment?*" Pryadkin said, leaning forward towards Zernov and raising his eyebrows theatrically. "Commitment Zernov?"

Zernov however refused to be intimidated. "My commitment's not in doubt," he said. "The problem's how we set targets."

He went on to argue that fixed targets were old-fashioned and inappropriate in a modern business. A suite of stretch targets would be better. These could be flexed as circumstances changed. That was how other international companies operated.

God help us, I thought – *is he trying to wind them up?* And sure enough the tone of the meeting changed noticeably.

"Stretch targets?" Pryadkin said with a humourless laugh. "Radayev – what do you think of that?"

Poor Radayev rose again and answered hesitantly. "It's something we'll think about and discuss of course. But I believe last year's targets were reasonable."

There was an awkward silence for a moment. Pryadkin scowled and invited comments from the other panel members. When nobody spoke, he looked at Zernov and said: "My colleagues will discuss your appeal – and you'll be informed in due course. For myself, I commend your desire to modernise our company – but would like to remind you that not long ago people were shot in this country for missing their targets."

Pryadkin was scrupulously civil towards those who followed Zernov, but there was no escaping a new hostility in his demeanor. Zernov's mild audacity had offended him, and his mood was dark for the rest of the meeting. What had been a soporific atmosphere was now tense, edgy and oppressive. Feeling the discomfort of my Russian colleagues, I too sat uneasily, inwardly lamenting the circumstances. I knew then that I'd had enough.

Yet depressing as it seemed at the time, this was not the breaking point for my Moscow adventure. It might have been, if left to myself – but events overtook me. Not long afterwards rumours of change began to surface. A reorganisation was whispered – which HR knew nothing about. This inclined me to believe it was true. As the gossip intensified, so did the scale of predicted redundancies. The world financial crisis of 2008 had hit Russia hard. Falling oil revenues had damaged the general economy, and our company had to cut costs. We all waited for the cloudburst.

Looking back, I wonder if at some unconscious level I had picked up signs of impending change, intuition stoking my unease and discontent. Whatever the case, when the rumours started, I sensed I was nearing the end in Moscow, and turned my attention to how I should use my remaining time in the city. I still had things to see.

***

After work one evening, while there was still enough daylight for photography, I took the metro three stops on the green

Zamoskvoretskaya Line, from Tverskai to Dynamo. My wife declined to accompany me.

"Why on earth are you going there?" she said. "It's derelict. And obvious from the road there's nothing worth seeing."

My response was low key. I did not feel like giving a full explanation.

"It's just something I want to do before we leave," I said. "I'll look around, take a few snaps and come straight back."

The Dynamo metro station is on Lenigradsky Prospect. We had passed often in the car on our way to Sheremetyevo Airport, or to one of the new superstores on the city's outer edges. As the name implies, the station serves the area around the Dynamo football stadium which stands just behind it, overlooking the highway. This was my destination: the home of *Moscow Dynamo FC,* a famous name from the past.

I knew the stadium was ramshackle – a graffiti-covered ruin reportedly scheduled for demolition. But my interest wasn't the arena itself, but the bronze statue of legendary goalkeeper Lev Yashin which stood near the entrance. Yashin was a figure from my schooldays, remembered for his acrobatic displays for the USSR – dressed in his habitual all-black kit – in televised coverage of the 1966 World Cup. Before my time he had also taken part in the 1958 and 1962 tournaments, and he was spoken of with awe by Scottish football fans of that era. Although they had no reason to wish the Soviets success, they recognized and celebrated Yashin's magnificent skills. Many experts consider him the greatest goalkeeper of the 20th century, perhaps of all time. His career with Moscow Dynamo, his only club, lasted from 1949 until 1971, and I reasoned that when they tore down the stadium they would surely preserve his memorial – to erect again in front of its replacement.

But inevitably the statue would likely be locked away for years, and if I delayed my pilgrimage, I would miss my chance.

Close-up the full extent of the stadium's decay was apparent: peeling paint, boarded windows, rusting metal, cracked concrete. The dilapidation echoed the club's recent lackluster reputation – it had not won a domestic league championship since 1976. Yet Moscow Dynamo was once one of the great names of world football, and the stadium, even in its current sorry condition, was loaded with historic resonance. From the 1930s until well into the 1960s Dynamo was Russia's foremost team, with both an unmatched reputation throughout the Soviet Union, and a respected international profile. As a schoolboy fan in 1960s Scotland, Dynamo was one of a few foreign clubs that claimed a place in our football folklore.

The club's subsequent decline mirrored the fortunes of Russian football in general. While other European leagues boomed thanks to television revenue and capacity crowds, Russia has not enjoyed similar growth, and most clubs are unprofitable. Television earnings are tiny, and gate receipts generally fail to cover running expenses. The typical attendance at a Dynamo home-game today is around 10,000, a decent enough number, but nowhere near the crowds of Europe's major leagues. Barcelona can regularly count on upwards of 84,000, Manchester United 75,000, and Bayern Munich 69,000. Unsurprisingly, for the past two decades, with rare exceptions, Russian clubs have failed to make an impact in international competitions. CSKA Moscow did win the UEFA Cup in 2005, and Zenit St. Petersburg repeated their success in 2008, but overall, the picture has been disappointing.

The low level of commercially generated revenue in the Russian game has led to a reliance on sponsorship by big business, or ownership by oligarchs. Zenit is sponsored by Gazprom and Lokomotive owned by Russian Railways. For a few years at the beginning of this century, the oil giant Yukos sponsored Dynamo, until the Kremlin destroyed the company and jailed its owner Michael Kodorovsky for corruption and tax offenses. In a way, today's business involvement is not so different from how Russian clubs have always operated. In their Soviet heyday each was aligned with specific sectors of society, from which they drew support and finance. CSKA Moscow was the army club, Lokomotive represented the railwaymen, and Torpedo the car workers. Spartak was supported by trade unions and co-operatives in industries such as textiles and food production and became known as the workers' club. Dynamo on the other hand, notoriously was controlled by the security services. For Dynamo the association has always cast a dark shadow. Felix Dzerzhinsky, the founder of the Soviet secret police, established the club in 1923 to encourage his agents to keep fit, and Laverenty Beria, his most infamous successor, became its honorary chairman just over a decade later. As a result, Russians even today refer contemptuously to Dynamo as the *Chekist Team*. During its most successful era, the club's fame attracted support from far beyond the security services, but at the same time the connection also made it the focus of hatred and fear. Clashes between Dynamo and Spartak in particular went beyond normal sporting rivalry and contained an existential element. Russians of the time recognised, but could not openly admit, that victories by Spartak over the team of the communist party's enforcers represented at some level a victory for the Russian people over the Soviet state.

The history of both clubs in the late 1930s and early 1940s makes this antipathy understandable. Until Spartak was founded in

1936, Dynamo was the undisputed giant of Soviet football. The newcomers however quickly challenged their dominance, as talented players were attracted to the club by a relaxed atmosphere that contrasted with the dour regimentation of the army and security teams. Spartak vs. Dynamo would become one of the great perennial sporting rivalries of the Soviet era. In 1936 Dynamo won the inaugural season of the new national football championship, but Spartak triumphed in 1938 and again in 1939.

In a footnote from the era of the Great Terror, the first direct meeting between the two clubs was scheduled to take place in front of Stalin in Red Square in 1936, to mark Physical Culture Day. At the last moment, Dynamo withdrew, fearful, it is said, of a ball sacrilegiously bouncing against the Kremlin walls, or even hitting Stalin. Instead, an exhibition match was arranged between two sides provided by Spartak. During the night before the game, three hundred Spartak volunteers covered the cobbles in the square with green felt to provide a playing surface, and Stalin and the Politburo watched the match from on top of Lenin's mausoleum. It was scheduled to last half an hour, but the organizers, worried Stalin would get bored, arranged a signal with a handkerchief to stop the play earlier if necessary. However, the opposite happened: Stalin was absorbed and the action continued for forty-three minutes.

As Spartak grew in strength towards the end of the 1930s, a faltering Dynamo drew on its secret police connections, and Beria began an off-field campaign of intimidation against Spartak players and officials. Warnings were issued about the inadvisability of bettering Dynamo, but to Beria's fury Spartak kept on winning. In the volatile and dangerous political atmosphere of the time, he succeeded in having Alexander Kosarev, Spartak's founder and head also of the Komsomol (the Young Communist League), arrested and executed as an "enemy of the people." Similarly, Spartak's best player, Nikolai Starostin, was arrested along with several other Spartak team-mates, including Starostin's three brothers. They were accused of "propagandising bourgeois sport," a ridiculous trumped-up charge that nevertheless resulted in sentences of ten years in labour camps. Starostin survived, and in an autobiography, published in the 1980s, wrote of his belief that he and his brothers had been saved from Kosarev's fate only by Spartak's popularity, which made Beria wary of provoking the outrage of millions of football fans, by executing their idols.

In his obsession with football, Beria was a rarity amongst senior Soviet leaders, most of whom had little interest in sport. In the years immediately following the Revolution all sport was viewed with suspicion, since competition of any kind was considered anti-communist. The Soviet football boom of the inter-war years marked a new attitude to sport in general. Beria had personally played senior level football in his native Georgia, and once even came up against a team that included Starostin, who recalled him in his memoirs as a "crude and dirty left half."

The Dynamo-Spartak rivalry continues to this day, if less lethally for those involved. Dynamo's relationships with other teams are not as explosively hostile, yet in the eyes of opposition fans the club has never shaken off its dark reputation. Its own supporters however remain unembarrassed by history, and revel in their notorious connections. *The Moscow Times* reported that at a match in 2006 Dynamo fans taunted Spartak supporters with a huge portrait of Beria, bearing the legend: *He Sees Everything.* In the perennial soap-opera of fan warfare, the theme was picked up by Zenit supporters when their club played Dynamo the following season. Displaying the same portrait of Beria, they added their own message: *You'll Pay for His Sins.* At the next game between the two clubs, the Dynamo reply was a portrait of a prominent St. Petersburg socialite, the daughter of a former city mayor, whose colorful personal life was receiving publicity. Their message read: *Even in 100 Years You Couldn't Pay for Her Sins.* And so, football goes on.

Personally, I once encountered the fearsome aggression of Russian fans first-hand, when I stumbled across a mob in Pushkin Square. I heard them before I saw them: a roar followed by loud chanting, then several hundred men surged up the steps of the metro entrance and scattered over the square, trampling flower beds and jostling people in their way. Their red and white banners and football scarves, proclaimed them Spartak supporters. I later heard they were fresh from a victory at Dynamo and had disembarked the train after a few stops to celebrate in the city centre. While I witnessed no serious violence, they were an intimidating crowd; largely young, with a fair measure of skinheads. Many had removed their shirts, and aggressively swaggered around bare-chested that warm evening. Like other passersbys, I gave them a wide berth, and I and retreated in the opposite direction down Tverskai Street.

The Beria-era rivalry between Dynamo and Spartak was the subject of a novel in English by British writer Tariq Goddard, who produced a fictionalised version of events in *Dynamo* (2003). I approached his book with hope and expectation, since the historical facts are ideal ingredients for a thrilling read – sporting heroism, chilling threats, spies, treachery, and life-or-death decisions. All played out against a shabby-exotic 1930s Moscow background. But Goddard's realisation is disappointing, and anyone familiar with the Dynamo-Spartak story will lament the waste of wonderful material. He tells a lurid tale – with plenty of sex, swearing and violence – which in the end is nevertheless curiously flat. The main weakness is characters which never come to life. They're crudely drawn, mouth stilted dialogue, and fail to convince as sportsmen or human beings. (The gothic oaths uttered by the emotionally tortured Spartak team-coach for example, sound phoney and ridiculous.) Equally important is a failure to depict real differences between the two clubs – in playing style, sporting values or political principles. We don't know who to root for – or why we should care what happens. There remains a fascinating book – or film – yet to be written about Dynamo and Spartak.

In November 1945, just months after the war ended, Dynamo entered British football's collective consciousness when it became the first Russian club ever to visit the West. The team arrived for a four-match tour that the British authorities hoped would mark sport returning to normal, while the Russians saw it as a propaganda opportunity at a time their alliance with the West was set to crumble. The Kremlin chose Dynamo to represent the USSR, as the security service connection reduced the risk of players and officials defecting when travelling abroad. Before the Russians left for Britain, the players were called to the Kremlin to be lectured by Stalin on the significance of their mission, and importance of their performances.

In an era before regular European tournaments, the tour was a huge event which captured the imagination of the sporting public. The FA proposed a match between Dynamo and England, but the Russians declined, arguing a club side should play only other clubs. Instead, fixtures were arranged against Chelsea, Arsenal, Cardiff City and Glasgow Rangers.

Politically, the series did little to foster friendship between the two nations. The visit was dogged by rows over administrative arrangements, and several times the Russians almost left for home in protest. (In truth the discord was largely the fault of the British – in particular the English FA, who proved shabby and mean-spirited hosts.) George Orwell at the time called the tour "war without shooting." As a football event, however, it was a great success. The Russians were a revelation – to the surprise of the British public and the sporting press, who assumed Dynamo would be no match for British professionals. Employing a fast passing game, and what was then an innovative 4-4-2 system, the Russians proved challenging opponents, demonstrating tactical awareness and teamwork – as well as impressive individual skills – that took their opponents by surprise. Their first game, against Chelsea, ended in a 3-3 draw, and impartial observers conceded Dynamo were unlucky not to have won. The next was a mismatch, against the part-timers of Cardiff City, whom they beat 10-1. This was followed by the Arsenal fixture – widely regarded as the highlight of the tour. The Gunners had been England's most successful club during the 1930s, and the Russians saw the tie as the most prestigious.

In the event it was farcical. Heavy fog spoiled the game, the Russian referee was erratic, and for almost 20 minutes Dynamo had twelve players on the pitch (due to a botched substitution missed in bad visibility.) Yet despite Arsenal having been beefed-up with several 'guest' players from other clubs – provoking valid claims that the Russians in reality faced an England select and not Arsenal's normal team – Dynamo, to the delight of the authorities in Moscow, triumphed 4-3.

The final match was against Rangers in Glasgow, in front of a crowd of 92,000, the largest of the tour. By then, the quality of the Russians was recognised, and it proved a hard, physical contest, which to the satisfaction of both sides ended with honours shared at 2-2.

Dynamo returned to Moscow with an enhanced reputation and their propaganda objectives achieved. They had outdone the British teams, and at the same time provided a football masterclass that cracked the self-regard of British football. Assumptions of superiority were shown to be unwarranted, and forward-thinking football heads began pondering how to modernise the British game. In the West of Scotland, the Dynamo tour became part of football folklore, remembered for decades by sections of the population who see the world through the lens of football. Naturally, this had a lot to do with Dynamo's failure to beat Rangers. The Arsenal big shots had fallen – but Scottish pride was unharmed. Legions of old men kept the Dynamo legend alive, burnishing their own sporting credentials with (often untrue) reminiscences of being part of the huge crowd that witnessed history when the Russians visited in 1945. Dynamo's profile was still high in Scotland well into the 1960s, and received another boost in 1972 when they met Rangers again – this time in Barcelona, for the final of the European Cup Winners Cup, the first time a Soviet team had reached a European final. (Rangers would win 3-2.)

Like most of Scotland I watched the game live on television. And as I stood in front of Dynamo's silent stadium that spring evening, I made a fleeting effort to recall it. Seeking some connection, I guess, however flimsy and fanciful, between my own past and the football history in front of me. In truth, I could recall little of the game itself. What stuck in memory was its aftermath, when celebrating Rangers fans staged a pitch invasion, and to the delight of viewers back home, fought hand-to-hand battles with Spanish riot police. The violence of course shocked the football authorities, but provoked no general shame. And for Scottish Stalinists it was even a measure of compensation. Their Soviet heroes may have lost, but in those days of Franco's dictatorship, the Glaswegian rampage was a blow for liberty, a deserved swipe at a fascist state.

Sadly, Yashin did not play in that European final. He had retired a year earlier, but the statue I'd come to see at Dynamo depicts him in his athletic prime. He's shown soaring high above the goalmouth, arms stretched, plucking the ball to safety with his right hand – his body held aloft by a triangular structure comprising a goalpost and the crossbar. On Yashin's head the sculptor has cast a bronze version of the familiar cap he so often wore during games. It's a genuinely evocative monument and captures, in a moment of action, the goalkeeper's bravery and agility. And there, in front of Yashin's goalmouth, I positioned myself and asked a friendly passerby to use my camera and photograph me with Yashin. The man nodded approvingly, raised his fist in salute and said: "Yashin!"

***

Exploring the streets of Moscow's historic centre, I once came across a wall inscription that propelled me back decades and awoke a more personal football memory. In a quiet lane between Bolshaya Nikitskaya Street and Vozdvizhenka Street, just minutes' walk from the Alexander Gardens and the Kremlin walls, there's an ornately handsome pre-revolutionary apartment block. Number five Romanov Pereulok was originally inhabited by wealthy middle-class Muscovites, but after the Revolution was seized by the state and became home to some of the most powerful figures in the Soviet elite. The memorial plaques on the exterior record the famous names who lived there, including Marshall Zhukov and generals Kliment Voroshilov and Semyon Budyonny. I later discovered there had beensome even grander occupants, although no plaques marked their tenure: Trotsky, Khrushchev and Molotov. These three relocated here when declining political fortunes drove them out of the Kremlin itself. The absence of acknowledgement was presumably part of the process of fallen stars becoming non-persons. As I scanned the building's inscriptions, however, one name caught my attention, and reminded me of an experience from my schooldays – Alexi Kosygin.

For historians and ordinary Russians of a certain age, Kosygin's a famous name – one of the highest profile personalities on the world stage during the Cold War. A fixture in the TV newsreels that were background commentary to life in the 1960s and 70s. He was Soviet Premier and number two in the USSR's collective leadership, when Brezhnev occupied the top post of General Secretary of the Communist Party. But I had not heard him mentioned in decades.

When I asked Valeria what she knew about him she grimaced.

"He was high in our government, I think. Before I was born."

"You know, I once saw him in real life?"

She looked at me doubtfully. Understandably – Kosygin had been dead since the early eighties.

"It's true," I said. "I saw him – in Scotland. More than thirty years ago. He came to a football match."

I broke off here and retreated into thought, keeping to myself the complex emotions I recalled from that day. Kosygin had been on an official visit to Britain, and it was announced he'd attend a game during the Scottish part of his tour. When I told Valeria the story, I'd been unsure about dates – and my thirty-year guess should have been closer to forty. But I still have the match programme and can now be precise – it was on the afternoon of Saturday 11 February, 1967.

The game chosen was Kilmarnock FC vs Glasgow Rangers, at the former's Rugby Park stadium. I went with my grandfather who was a Rangers fan, although in those days he rarely attended live games. Kosygin's presence was surely the attraction, which I found odd as my grandfather wasn't a man interested in celebrities. He wouldn't have crossed the street to see a Hollywood star. But Kosygin was different – he meant something to him. Children grasp more than adults imagine, and as we waited for kick-off, I sensed in him an unusual nervousness. I understood, even as a schoolboy, that it wasn't about football. But the kind of welcome the Rangers fans might give a Soviet dignitary.

Football rivalry in the West of Scotland is living history – the tail-end of forces that once shaped Britain. As much about age-old religious and political antagonisms as the game itself. In a divided city, Glasgow Rangers are the club of the indigenous Scot, the protestant working man, and in the eyes of some, the old Scottish establishment. In contrast, city rivals Glasgow Celtic, were founded by Irish Catholic immigrants, and are still regarded by many Scots as outsiders. Scottish by location only – but Irish in sympathy. The symbolism displayed by both clubs underlines their different traditions. Rangers proclaim their Britishness. The union flag flutters over their stadium, and fans routinely sing the national anthem as an expression of loyalty to queen and country. Celtic on the other hand fly the Irish tricolor, and the crowd celebrates with Irish rebel songs that scorn the British state.

Along with the rest of the 35,000 crowd that day I witnessed a sliver of history. To welcome the guests, the red Soviet flag flew over Kilmarnock's Rugby Park stadium. The Soviet Premier was to take to the pitch and shake hands with players and officials. I was aware also of a personal drama taking place beside me on the terracing. My grandfather had become increasingly tense, and I knew that deeply-held, but contradictory, feelings were at war in him. As a socialist and atheist, he had no truck with royalty or religion. Philosophically he supported the Soviets. Yet emotionally he'd never shaken off a tribal allegiance to the football club of his youth and his Victorian father. And so – like a child who fears his family might embarrass him in front of a new friend – he waited for the Rangers support to shame Scotland with a display of bellicose monarchism. And sure enough, when the dignitaries emerged from the tunnel on to the grass, the crowd burst into God Save the Queen.

My grandfather sighed. "Ach, here they go!"

But Alexi Kosygin saved the day. As he walked to the centre of the pitch, he raised his hat and saluted the crowd, who responded in kind, with enthusiastic applause. As the cheers subsided my grandfather relaxed. Rangers beat Kilmarnock 2-1.

Kosygin's Scottish tour had included the usual dull formalities: a civic reception in Glasgow and a visit to a nuclear power plant. But according to reports, on the drive to the football match the curious statesman, spotting a surprising road sign, ordered his entourage to take a detour four miles east of Kilmarnock – to visit the tiny Ayrshire village of Moscow.

***

A few days before leaving Moscow, my wife and I made a final pilgrimage. We took the metro to Park Kultury, then made our way along Komsomolsky Prospect, turning off into the backstreets of the Khamovniki district. According to my guidebook our destination had once been called Dolgohamovnichei Street, but it's now Tolstoy Street – and the location of the writer's Moscow house.

Tolstoy bought it in 1882 at the urging of his wife Sofia, who had tired of country life at their Yasnaya Polyana estate 120 miles south of Moscow. She insisted the city would provide better educational opportunities for their children, and between 1882 and 1901 the family spent their winters here. The house, which sits behind a high orange-coloured wall, is a comfortable family home rather than a grand mansion – a two storey wooden building dating from the 1800s, and already old when Tolstoy took possession. It's another of those rare wooden houses that were fortunate enough to survive Napoleon's invasion. Tolstoy was reportedly attracted by the location rather than the house itself, as it was then a peaceful, semi-rural spot in the city's outskirts, with an orchard and a generous garden. Today the garden is smaller, but it remains a tranquil haven in Moscow's bustling centre. The house is still bordered by bushes and mature trees, and with its stable yard, outhouses and plentiful foliage (and shutters and doors painted green to blend the structure with its surroundings) has an air of having been transplanted from an old-fashioned country estate. A year after Tolstoy's death in 1910, his widow sold it to the Moscow city authorities, intending it become a museum, and a decade later, fearing for its future under the Bolsheviks, she successfully petitioned Lenin to have it taken it into state care. It has been a museum ever since.

We paid our entrance money at the ticket office in the old gate-house and crossed the yard to the main door. Here, as usual in

Moscow's house museums, an attendant provided us with felt overshoes. They protect the wooden floors, but at the same time kindle feelings of reverence – like donning white gloves to open an antique book or removing hats at a church door. In places once inhabited by great artists there's often a sense of the sacred – if only in the imaginations of their followers – and in Tolstoy's house it's compelling. To my mind, it's the best of all Moscow's traditional house museums. (The Bulgakov one I exempt as a different model.) Just before Sofia left, she made detailed descriptions of the layout and contents of each room. Her records of the furniture, wallpaper and colour schemes are used to preserve the interior as it was in Tolstoy's lifetime. The contents are not just period props, but artefacts that belonged to the family, including personal items like family photographs and original crockery. There are curiosities, such as the bicycle Totstoy learned to ride in his late sixties, and lying where he kept them, in a back corridor, the dumbbells he used daily to keep fit well into his 80s. Each room displays a card explaining in English its contents and their significance. Surprisingly, the house has no electricity or running water. Both were available in Moscow in Tolstoy's day, but he wanted to live simply and refused to have them installed. Respecting his wishes, the museum has left the house unchanged, and continues without them. It means though, that there's an undeniable whiff of dampness throughout the building.

Tolstoy's study is roped-off at the door, allowing visitors to look in, but not enter. His desk is there, and a chair with shortened legs that drew him close to the desktop, and allowed him to read without wearing spectacles. It's a small room and the desk is so near the entrance you can stretch out an arm and touch it. I was poised to do this when I heard the shuffling steps of the attendant approaching behind me and drew back.

***

I left Moscow in 2009. Rumours of staff cuts had circulated for months, but when the end finally came to my Russian adventure it was abrupt. Without warning or ceremony, the President suddenly announced the immediate elimination of twenty percent of jobs. At the same time, staff being retained were to have their salaries reduced. In a wise political gesture, the President decided all expatriates should have their contracts terminated. This resulted in negligible financial savings, as the company honoured them to the letter, and paid us off with everything we were due.

Grishin became head of HR and Valeria his secretary. Norman found a job in Kazakhstan on less money, while Morrison, cushioned by the fact his wife was in well-paid employment, stayed on in Moscow. Berkovich was deemed a foreigner and dismissed with the rest of us. On my last day Nikolai drove me to the airport. He had also lost his job and was pondering a career as a taxi-driver.

I departed with mixed feelings. Fed-up at work, I was ready for a change. Yet I was sorry to leave Moscow itself, and recognized, too late to matter, that what I thought frustrating in the bureaucracy and irritations of office life, were trivial in the scheme of things. Worth enduring for the privilege of discovering the city. In any case, annoyance was a luxury for fortunate westerners like myself, who had choices unavailable to my Russian colleagues. Some of them now a faced life-changing upheaval that echoed the troubled 1990s.

Further Reading

While the book's core is personal experience, I used various published sources for background on Moscow's history and literary heritage. In particular, I drew liberally on the local Russian press, and owe a special debt to the *Moscow Times,* the city's English language daily. Well-written, serious, and informative, it not only kept me up to date with current events during my years in Moscow, but gave me a wider education on contemporary Russia, as well as a critique of the Soviet past.

In addition, I found the following histories particularly useful:

Lenin's Embalmers – Ilya Zbarsky & Samuel Hutchinson (1998)
Natasha's Dance – Orlando Figes (2002)
Stalin: The Court of the Red Tsar – Simon Sebag Montefiore (2003)
Gulag: A History – Anne Applebaum (2003)
Stalin & His Hangmen – Donald Rayfield (2004)
Moscow 1941 – Rodrick Braithwaite (2006)
The Greatest Battle: The Battle for Moscow – Andrew Nagorski (2007)
Absolute War: Soviet Russia in the Second World War – Chris Bellamy (2009)
Russia's War: 1941-45 – Richard Overy (2010)

Many creative works – books and films – contributed to my imaginative grasp of Moscow and the Russian experience. Some are mentioned in my narrative itself. Below are those I found the most interesting.

Books:

A Hero of Our Time – Mikael Lermontov (1840)
Dead Souls – Nikolai Gogol (1842)
Quiet Flows the Don – Mikhail Sholokhov (1928-40)
The Master and Margarita – Mikhail Bulgakov (1973)
Dynamo – Tariq Goddard (2003)
The Coast of Utopia – Tom Stoppard (2003)
Stalin's Ghost – Martin Cruz Smith (2007) *
Snowdrops – A. D Miller (2011)

* *Stalin's Ghost* is the sixth in a series of nine crime novels featuring fictional Moscow detective Arkady Renko. Renko first appeared in the bestselling Soviet-era *Gorky Park* (1981), and continued in his career through communism's collapse, into the contemporary period. Dramatising crime, corruption and social issues typical of the times, Smith's novels seem to me to capture the spirit of Moscow in transition as well as any conventional history.

Films/ TV shows

An Englishman Abroad (1983) – BBC TV
The Inner Circle (1991)
The Mark of Cain (2000)
Enemy at the Gates (2001)
Who Killed Stalin? (2005) – BBC TV
Eastern Promises (2007)

The Last Station (2009)

More recently, Armando Iannucci's satire, *The Death of Stalin (2017),* delivers both hilarious black comedy and serious commentary on the Soviet era. We see that behind the façade of omnipotent power, Stalin's monstrous regime is not only vicious and deceitful, but inherently fragile, ridiculous, and incompetent.

Acknowledgements

I would like to thank my editor at Vulpine, Enda Kenneally, for his support and guidance in getting the book ready for publication, and Gordon Welsh for his comments on an earlier draft which prompted some necessary changes.

The author studied history and literature to Ph.D. level, but has never worked as a professional academic, enjoying instead a diverse career in a variety of industries in the UK, Europe, the Middle East and Asia. *Conversations with Valeria* is his first book, and reflects the four years he spent in Moscow during the first decade of this century. He lives in Scotland.

*9 7 8 1 8 3 9 1 9 4 7 2 6 *